Inventing Secularism

Inventing Secularism

*The Radical Life of
George Jacob Holyoake*

RAY ARGYLE

Foreword by ROBERT FORDER

McFarland & Company, Inc., Publishers
Jefferson, North Carolina

Also by Ray Argyle

Scott Joplin and the Age of Ragtime
(McFarland, 2009)

Frontispiece: George Holyoake attained status of one of England's "Grand Old Men" (courtesy Bishopsgate Institute).

ISBN (print) 978-1-4766-8421-5
ISBN (ebook) 978-1-4766-4229-1

Library of Congress and British Library
cataloguing data are available

Library of Congress Control Number 2021003063

© 2021 Ray Argyle. All rights reserved

No part of this book may be reproduced or transmitted in any form or by any means, electronic or mechanical, including photocopying or recording, or by any information storage and retrieval system, without permission in writing from the publisher.

Front cover: *Holyoake at Forty: An Impression,*
by Sarah Watson © 2021.

Printed in the United States of America

*McFarland & Company, Inc., Publishers
Box 611, Jefferson, North Carolina 28640
www.mcfarlandpub.com*

Acknowledgments

An author's first acknowledgment in biography, I believe, should be to your subject for having lived an important and interesting life. This is especially true of George Jacob Holyoake, who made a major contribution to the modern world by his creation of Secularism and through his pioneering development of its core principles.

In addition to having lived an eventful eighty-eight years, George Holyoake left a voluminous accounting of his life and times, recorded in his newspapers, books, pamphlets, journals, and letters. Compared to the six trunks stuffed with letters and other documents that Joseph McCabe had to sort through when he began work on Holyoake's biography of 1906, my task has been much less formidable. The digitization of Holyoake memorabilia at the Bishopsgate Institute in London and the National Co-operative Archive in Manchester has opened a trove of material to quick and easy access. Unfortunately, Holyoake had no convenient means of making copies of his own correspondence, so we are left in the main to infer much of our understanding of him from the letters he received.

Historians have been aware of George Holyoake's achievements, but they have not brought them to public notice. I am amazed I am the only biographer in a century to have unearthed the largely forgotten story of a man who had such a transformative effect on modern history. There is much about Holyoake's life I have had to leave out, as a fuller accounting of his challenges and achievements would take at least a second volume. This is a demonstration, I think, of the theory that a good story is like an iceberg; the reader sees only the tip of it. The Notes and Bibliography that follow offer further reading for those who wish to go deeper into Holyoake and his times.

I am grateful to the staff of the archives I visited for their generosity of time and expertise. I especially wish to thank Stefan Dickers at the Bishopsgate Institute and Sophie McCulloch at the Co-operative Heritage Trust. My thanks also to Helen Glenn and Geoff Burns at the Birmingham

Public Library and Archives for assistance in tracing George Holyoake's family background. Researchers at the British Library also were very helpful. Appreciation is also due the Internet Archive, the non-profit digital library of more than 300 billion pages of material, including many works of dead authors, by and about George Holyoake. I am not so appreciative however, of their posting two of my books for all the world to read free of charge.

I would likely not have taken on this challenge without the encouragement of Andrew Copson, CEO of Humanists UK, who was enthusiastic in his support from the beginning. I received invaluable assistance from Bob Forder, historian of the National Secular Society (UK) who read my drafts and was most helpful in his comments. I am particularly pleased that Bob consented to write the foreword to this book.

My special appreciation goes to Layla Milholen, Managing Editor—Operations, of McFarland. Her guidance, encouragement, and support made it a privilege to work with her and her team.

My daughter Sharon Norman accompanied me on my archival visits and has been most helpful as a researcher and traveling companion. She also contributed the map of Great Britain facing Chapter 1. My granddaughter Sarah Watson created the cover portrait of George Holyoake, which makes me both proud and grateful. As always, gratitude goes to my partner Deborah Windsor for her unfailing support and encouragement.

Table of Contents

Acknowledgments — v
Main Dramatis Personae — ix
Chronology — xi
Foreword by Robert Forder — 1
Introduction — 4

Part I—Reform and Rebellion

1. An Inge Street Boy and the Capitalist Who Preached Socialism — 11
2. The Roar of the Blast Furnace in a Time of Turmoil — 21
3. In Which It Is Hard to Change the Mind of a Midlands Man — 29
4. Is It Possible to Be Rational About Religion? — 39

Part II—Dare to Be an Atheist

5. An Honest Answer to a Difficult Question — 50
6. The Lure of London and a Trial by Tyranny — 61
7. How a Prisoner Became the Watchmaker's Nemesis — 72
8. The Light of Freedom Shines on a Liberated Blasphemer — 81

Part III—Discovering Secularism

9. Fleet Street Ink and the Fight for an Unstamped Press — 92
10. Throwing Bombs in the "Springtime of the Peoples" — 105
11. How the Idea of Secularism Came Into Being — 115

Part IV—A Respectable Man

12. Finding Yourself in Company of the Famous — 128
13. She Heard No Evil, but Saw Much — 136
14. A Funeral in Wales and Rallying the Faithless — 143
15. The High Cost of a Clash of Ideas — 152
16. The Co-operative Man Makes a Change of Direction — 162

Part V—Goals Gained

17. Charles Bradlaugh, Birth Control and Mrs. Besant — 172
18. Going Blind, but Keeping the Vision of a Secular State — 183
19. An Innocent in America Finds the Ties That Bind — 192
20. "The Queen Is Dead, Long Live the King!" — 202
21. A Life, a Legend, a Legacy — 211

Epilogue: In Our Time: Secularism Under Siege — 221
Chapter Notes — 233
Bibliography — 247
Index — 251

Main Dramatis Personae

Besant, Annie (1847–1933), British author, activist, and secularist; confidante and close friend of Charles Bradlaugh, prosecuted with him for publishing book on birth control; abandoned Secularism to take up spiritualist religion of theosophy.

Bradlaugh, Charles (1833–1891), English political activist, founder of National Secular Society; his insistence on atheism as basic to Secularism led to conflict with George Holyoake, splitting secularist movement. First avowed atheist elected to Parliament.

Carlile, Richard (1790–1843), advocate for universal suffrage, freedom of the press, and atheism; befriended George Holyoake during his trial for blasphemy; turned to mystical Christianity; subject of biography by Holyoake, *Life and Character of Richard Carlile*.

Foote, George Wm. (1850–1915), secularist leader, occasional ally of George Holyoake; founder of *The Freethinker* in 1881 (now online); jailed one year for blasphemy; succeeded Charles Bradlaugh as president of National Secular Society in 1890, serving for 25 years.

Garibaldi, Giuseppe (1807–1882), Italian general and patriot, campaigned for creation of Kingdom of Italy; supported by George Holyoake who served as secretary of the London Garibaldi Fund Committee; escorted him on English visits.

Gladstone, William E. (1809–1898), Liberal party leader, four times Prime Minister of Britain between 1868 and 1894; known as "The People's William"; introduced secret ballot, advocated Irish Home Rule, secured disestablishment of the Church of Ireland.

Holyoake, George Jacob (1817–1906), social reformer and atheist in nineteenth century Britain, author and editor; convicted of blasphemy in last jury trial for atheism in England, 1842; created terms "Secularism" and "jingoism"; advocate and historian of UK Co-operative movement.

Huxley, Thomas Henry (1825–1895), English biologist and supporter of Charles Darwin and George Holyoake; coined the term agnosticism in 1869; fought extremism in religion and promoted scientific education.

Main Dramatis Personae

Ingersoll, Robert G. (1833–1899), American freethinker and author, known as "the Great Agnostic"; Civil War colonel in Union Army; met Holyoake in 1883 during Holyoake's second visit to the U.S.

Martineau, Harriet (1802–1878), British writer, atheist; deaf at an early age; regarded as first female sociologist; authored many books; secularist, friend of George Holyoake.

McCabe, Joseph (1867–1955), Catholic priest turned freethinker, prolific writer, author of the definitive although not impartial 1908 biography, *The Life and Letters of George Jacob Holyoake*. In 1920 McCabe debated Sir Arthur Conan Doyle, debunking the claims of spiritualism. Author of *Twelve Years in a Monastery*.

Owen, Robert (1771–1858), capitalist turned socialist Utopian reformer; denounced religion in 1817 London Tavern speeches; founder of Universal Community Society of Rational Religionists; fostered Utopian communities New Harmony in U.S. and Queenwood in England; was eulogized after death by George Holyoake.

Southwell, Charles (1814–1860), British freethinker; one of thirty-three children fathered by William Southwell; bookseller, ally of George Holyoake, editor of atheist newspaper *Oracle of Reason*; served one year in jail for blasphemy; emigrated to New Zealand.

Tennyson, Lord Alfred (1809–1892), renowned poet of the Victorian era and Poet Laureate of Great Britain; noted for such poems as "Charge of the Light Brigade" and "Ulysses"; friend of George Holyoake.

Chronology

	George Jacob Holyoake	Historical Events
1817	b. April 13, Birmingham, England, 2nd of 13 children of foundry worker father; mother, a button maker	England victory over Napoleon 1815; aristocrats prosper, poor suffer; Habeas Corpus Act suspended
1821	Attends Dame School and Wesleyan, Baptist and Unitarian Sunday schools	First Mechanics' Institute begun in Edinburgh; in London 1823
1825	Solders handles to tin pots; age 9 begins work in Eagle Foundry	Robert Owen buys town in Indiana for New Harmony community
1833	Attends classes at Birmingham Mechanics' Institute, age 17	England's political structure shaken as result of 1832 Reform Act
1838	Joins Chartist Union; meets Robert Owen; goes on 5-week walking tour	SS *Great Western*, first steamship built to cross Atlantic Ocean
1839	m. March 10, Eleanor Williams; quits Eagle Foundry, teaches at Mechanics' Institute	First Henley Regatta held
1840	Takes position as lecturer in Worcester for Robert Owen's Rational Religionists; transferred to Sheffield May 1841	First postage stamp issued in UK; "Penny Black" bears portrait of Queen Victoria
1842	Becomes an atheist; sentenced to 6 months jail for blasphemy after denying existence of God	China cedes Hong King to Britain; regains control of island in 2003
1846	With aid of £50 prize, launches *The Reasoner*, weekly paper of atheistic and secular views	Potato famine in Ireland causes 1 million deaths, another million emigrate to colonies and U.S.
1851	Creates term Secularism; comes to mean public sphere free of religion	Astronomer George Airy places prime meridian at Greenwich, Eng.
1853	Debates the Rev. Brewin Grant for 6 nights at Cowper St. School Rooms in London	Crimean War pits Britain against Russia, ends in Treaty of Paris 1856; makes Florence Nightingale famous
1859	Ill most of year, spends time at Turkish baths and 3 weeks in Paris	Big Ben rings out over Houses of Parliament for the first time; Charles Darwin publishes *Origin of Species*

	George Jacob Holyoake	Historical Events
1864	Welcomes Italian Gen. Garibaldi to Britain celebrating establishment of Kingdom of Italy	U.S. Civil War at its height; ends in 1865 followed by assassination of President Lincoln
1866	National Secular Society founded by Charles Bradlaugh with strong emphasis on atheism	Swedish chemist Alfred Nobel invents dynamite; on his death in 1896 funds Nobel Prizes
1876	Founds *Secular Review*; Secularism promoted as standing for neutral public sphere free of religious control	Telephone patent issued to Alexander Graham Bell; German engineer N.A. Otto invents internal combustion engine
1877	Splits from NSS over atheism and birth control, backs rival British Secular Union	Queen Victoria becomes Empress of India; British Empire at its height of power
1878	Creates word Jingoism to decry bellicose British policy toward Russian Empire	Second British-Afghan war waged from 1878 to 1880 as part of "Great Game" vs. Russia
1879–1882	Holyoake makes two journeys to America; publishes two books	French education system undergoes secularization
1886	Marries Jane Parsons May 25 in Brighton, having moved there before Eleanor's death in 1884	First automobile patent taken out by Karl Benz in Germany
1887	Serves as president of Co-Operative Congress; publishes several books on co-operative movement	Eiffel Tower under construction, will open for Exposition Universelle in Paris, 1889
1893	Publishes *Sixty Years of an Agitator's Life*; elected Hon. Member of National Liberal Club	Thomas Edison's invention of kinetoscopes provides world's first motion pictures
1896	Union of Ethical Societies formed, becoming British Humanist Assn. in 1967, now Humanists UK	Inaugural games of modern Olympics held in Greece, with 280 male athletes from 12 countries
1901	Becomes president of Rationalist Press Association, pamphlet publisher	Queen Victoria dies January 22, after sixty-three years on throne
1905	Publishes two vols. of reminiscences. *Bygones Worth Remembering*	Mediation by Pres. T. Roosevelt settles Russia-Japanese war
1906	d. January 22, Brighton, England, hailed as "man who fought and won for Englishmen freedom of speech."	Earthquake of 7.8 force shakes San Francisco, 3,000 dead

It is part of a good man to do great and noble deeds,
though he risk everything.—Plutarch

Modern society requires and deserves a truly secular state,
by which I do not mean state atheism, but state neutrality
in all matters pertaining to religion.—Richard Dawkins

Foreword
by Robert Forder

A biography has merit not only for what it tells us about an individual's fame but also what it reveals of their influence, ideas and legacy. Nowhere is this more apparent than in the life and career of George Jacob Holyoake, the subject of Ray Argyle's inquiring and lively biography. Relatively few have heard of Holyoake, yet his influence on Western thought endures and many of his ideas, prescriptions and suggestions remain as relevant today as when first proposed. In fact, we might go further and suggest that in times when liberal democracies are facing challenges from a populism that seeks to bypass hard won rights and freedoms, in ways that only recently seemed unimaginable, Holyoake's teachings take on an increasing and more urgent relevance.

Liberal democracy is a form of representative government characterized by a separation of powers into different branches of government; the rule of law and the protection of human rights, civil rights, civil liberties; and political and religious freedoms for all. It is underpinned and given legitimacy by free and fair elections and equal access to the political process regardless of race, creed or religious (and non-religious) belief. While the significance of elections is generally accepted and understood, the importance of equality of access to the machinery of government is less often acknowledged, despite its centrality to the freedoms and rights fundamental to Western democracies. The first step toward protecting and enhancing such rights is to give that protection a label coupled with a clear definition. That service we owe to George Holyoake. The label is Secularism, although to Holyoake, Secularism did not stand alone but was related to other "advanced causes" he championed during his long life.

Holyoake's roots lay in the English working class, although as Argyle makes clear, he never suffered the grinding poverty of many of his countrymen. Nevertheless, it was this background that led him to the socialism of Robert Owen and it was from this that he learned a fundamental tenet. Human beings are the product of the environment in which they live, work and, in particular, are born into. Once this is understood, religious concepts such as sin and evil lose their meaning and are replaced by the optimism of the reformer who works for the benefit of humankind at large. Here lies the optimistic thread that connects Owenism, Chartism, liberalism, Co-operation and Secularism, all of which Holyoake held dear and championed. That the lives of ordinary men and women could and should be improved.

Victorian England was an age of demographic, industrial and social change that entailed a rapid urbanization and the growth of the first modern cities. The political fulcrum of the country and Empire was London, which despite Holyoake's Midlands origins was to become the focus of his work and activities. London was not only an international economic powerhouse and political hub, it was a breeding ground for the generation of political ideas of liberalism, socialism, democracy and Secularism. Ray Argyle paints Holyoake's portrait against this backdrop, bringing to life the environment in which his subject worked and lived and how this helped form the man and his ideas.

Although the author expresses great admiration for the man and his achievements, this is no hagiography as Holyoake's failures, limitations and shortcomings are recognized. He was never elected a Member of Parliament and he was a poor platform speaker in a day of great orators. He aspired to leadership without possessing the requisite organizational skills and reacted badly when he detected personal slights. These factors came together to see him replaced as the leader of the British Secularist movement by the younger and more flamboyant and eloquent Charles Bradlaugh who succeeded in establishing a national organization for British freethinkers and Secularists, the National Secular Society. In so doing, Bradlaugh adapted the meaning of the term Secularism away from Holyoake's more inclusive ideal toward something less compromising and closely related to atheism. It is interesting to note that it is Holyoake's ideas, rather than Bradlaugh's, that are best encompassed by the term today.

Argyle also traces how during Holyoake's lifetime views of religion and civic duty evolved and moderated. The firebrand of 1842 who fell out with the Owenites over their moderation, who was imprisoned for blasphemy and admired the militant Richard Carlile, evolved into the sober elder statesman who opposed Bradlaugh's publication of a birth control pamphlet, admired Christian Socialists and counted England's prime minister, William Gladstone, among his associates. Such perceived compromises and apparent search for respectability cost him the support of former allies.

While recognizing these limitations, the author stresses some impressive achievements, in addition to his championing of Secularism. Holyoake was the foremost radical journalist during the period after the collapse of Chartism, when radicalism was in danger of losing momentum. His longest lasting journal, *The Reasoner*, acted as a point of reference and focus for radicals. Today its pages are a reminder of working-class political activity of its era. Holyoake was a champion of Co-operation and emerged as the historian of that movement. His championing of freedom of speech and a free press resulted in six months of imprisonment for blasphemy, although for a time this elevated him to heroic status.

One aspect of Holyoake's career that distinguishes him from most other reformers was his ability to engage in both political and economic reform. For example, Charles Bradlaugh may be regarded as an extreme liberal individualist whose guiding belief was that if the working class could be made free, then each individual would be made good. In contrast, Holyoake understood that freedoms needed to be coupled with economic reforms to support the poor and needy, hence his promotion of Co-operation.

Ray Argyle's writings are distinguished by his lively descriptions of people and places. The issues that motivated nineteenth century radicals are not always easy for us to appreciate. Argyle highlights, illustrates, colors in, explains and brings to life the challenges of yesteryear and demonstrates their relevance to our world. This much needed and balanced biography reminds us that the gains made by those who champion secular, liberal democracy are hard won and never permanent. While its champions often remain anonymous, Ray Argyle demonstrates we must be grateful for their lives and sacrifices and must remain on guard to protect their legacy.

Robert Forder is an historian of the National Secular Society, London. His great-grandfather, Robert Joseph Forder, became the first paid employee of the NSS in 1877.

Introduction

> The thinker who is really free, is independent; he is under no dread; he yields to no menace; he is not dismayed by law, nor custom, nor pulpits, nor society, whose opinion appals so many. He who has the manly passion of free thought, has no fear of anything, save the fear of error.
> —George Jacob Holyoake, *English Secularism: A Confession of Belief*, 1896

To know in the twenty-first century of the nineteenth century life of George Holyoake is to know two different worlds. Although vastly dissimilar, they are in some manner much alike. Our century enjoys access to a broader range of knowledge but our ability to apply what we know seems no greater. The Victorian Age was loath to accept human existence as a biological phenomenon unaffected by any higher power. We are reluctant to act on what we have learned about the precarious balance of life on a small, blue planet that is subject to plagues, tsunamis, and climate change.

George Jacob Holyoake was born in Birmingham, England, in 1817 and died in Brighton, England, in 1906. Notwithstanding his origins in the nineteenth century, Holyoake was a man for the modern age. His vision encompassed ideals of social justice that would become universally accepted nearly two hundred years after he first expressed them. Through a long, controversial, and conflict-filled life, marked by as many mistakes as triumphs, he was in the vanguard of almost every struggle to improve the lives of ordinary people—public education, the Co-operative movement, freedom of the press, trade unions, women's rights, and universal suffrage. He was hailed after his death as "one of the men who fought for and won for Englishmen that freedom of speech which we take as a matter of course today."[1] For a man largely neglected in popular history, he played a transformative role in the evolution of modern life and the rise of democratic rule in Britain and the West.

Holyoake's great, original idea—and the one for which he is primarily recognized—was that our first duty is to look to the well-being of our fellow citizens in this life, rather than to an imagined life after death. He called his concept Secularism and announced it to the world in 1851.

Holyoake came to the idea of Secularism after enduring hardship, persecution, and imprisonment as a social missionary for capitalist turned reformer Robert Owen and his Socialist utopian movement, the Society of Rational Religionists. After a Christian upbringing, George Holyoake fell into atheism with the imprisonment of a friend for blasphemy and his own arrest for a speech in which he declared he no longer believed in such a thing as a God. Convicted of blasphemy, Holyoake reflected on the conditions of English life during his six months in the Gloucester County Gaol. He came out convinced of the need for a new social order that would release the individual from the grasp of enforced religious doctrine.

Having originally seen Secularism as an alternative to Christianity, Holyoake came to embrace the coexistence of the secular and the religious: "Secularism divides life into what is secular and what is religious and would consign all matters of religion to the sphere of private interests."[2] With separation of state institutions from religious institutions, Secularism would become the universal model for social organization throughout most of the world.

The idea of atheism, Holyoake had realized, was weighed down by a public misconception that in rejecting God, one was left with a devilish alternative of immorality and indecency. He struggled for the next decade to articulate a more acceptable vision. After much reflection, he created the word Secularism. He was acting on principles set out as early as the Greek philosopher Epicurus and as recently as the Enlightenment thinker John Locke, who inscribed a difference between civil society and religious life; the one concerned with "free and peaceable enjoyment of all good things," and the other dedicated to gaining "happiness after this life."

For the word itself, Holyoake drew on the English adjective secular, descended from Late Latin—*saecularis*, "worldly, of an age"—and Old French—*seculier*—to create the new English noun, Secularism. Over the next one hundred and fifty years, extending into the twenty-first century, variations of Secularism would become central to not only how Western countries govern themselves, but of some of the oldest societies of the Eastern world.

After inventing the word Secularism, Holyoake wasn't entirely sure what to do with it. Was it to be an alternative to Christianity, open only to atheists, as some advocated? An ethical creed or ideology setting practical moral standards for daily life? Or a social movement that would recruit thousands—or millions—of adherents? It would take years of conflict among secularists and a slow change in public attitudes for Secularism to emerge in various forms—its most notable variant based on a public sphere free of religious intrusion.

Holyoake's views led him into fierce controversy with Charles Bradlaugh, a young and militant rival who envisioned Secularism as a mechanism for the abolition of religion and the replacement of superstition with rational thought. Holyoake, an indifferent organizer and a diffident speaker, lost the battle to control the secularist movement. But the principles of Secularism and rational rule were being adopted with the decline of religious influence in English law, morality, politics, and society. Bradlaugh became the first avowedly atheist Member of Parliament and founder of the National Secular Society, while Holyoake, his secularist work largely done, became an advocate and historian of the Co-operative movement.

Holyoake married twice, fathered five children—two of whom died at an early age—and led an enormously productive literary life. He popularized Secularism as a radical journalist, author, and tireless lecturer. He wrote for many newspapers, authored 160 books and pamphlets, and was editor of eighteen radical papers. The longest-lived of these was *The Reasoner*, his chief exponent of Secularism between 1846 and 1861. His writing style was eminently Victorian: excessively formal, unduly polite in its arguments, and verbose to an eye-dazzling degree. His appeal to modern readers is limited although there is much that is enjoyable in his use of metaphors and epigrams: "A page of laughter is a better defence against a worthless adversary than a volume of anger."

Biographer Joseph McCabe knew Holyoake during the last years of a long life that spanned the entire reign of Queen Victoria when the British Empire was at its height. "Though weak in voice, well trained in delivery, witty, and never sententious ... his refined and dignified bearing won all who met him," McCabe wrote.[3] "His grave, well-cut features, framed in dark long hair, did much to disarm those who came to hear him retail the 'horrid blasphemies'" of disbelief.

Upwards of one hundred countries now affirm support for Secularism. The United States has functioned as a largely secular state despite a continuing presence of religiosity in its public life; the United Kingdom, secular in many respects, retains an established church with appointed bishops in its House of Lords, religious schools, and a monarch who is head of both the church and the state. Canada, nominally secular, recognizes "the supremacy of God" in its constitution and provides public funding for Roman Catholic schools. Its French-speaking province of Quebec bans wearing of hijabs by public sector workers in positions of authority. British-controlled

India adopted Secularism for its promise of harmony between Hindus and Muslims, a hope that has receded under the long-reigning Modi government. Other countries such as Israel, Turkey, and Indonesia are more ambiguous. Three states that were once secular—Iran, Iraq, and Afghanistan—have enshrined Islam as their official religion.

As demonstrated in recent soundings of public opinion, religious belief is in free fall everywhere in the West. People of no religion (the "nones") account for 52 percent of the population of England and Wales, and one-quarter of the population of the United States and Canada.[4] Only 12 percent of Britons are affiliated with the Church of England, down from 40 percent in 1983. There is almost universal support for Secularism in France, along with the Netherlands, New Zealand, and Australia. China pays lip service to Secularism but uses its atheist ethos to oversee its Christian citizenry and oppress its Muslim minority.

In contrast to these trends, Secularism finds itself in a state of siege in many countries. Christian evangelists are pushing to have their religious ideas enacted into public policy in fields as diverse as health, education, foreign aid, and law. Islamic fundamentalism uses the blunt force of terrorism to attack rival faiths and the infidel idea of Secularism. Secular states must respond to the pressures of twenty-first century migrations and the accommodation of non-secular traditions. I address these challenges in my Epilogue.

I have written this book in the hope it will give readers a greater appreciation for George Holyoake's achievements in widening our horizons and freeing people to seek their own truths. If it also deepens our commitment to defend democratic Secularism—and its philosophical cousin, Humanism—from the challenges ahead, my purpose will be amply fulfilled.

Part I

Reform and Rebellion

George Jacob Holyoake campaigned for Secularism across the United Kingdom (courtesy Sharon Norman).

1

An Inge Street Boy and the Capitalist Who Preached Socialism

> The straggling cottages by the road-side, the dingy hue of every object visible, the murky atmosphere, the paths of cinders and brick-dust, the deep-red glow of furnace fires in the distance, the volumes of dense smoke issuing heavily forth from high toppling chimneys, blackening and obscuring everything around; the glare of distant lights, the ponderous wagons which toiled along the road, laden with clashing rods of iron, or piled with heavy goods—all betokened their rapid approach to the great working town of Birmingham.
> —Charles Dickens, *The Pickwick Papers*, 1836

George Jacob Holyoake enjoyed a more comfortable childhood than most who grew up in England in his time. His working class parents were descended from families of substance in nineteenth century Birmingham, a city that had seen the invention of the steam engine and the launch of one of England's great financial institutions, Lloyds Bank. The family was close and comforting; George's father sober and hard working, his mother loving to her children and faithful to her husband and her God. Their foothold on the ladder of English social life gave them a sense of bearing and belonging. The Holyoakes were determined never to surrender that standing.

Young George Holyoake's father, also George, was a younger son who under the rules of primogeniture could not inherit family property in the nearby community of Selly Oak. An earlier George Holyoake was a solicitor and evidence of his affluence is to be found in the invoice for five pounds—a substantial amount for the times—he sent to the Gough family of Perry Hall for legal services in 1752.[1] There is an account of his purchase of servant's livery in 1739 and a record of a land transaction of George Holyoake, Gentleman, as early as 1730.

Our George's grandfather, Jacob Holyoake, operated a forge on the old River Rea in the early 1800s. He fashioned iron implements an elbow's length away from the miners and blast furnace workers who were building Birmingham's first industries. Jacob trained many a famished farm laborer in flight from a series of brutal winters and chilled summers that devastated the countryside. One night, Jacob Holyoake disappeared after high water washed away his premises and all his possessions. They were few enough in the wake of a partner's lawsuit that left him with reduced means and an uncertain future.

Not until forty years later, in an encounter with "an old artisan" who had shared a house in Manchester with Jacob, did George Holyoake learn of his grandfather's fate. George was told how Jacob, "a powerful, wilful man," knowing his wife and children enjoyed a measure of protection in property the family owned, had slunk away to that city to begin life anew. In due time, having decided to return to Birmingham, he tarried at a hospital while waiting for a coach. Leaning over a low stone wall, deep in conversation with a patient allowed to walk the grounds, he caught an infectious fever and fell ill. Refusing medical assistance, he died.[2]

George's maternal grandfather, Richard Groves, like many Birmingham artisans ran his own business, a buckle making establishment. He provided his family with a comfortable living but lost his life savings when the beneficial "friendly society" to which he had entrusted his funds evaporated as he was about to retire. George inherited the spiral-shaped walking stick that Grandfather Groves had wielded as a symbol of his position as a beadle of the Anglican Church of St. Martin's, a minor functionary who strode at the head of funeral processions. George looked with wonder at the "fine long blue coat, red collar, brass buttons" that set off his grandfather's outfit when they wandered through the church cemetery inspecting gravestones.

George's greatest delight was to accompany the old man to his garden on the Bristol Road, a short distance from the Holyoake home at No. 1 Inge Street. They would set off as early as four o'clock on a midsummer morning. It "seemed a paradise of fruit, flowers, and vegetables."[3] George would light his grandfather's pipe with a "lucifer's match"—a spark from a flint. Richard Groves lost his sight in his old age, as many people did then, and George remembered reading evening prayers for him, his grandfather "bowing his head reverently as I read to him." George knew neither of his grandmothers; he was aware, however, that Grandmother Holyoake, Jacob's wife, died shortly after her husband's disappearance, as much from heartbreak as from any disease. From her, he

1. An Inge Street Boy and the Capitalist Who Preached Socialism 13

had inherited another walking-stick: an inlaid, ivory-headed cane bearing the date 1699.

~~~

It was in the house on Inge Street, on the southern edge of Birmingham but within sight of the spire of St. Martin's, the original parish church of the city, that George Jacob Holyoake was born on April 13, 1817. He was the second of thirteen children and the eldest son of George Holyoake and his wife, Catherine Groves. It was his mother's wish that he be called George after his father; the new arrival's aunts insisted on Jacob, after his grandfather, and so they compromised and he acquired both names.

As a child, George was sent to work alongside his father in the Eagle Foundry but he had a hunger for learning and was diligent in his night school studies at the Birmingham Mechanics' Institute. George tells us that his father conducted himself with great dignity in the forty years he worked there as a skilled whitesmith, filing and polishing white iron and burnished

An 1817 rendering of Inge Street, Birmingham (Birmingham Public Library, Department of Archives and Manuscripts).

steel from six o'clock in the morning until as late as nine o'clock at night. He was a "tall and comely man" with an honest voice, a way of looking at you directly, and one who was not quick to doff his hat to a boss.[4] His skills in metalwork set him a cut above his fellow workers. The foundry's owners, Samuel Smith ("a placid gentleman") and William Hawke ("to whom no workman made any request") treated George's father with respect.

With only a few dozen workers—most Birmingham plants were on the small size—a casual affinity developed between bosses and employees. Mr. Smith sometimes advanced small loans between paydays. Still, the Eagle Foundry paid its workers by piecework at whatever price seemed compatible with the owners' aims. As the workers queued to collect their pay on Saturday nights, they often had little idea how much they'd pocket. Their first task on leaving the Foundry would be to visit the coal shed of Mrs. Gillybrand and buy a barrow load of coal; that is, if they weren't deterred by the convenience of the Fox Tavern.

Of religion, George never heard his father speak a word. "He left all that to mother … she had enough religion for both of them."[5] Perhaps George saw something of himself in his father's disdain of churchly ways. "He had a pagan mind, and his thoughts dwelt on the human side." His mother, especially after his father's death in 1853 at the age of sixty-two, took on what was respectfully referred to as "convictions" and attended faithfully, for the remaining fourteen years of her life, the Wesleyan Church of the Rev. John Angell James, where George spent much time in Sunday School.

Catherine Holyoake had conducted a button-making business before her marriage. She kept it going from a lean-to attached to the Holyoake house, in competition with twenty-five such establishments recorded in *Bissett's Magnificent Guide to Birmingham*. She employed several hands in the task of cutting, grinding, and polishing the horn buttons that she sold from the front door; buttons for long tailcoats, for breeches buttoned at the knee, for shirts and skirts, and for sailors and their bell-bottom trousers. Catherine ordered the cattle horns and hooves from which the buttons were carved, kept the accounts, and collected the money from her customers. She raised eleven children who survived infancy and juggled her days to meet the demands of business and home, a challenge that women of a later century would find equally daunting.

From the profits of his mother's button-making and the wages of his father's foundry job, George and his siblings enjoyed more comforts of living than did most Birmingham children. Their larder in his early years was always well stocked. He remembered stepping from his bedroom and peeking down from the top of the stairs one evening, his eyes catching sight of a roast suckling-pig about to be served to a gaggle of guests.

1. An Inge Street Boy and the Capitalist Who Preached Socialism

George Holyoake was born at a pivotal moment in British history. In the first decade of his life, England was struggling to recover from the economic distress brought on by disruptions in trade during the Napoleonic Wars and the collapse in domestic markets following their end. With Napoleon's defeat at Waterloo on June 15, 1815, the demand for military supplies collapsed, an especially hard blow for the gun-makers of Birmingham whose hand crafted weapons were considered the best in the world. Three hundred thousand soldiers and sailors were dumped into a British labor market that had little demand for their services. The Corn Law of that year restricted the import of grain and bread prices rose steeply in the cities while the countryside struggled with near-famine. The terrible spring of 1816—snow late to melt, rivers in flood, seeding next to impossible—was followed by an equally disastrous summer. Agitators campaigned against the monarchy and riots broke out from Newcastle to Bristol.[6]

Within a few months of George's birth, two events that were to imprint themselves on English history came to pass. On March 4 the British Parliament, terrified at the outbreak of civil unrest, suspended for a year the Habeas Corpus Act, that guarantor of British justice which required accused to be brought promptly before the courts. The authorities could imprison anyone they wished without a trial, for as long as they wished. It was not the first time such a draconian decree had been loosed on England; three times in the past quarter-century Parliament and King, fearful that the country was slipping into armed rebellion, had suspended habeas corpus, banned public meetings, and prosecuted dissidents for sedition.[7] This latest blunt instrument wielded in the interests of maintaining order, failed to forestall the quarrymen and ironworkers who set out on the night of June 9–10, armed with pikes and scythes, to march from Pentrich, Derbyshire to Nottingham to rally support for better wages and working conditions. Slightly comic opera except for its deadly outcome, the incident became known as the Pentrich Revolution, one of the last rebellions to take place on English soil. Oliver, a government agent embedded among the marchers, alerted the authorities and the 15th Regiment of Light Dragoons met the men on the road in pouring rain. Eighty-five were arrested; three were hanged and then beheaded, and thirty transported.

~~~

George Holyoake held tight to his memories of life as an Inge Street boy. Years later, he observed that the house where he was born "still stands, but in a dead street now. The grime of smoke, of decay and comfortlessness, are upon it. Then it was fresh and bright," a world away from the industrial grime of Birmingham.[8] An arbor of oaks and elms stood opposite the Holyoake home, sheltering a hat maker's craftshop. The family felt a natural connection to this small wood. George's aunts had inherited property at Selly Oak, a village just outside Birmingham famous at the time for its hundred-year-old oak tree that stood at the intersection of the Bristol Road and Oak Tree Lane. The family was spoken of as "the Holyoakes of Selly Oak." And so, as with many English names, theirs likely evolved from family associations; in this case in recognition of their Christian faithfulness and their long association with the stout trees that came to symbolize the strength and stability of the English nation.

Inge Street was a minor mark on the map of Birmingham, a city already of more than one hundred thousand people. The street ran but a block between two more important thoroughfares a few hundred yards south of St. Martin's. It was roughly paved, possibly with boulders known as "kidney stones" for the pain they could induce when you had to walk on them. The street, like most in Birmingham, was also smelly and dirty; soiled ashes collected from outhouses overnight were dumped in the street to be cleared away in the morning. Manure from horses pulling carts and wagons fell incessantly. Romping across the stones and into the fields, George saw himself at "the entrance of a sylvan glen," filled with tall red brick houses, vine-covered wooden fences, gray garden sheds and out houses, but most of all gardens—gardens of vegetables, of flowers, and of pear and apple trees.[9] As he grew older he made almost daily crossings of a meadow leading to Lady Well Walk where "more gardens lay, and the well was wide, clear, and deep."[10] His task was to collect a pail of water—purer water than that which flowed from the Holyoake's own well at home. Whenever he looked up, he saw the spire of St. Martin's church.

Alone or with his siblings, George explored every corner of this small world. As the eldest son, it was his job to keep peace between the children and to return them home safely when they ventured out. They bonded closely, a mark of their sharing small rooms, and beds, throughout their childhood. Their parents had little time or energy to lavish them with care; children were still considered, at best, little adults who would be put to work, as George was, at an early age.

At the back of the Holyoake house stood St. John's Church, and next door, at No. 2, lived Mrs. Massey, "a very large old lady" who sold cakes and tarts.[11] At No. 5, sheltered behind green silk curtains, the "wart lady" held forth with exotic cures for everyday maladies. A man George thought looked like God, Mr. Hawksford, a miller, lived close by; opposite was a Mr. Roberts who made his living grinding glass for opticians. Another neighbor, Sally Padmore, "The only old woman I knew in my youth whose kindly voice never changed," nursed the Holyoake children when they were ill.[12] The house George liked most to visit was that of a "plain, busy, rosy faced widow"—he does not say her name—who kept shop in a house with no front window but who sold the best butter in the neighborhood. The lack of a window was probably intentional; there was a tax on windows.[13]

At the top of Inge Street was Hurst Street, a short walk for George to reach the local "dame school," the famously inadequate substitute for the real schools that England failed to provide its children during Holyoake's early years. A housewife, often illiterate, charged a small fee to gather neighborhood children about her, usually in a circle on the floor. It was not much more than rudimentary day care. George would have played games and socialized but received little in the way of instruction. After school he helped his mother in button making; his job was to wind copper wire on a lathe, cut off pieces and rivet them into the buttons. This led to his first real job of soldering handles onto lanterns for a tinsmith. He burned his fingers often but earned up to three shillings and six pence per week, a princely sum for a child and a compelling reason for parents to send their offspring into labor.

George was nine when he convinced his father to let him work with him at the Eagle Foundry. He confesses he was often half asleep as he was dragged up Easy Hill to the Broad Street works, in sight of the Birmingham Canal, before six o'clock in the morning. He learned his father's whitesmithing trade and would work there, small child and gangly youth, for thirteen years. An early accomplishment, at the age of twelve or thirteen, was forging a fire grate as a chimney ornament for his mother. He missed many days because of illness, spending a childhood filled with dire predictions that he had not long to live. At seven or eight, "it was doubtful he should be reared."[14] At twelve, it was said his teens "would try me," a decade later, that the "critical time" was at hand, and that if he lasted to thirty, it would be a remarkable achievement.

Religious influence entered George's life at about the age of eleven when his mother enrolled him in the Sunday School of the Rev. John Angell James at his Wesleyan chapel on Carr's Lane. The pastor gave a public address one night a week. His main point was always his advice to young men to be content in the station and with the lot assigned to them by Providence. James was no less dogmatic in his directives to young women in his flock, writing that their strongest quality was their "gentleness" and that their influence came in "passive power ... the power that draws, rather than drives, and commands by obeying."[15] George spent five years at Carr's Lane "yet save hymns and reading in the Bible, I had learned nothing."[16] He attended a "sand class" where children learned to write by copying figures in the sand. George came out, however, equipped to teach Sunday School to other children. He ventured to several chapels of dissenting faith—Congregational, Unitarian, and Baptist, where he taught Sunday School.

Buckle manufacturing and button making were the kinds of businesses the Industrial Revolution, with its emphasis on factory production, would soon demolish. The Holyoakes encountered economic distress in the late 1820s when factories like John Taylor's, where five hundred employees were mass-producing cloth-covered, gilt, and metal buttons, forced Catherine out of business. Adding to the family's distress, a general downturn in the economy led to cuts in the piecework wages paid to George's father. Only the Holyoakes' strong sense of pride and their capacity to accept whatever privations might be forced on them kept the family going.

For as long as they could remember, the Holyoakes had been respectable citizens and faithful payers of the mandatory tithe to the Anglican Church. When the new rector of St. Martin's, the Rev. Mr. Thomas Mosely, sent his Easter demand of four pence, the notice went unheeded. The next week, a late charge of half a crown was added. George's mother left the bedside of her ill daughter Eliza to hurry to St. Martin's to make the payment. She knew that agents of the church could come to her home armed with a warrant of distraint and seize whatever they liked. Only recently, a bed had been taken from under a sick neighbor. Catherine was kept waiting at the rector's office five hours before anyone would take her money. George and his elder sister Matilda had the sad duty of telling their mother, on her return home, that little Eliza had died. George, then twelve, developed rheumatic fever after attending his sister's funeral, almost fulfilling the dire expectations of a short life. This experience of Christian charity to neighbor would not be lost on him.

～～～

New nostrums of socialism, workers' cooperation, and demands for a widening of the franchise began their incessant seep into British working class thinking. Britain was deep in the Regency period, first under the Prince Regent, son of the insane George III from 1795 to his father's death in 1820, and then through the reign of the Prince as George IV until he died in 1830. George Holyoake would have been scarcely aware of these faint shifts in the social structure of England, but there was one man who understood what was happening and who strove to hasten the day when Englishmen might meet as equals in the economic and social order.

Robert Owen was a man who made good at an early age. He had the rare ability to win the confidence of older, better off men and to win their financing for his projects. Born in the Welsh village of Newtown in 1771, son of a saddler, he endured a variety of life-threatening escapades. Always in a rush, he swallowed a spoonful of boiling flummery (a breakfast meal of flour and water) leaving his stomach "deeply injured in its powers of digestion.... I could not eat and drink as others of my age."[17] At the age of six or seven, he rode a horse across a narrow wooden bridge on the Severn River, collided with a passing cart, and fell unconscious. "How I escaped I know not; but on recovering. I found myself on the footpath of the bridge, the mare standing quietly near me, and I was unhurt."

Owen was an omnivorous reader, devouring *Robinson Crusoe* and *Pilgrim's Progress*. He was sent at the age of ten to live with his brother in London. He worked for a series of drapery retailers, including one with a shop over the London Bridge that served upper class customers. Along with other staff, Robert had to be ready in formal dress, a hairdresser having powdered and curled his hair, before breakfast. These early life experiences taught him the discipline of work, but also gave him a precocious skepticism toward religion:

> The more I heard, read, and reflected, the more I became dissatisfied with Christian, Hindoo, Chinese and Pagan. ... It was with the greatest reluctance that I was compelled to abandon my first and deep-rooted impressions in favour of Christianity. I discovered that all [religions] had been based on the same absurd imagination. Thus I was forced, through seeing the error of their foundation, to abandon all belief in every religion which had been taught to man.[18]

Owen made his way to Manchester where he borrowed one hundred pounds from his brother to enter into a partnership making spinning mules, used to make cotton thread. Successful, he became managing partner of a cotton mill at the age of twenty, then moved on to Scotland where he married the daughter of David Dale, the owner of a large textile mill at New Lanark. Owen and his partners bought the mill in 1799 and set about improving conditions for the workers. He opened a school for their children, instituted an eight-hour day, sold goods at the company store for only slightly above wholesale, and discouraged the heavy drinking that was endemic at the time.

> The evil conditions which I had to contend against were the ignorance, superstition, and consequent immoral conduct and morality of the great majority of the population; the long day's work which they had to undergo; the inferior qualities and high price of everything which they had to purchase for their own use; the bad arrangements in their houses for the rearing and training of their children from their birth and through infancy and childhood; and their prejudice against an English manufacturer becoming a hard taskmaster as they imagined I was going to be, because they saw I was going to adopt what they called new-fangled measures.[19]

Owen submitted a plan for the elimination of poverty to a committee headed by the Archbishop of Canterbury. When Parliament refused to hear him, he organized a series of protest meetings. At the City of London Tavern, the chief site for public gatherings in the capital, Owen addressed an audience on August 14, 1817, that overflowed into the hallways and on the steps. Thousands, he claimed, were turned away. He used the occasion to denounce "all the superstitions [then called religions] which were forced upon different nations over the world."[20] All the London newspapers carried his speech; they had probably been bribed, as Owen bought thirty thousand copies that he sent to leading figures in Britain and Europe. The Post Office was kept so busy it had to hold up other mail for three days.

In a second talk a week later, Owen asked: "Why should so many countless millions of our fellow creatures, through each successive generation, have been the victims of ignorance, of superstition, of mental degradation, and of wretchedness?"[21] He hoped to win people to a rational view of religion: one where the literal truth of the Bible would give way to Christian compassion toward the working poor "who should be treated as human beings and not as the outcasts of society."

Owen's approach to beneficial capitalism attracted support, but his partners did not always approve of his easy ways that cost the company profits. He sold his controlling interest in the New Lanark mill in 1824 for today's equivalent of around £50,000,000, or US$65,000,000, and began writing books in which he attacked religion and preached the virtues of socialism.[22] He conceived the idea of "cooperative communities" where workers could live utopian lives, sharing equally in the product of their labor.

Owen put much of his wealth into establishing a collective community at New Harmony, Indiana, buying the property of a German religious collective.[23] Problems of every sort arose and when it failed, having squandered four-fifths of his capital, he returned to London in 1829. He was still convinced that organized religion was harmful to civilization, and he still believed in the merit of worker-run communities. With George Holyoake about to become a teen-ager, such a message was bound to interest an inquisitive boy who, though firm in his Christian beliefs, would have wondered about the meaning of nature, of God, and of the forces that drove people to act as they did. The Inge Street boy was beginning to think about the man he was going to become, and what he would be able to make of himself.

2

The Roar of the Blast Furnace in a Time of Turmoil

The Eagle Foundry was a noisy, dirty, and demanding place. Working alongside his father, George Holyoake learned to endure its sulphurous stench and the roar of its great coal-fed blast furnace. Molten iron ore oozed with a hiss as it poured forth, a ton to cast a single machine part. The three floors of the Foundry resounded with the forging of bridge girders and street cranes, machine gears and fireplace grates, kitchen ranges and black iron stoves. George toiled near one of the five large windows on his floor. Weak shafts of light penetrated the grime-encrusted glass. A turret atop the building housed a large clock. Above it stood a weather vane whose direction might give clue to the next squall or storm.[1] These were the most formative years of young Holyoake's life, establishing patterns of thought and inquiry that would remain always with him.

When George began work at the Eagle Foundry, the grit and soot accumulated over forty years gave assurance no workman would go home without bearing evidence of his day of labor. The Eagle Foundry was hot and hazardous, to George a place as fearful as it was fascinating, where "the sunshine always seemed apart from us." As he grew to manhood, he would swing the striking hammer for his father at the anvil. George felt he had been "born with steel and books in my blood." He retained vivid memories of his thirteen years at the foundry, from when he started in 1825 at the age of nine, until 1839 when, having reached twenty-two, he sought out a wider world.

> I see now the long, dull foundry yard as I saw it from the window at which I worked. On the right is the little house where the warehouseman lived, who had charge of the premises at night; and on the same side the wagon-way leading to the furnaces, the mills and casting shops. On the left were ramshackle sheds for storing sheet iron. Piles of wrought iron bars lay on the ground. The foundry cart is loading near the stable door, and at the top, through the open gateway, the people are passing, and the distant sunshine falls upon the broad road outside.[2]

George remembered a tall, lean old workman whose hand-made "pliers and tongs were the most perfect of anyone's." He had a daughter, Esther, who worked in the Foundry. She was the only woman in the place, and she had a little shop with its own fireplace where she black-leaded stoves, giving them their final finish before sending them to market. She was tall, like her father, and always ready for work. George never remembered seeing her sit down.[3]

George worked in dangerous surroundings and he had several close calls. One time, working with a steam-driven machine for turning bone buttons, the silk handkerchief he wore around his neck became entangled in the mechanism. Mr. Roberts, the optician neighbor on Inge Street, happened to be present and he heard George's calls for help. He stopped the machine just in time to save the boy from being strangled. The fact he wore a silk handkerchief suggests the comfortable circumstances of the Holyoake family.

The Eagle Foundry was a place of tough justice as well as hard work. George was filled with indignation when a young man, accused of stealing a file, was transported for ten years' exile in Australia. George thought a week's imprisonment would have been sufficient. It was such incidents, he believed, that filled the English workingman with rage and embittered successive generations at the domination of the land-owning aristocracy, the church, the nobility, and the government. By the 1830s, angry voices among the bourgeois-thinking mercantile and rising middle classes were demanding reform. The workingman had no voice in Parliament, and it was time to give him one.

~~~

Never before had a crowd so large been seen in Birmingham. By mid-afternoon on Sunday, May 13, 1832, two hundred thousand men and boys—and a scattering of adventurous women—filled the natural amphitheater on Newhall Hill. It was the culmination of the "Days in May," a torrid two weeks in which rallies across England demanded speedy passage of the Great Reform Bill. In common with other British cities and towns, there was thirst for reform in Birmingham. The demonstrators had come by the thousands from surrounding towns and villages, infiltrating the city through every roadway and alley. They roared their approval when Thomas Attwood, economist and banker and founder of the Birmingham Political Union, called on Parliament to extend the vote to every man who paid taxes and to open the House of Commons to fair representation of all the English people. The mood of the crowd was exultant and George Holyoake's cries of support were among the loudest heard that day.

Holyoake, a "thoughtful and impressionable lad," had watched a week of mounting frenzy from within a few yards of the offices of the Union on Great Charles Street.[4] Growing up in the 1830s—he was fifteen when the "Days of May" broke—George was facing one of England's most tumultuous decades. As young as he was, he had become one of the Union's first members. Now, Parliament was voting on legislation to wipe out the "rotten boroughs" such as Bramber, a hamlet of ninety-seven souls that held two seats in the House of Commons while Birmingham, the world's leading industrial city, had none. The rally, enlivened by the martial airs of two hundred bands and by marchers carrying seven hundred banners, was a hurried substitute for a more reckless march on London. It had been called off at the last minute.

This great demonstration, orchestrated by a coalition of businessmen, manufacturers, and middle and working class representatives, could have happened only in Birmingham. In no other English city was there the accord between workers and their employers that existed here. Unlike Manchester and other cities where textile mills groaned under the mistreatment of thousands of workers, or the Black Country where coal miners toiled underground for a pittance, Birmingham had found a tolerable balance between the owners of its hundreds of mostly small manufactories and the skilled workmen whose ingenuity and reliability were its lifeblood. It was this sense of common interest and shared benefits, however unequally weighed in the interests of employers, that created such unanimity of support for Thomas Attwood and his Birmingham Political Union.

To George Holyoake, Attwood was "The most remarkable Birmingham man of that day.... Royalist and Radical, not remarkable for intellectual strength, but had dignity of presence and a persuasive manner of speaking. A small, rotund man, with fire and purpose, and a ruddy complexion."[5] Few resented the fact his house, The Grove, was one of the finest in Birmingham. Attwood was sincere in his belief in equal representation and expanded manhood suffrage, but his main interest was economic reform. He believed prosperity would be found by abandoning gold coinage as the bedrock of the nation's currency, and instead circulating paper money, lots of it. He recognized that only a reformed Parliament, more receptive to the people's needs, would give consideration to such a radical change.

Two days after the rally, the House of Commons, following much recrimination, passed a third version of the Representation of the People Act. It had the solid backing of the Whig Prime Minister, Lord Earl Grey. London's *Morning Chronicle* reported that the Lord Mayor of London tendered a dinner—"a splendid entertainment"—for Attwood and a blue ribbon list of MPs and assorted reformers. Attwood was hailed for having "upheld and secured the liberties of the people without shedding one drop of blood, and without committing one act of violence."[6]

The House of Lords did what it could to derail passage of the bill. It took a threat from King William IV to pack the upper house with Whigs to convince the Tory majority to allow it to pass. They at last approved it on June 7. Gone were the "rotten boroughs," replaced by 130 new seats. Birmingham was to have two, and the electorate was increased from 400,000 to 650,000 men. But four out of five adult males were still off the voters' rolls. When the reality sank in that the Great Reform Act wasn't so great, further protests were organized around the country. They were put aside when an election was called in December under new electoral rules. The Whigs came back with a comfortable majority and Attwood easily won a Birmingham seat. For a banker, Attwood was a down-to-earth campaigner, according to Holyoake. "He not only kissed the children, he kissed their mothers. At one election, he was reputed to have kissed eight thousand women."[7] Kisses alone would not change who was permitted to vote nor would it lift millions of Englishmen out of poverty or rescue children from fetid factories and pitch-black coal mines. It would take a new mass movement of Chartists, waving a Charter of the People, and many more years of struggle, to bring about universal male suffrage.

The Chartists were the inheritors of the protest movement that had been initiated by Robert Owen with his push for co-operative communities. He began his agitation while still operating the New Lanark textile mill in Scotland. By 1828, his great experiment at New Harmony in America was in failure mode; he blamed the fact "families trained in the individual system, founded as it is upon superstition, have not acquired those moral qualities of forbearance and charity for each other which are necessary to promote full confidence and harmony."[8]

George Holyoake's desire to challenge society had its seeds in what he'd seen in his workplace, buttressed by his reading and the speeches he'd heard at meetings of the Birmingham Political Union. His habit of frequenting chapels and missionary meetings, keen to hear whatever fresh views of the Gospel might be on offer, "led me to attend political assemblies. These sessions, always lively and sometimes riotous, enlarged my views of life and duty, which the religion taught me had hidden from me."[9]

Naïve as he was, George was maturing emotionally as well as physically. His ambition was to be a prizefighter but a lame wrist suffered in his first bout "cut me off from any prospect in the renown of that pursuit." It was just as well, because George, frail as he was, would not have lasted long in an era of bare-knuckle fisticuffs. What other interests did this young man have? Aside from his work and his studies, Holyoake tells us little of his personal life in his four volumes of memoirs. He records some romantic failures, but did he have hobbies? Did he drink or smoke? The answer appears to be yes; he talks of having "a pipe" with his father the day before his father's death, and writes of enjoying the "famous ale of Burton." We assume he would have joined his fellow workers in their "local" public inn, if only to establish his manliness among them.

He was learning that not all men are to be trusted in everyday, practical matters. Phrenology, an old art that swept through Victorian England and had proponents examining head bumps to determine character and intelligence, came to Birmingham in the person of George Combe.[10] He had written a book that sold two hundred thousand copies. Combe was in town to conduct a two-week course in this new "science" and needed an assistant. A friend from the Mechanics' Institute, Frederick Hollick, introduced George to the visitor. George took off his hat, Combe passed his hand over his head, and declared he was "sure that I should suit him well." George was too shy to ask about pay, but he gave up his studies and spent four hours every night for the next fourteen nights handling props for Combe's lectures. On his departure Combe gave George a book on phrenology but offered no pay. A friend inquired why; a letter came back from the phrenologist stating George had "no claim on him and that further, he had done his work imperfectly."

There would be more cheating. A Swiss named Bally who made plaster casts for Combe's customers also engaged George. His pay was to be a free cast of his own head. The day he went to Bally's rooms for the casting, he found the man had absconded to Manchester. Reticence about money proved costly to George when "a portly, respectable-looking gentleman dressed in drab" arrived at his door in the Sandpits.[11] He wanted to know if this was where he could receive lessons in mathematics. George assured him he could, "at a moderate rate," and over the next two weeks he drilled the man in Euclid two hours a day. When he asked for pay, George was told that because he had made "no bargain" at the beginning, he would be paid nothing. The scoundrel left, saying, "Young man, let this be a lesson to you."

In January 1834, George Holyoake enrolled in night classes at the Mechanics' Institute in Birmingham. It was one of many set up throughout the United Kingdom at a time when schools for the general public were rare and costly to attend. He was sixteen. Public-spirited businessmen, recognizing that doing good can be good for business, raised the funds to educate workers in keeping books, reading manuals, and spreading literacy. The fact they were called Mechanics' Institutes reflected the considerable status of the mechanic or artisan—one who worked with tools or machines. They were at the top of the working class hierarchy. George paid three shillings per quarter to attend the Institute's evening classes and use its library, its reading room, and inspect, if he so chose to spend the time, an exhibit devoted to medical models and scientific specimens.

George was determined to make up for the schooling he'd lost while working at the Eagle Foundry. He made rapid progress in his studies, combining mechanical skills with an inventive mind. When he fashioned a set of compasses out of bits of scrap iron, a distinguished visitor to the school—Isaac Pitman, the inventor of shorthand—presented him with a case of mathematical instruments. He thought mechanical employment was far preferable to any other. But for himself, he knew he had to escape the "personal subjection" of the workshop. In September of his first year, George was elected secretary of his class and later, he was appointed to the Committee of Examination, a posting that put him a notch above older students.

George Holyoake entered the Mechanics' Institute as an untutored, unsure, and uneducated boy, although well read in the Bible, classical literature, and the popular press. Holyoake confesses in a memoir that as a youth "Christianity was a very real thing to me."[12] Every evening after work he attended one or another of the churches in his neighborhood—Wesleyan, Congregationalist, Baptist, Unitarian—in search of the key to salvation. On March 30, 1835, he drew up a list of ten things a Christian must believe, starting with "the Bible is true." He added a dozen articles of faith, ranging from "God governs this world by his providence," to "the most acceptable service to God is doing good to men."

Holyoake's faith was challenged when an itinerant preacher, a Mr. Cribbace, showed up in Birmingham. He was "a middle-aged man with copious dark hair, pale, thin face, threadbare dress [and] a half-famished look." He rebuked the churches for their failure to take literally the promise of Christ that "Whatever ye shall ask in My name, that will I do."

Anxious for a better understanding of the sermon, George sought out the preacher at his lodgings. "Is it true that what we ask in faith we shall receive?" George asked. Mr. Cribbace "parried his answer with many words," finally allowing that prayers would be answered "if God thought it for our good." George's heart sank as he heard these words of evasion. To a literal minded boy, they contradicted everything he'd ever heard in church. "I was never again the same Christian I had been before."[13]

George Holyoake's social skills were limited but acceptable for the time; he was polite and showed deference for his superiors. At the Mechanics' Institute, he excelled in every course he took. When he came to realize his intelligence outstripped that of his fellow students and he knew as much or more about his courses than his instructors, his attitude changed. For all his physical frailty, he became self-confident and assertive. He was an effective debater, a compelling writer, and showed a capacity to master all

2. The Roar of the Blast Furnace in a Time of Turmoil 27

branches of mathematics. He also studied grammar and logic and his favorite subject, astronomy. He was so carried away with studies of the stars that every year from 1837 to 1839, he spent three long November nights on the roof of the Eagle Foundry, making notes for the Philosophical Institution on the annual Leonid meteor shower. William Ick sent George one Guinea in 1838, enclosing notes of praise from Institution managers for his "valuable report."[14]

~~~

A young man like George Holyoake, filled with energy and pumped by a high metabolic rate, would have thought about other things than politics. His mind would have turned often to romance or sex and its inevitable consequence, marriage. But shy as he was, he would have had difficulty—despite having grown up with five sisters—in approaching girls. His first experience with an appealing young woman turned into tragedy. He described his pain in his memoir, *Sixty Years of an Agitator's Life*.

> One day when I was eighteen a young Lichfield girl came into my workshop to speak to a relative—a relative by kindness rather by blood as she was kinless. She had a gipsy kind of beauty, but with an instinctive shyness not common to that tribe. As I looked up at her, the sunlight was pouring into the place, The crimson rays seemed to pass through her hands and face.... I had never seen anything like it.... For two years, I sought her company as a lover.[15]

Holyoake admits he was a "very unengaging though not unpersistent suitor." No matter what he said or did, he couldn't entice the girl to accompany him on even a simple stroll. Hopeless, he wrote her to say he would woo her no more, and instead was going to "give myself to learning." Two Sundays later, she arrived at his door and without saying a word, dropped the letter at his feet. He took it as a signal he should never have sent it. Perhaps there was hope, after all. He walked in silence by her side and left her at her cottage door. "I never saw her again until she was dying. I might have won her ... but I had no experience, no skill."[16] George was given an acorn-shaped jewel of china that had belonged to her. He never lost it, nor did he ever look at it.

Holyoake was not the only young Victorian to be dismayed by love. He tells of a girl who was visiting his house when a young friend arrived from London. She later received a crude and vulgar Valentine card, postmarked London, and assumed it was from the friend. "She imagined the Valentine had been meant to deride her, that she had been played with."[17] A second, genuine and respectful card, arrived a few days later. The girl thought both had been sent by George's friend. She returned it. Neither knew that the poor young man had written to the girl's father seeking permission to contact her. The letter, misaddressed, went astray. "The returned Valentine made him hesitate what to do, and he did nothing." Too late it was learned "the mischief-making valentine had been the act of a silly phrenologist who had been a guest in the house."[18]

No more tortuous plots could have been invented by Jane Austen or George Eliot. Both incidents illustrate the conflicted feelings on sexuality that affected many Victorians. It was no myth that some matrons covered the legs of their tables and spoke of such human appendages only as "limbs." Prostitution was considered the biggest social problem of the nineteenth century, partly because it allowed girls and women to escape the authority of their families or employers. Most, however, were driven to prostitution by poverty and clutched at it as their only means of survival. These whores, or "fallen women" as the Victorian euphemism had it, had to be shamed and driven from the streets, exposed as depraved and dangerous. George Holyoake took such prophecy as a warning to all young women of what could befall them.

3

In Which It Is Hard to Change the Mind of a Midlands Man

George Holyoake's view of the world was shaped by his working class origins, his exhausting studies across a range of subjects, and by the contradictions and complexities of Victorian society. His first trips away from home took him to the nearby towns of Worcester, Cheltenham, and Sheffield as an Owenite missionary, and when he was twenty-five he walked the ninety-seven miles from Birmingham to Bristol to visit his imprisoned friend, Charles Southwell. He made his first visit to London in the same year. Holyoake watched with keen interest the rise of the co-operative movement in England; he followed the debate over the 1832 Reform Act, and he was stirred by the fusillades that Robert Owen fired at organized religion. George regarded himself as a Midlands man, emerging from one of the four great sectors of England—the North, the South, London, and the Midlands. But more notably, he was a *Brummie*, a native of Birmingham, whose people spoke not with a common accent, but in variations of dialect according to where in the city they had grown up. Holyoake examined the Birmingham personality and the Midlands mind with a close lens:

> Birmingham being in the heart of the Midlands of England, its people have insularity of character as well as of race. The various nations of invaders who, for more than a thousand years, bestowed on England their malevolent presence, no doubt penetrated more or less to Birmingham. But the British founders and their descendants probably kept substantial occupancy of the interior of the country. Our furious incursionists doubtless left behind them turbulent additions to the population—perpetuating a like spirit along the invaded shores. Thus to this day the coast-land population show energy and unrest of character. The Midlanders have steadier attachment to independence and to ways of their own.[1]

Few foreigners came to Birmingham during Holyoake's youth, which is perhaps why he so mistrusted "all people not English." He is unclear whether this prejudice extended to the Scotch, Welsh and Irish, but his attitude spoke to the narrow lives of most nineteenth century Britons. The Midlands mind, Holyoake would observe, "sees clearly what is before it, and nothing escapes it within its own range but it sees nothing beyond it."[2] It was hard to change the mind of a Midlands man and it would take many years for Holyoake to amend his thinking. Only after traveling to the Continent and to the United States and Canada did he develop an appreciation for the culture and customs of the stranger next door.

The teen-age ironmonger was a careful observer, however, of all that was happening around him. He would have given close attention to Robert Owen's four essays on *Formation of Human Character*. These papers addressed the nature of the working class population, knowledge gained from Owen's operations of mills in Manchester and Scotland. None of this stopped Owen from spending most of his time with members of the upper class. He cultivated MPs, nobles, and royalty, even hosting the future Tsar Nicholas of Russia at New Lanark. Nicholas offered him Russian citizenship if he would bring his ideas for social reform to Russia.

Like all inspired men, Robert Owen was convinced he had the answer to the ills that beset society. He offered a rational approach to religion and a new moral order, free of the superstitions that had oppressed mankind. Despite the failure of his New Harmony project he stood by his scheme for resettlement of workers into new communities of five hundred to three thousand people. Owen had at least one other unfashionable idea: he believed character was formed chiefly by environment; it was a mistake to condemn poverty-stricken, uneducated masses for their dissolute behavior when it was a predictable response to the dire circumstances

Robert Owen inspired George Holyoake with his vision of social, economic, and religious reforms (Pictorial Press Ltd./Alamy).

3. In Which It Is Hard to Change the Mind of a Midlands Man 31

of their lives. Owen's idea, if cast into the modern debate of nurture vs. nature, would land him solidly in the nurture camp.

Holyoake would have applauded Owen's scheme for a National Equitable Labour Exchange. Using a combination of barter and alternative currency, the Exchange issued notes based not on price but on time—the time a worker had spent at his forge or his cotton machine. Owen's intent was to end the tyranny of company stores that kept workers indebted to their masters. Exchange notes were soon circulating widely in London. An Exchange office set up on Gray's Inn Road was crowded from morning to night after its opening on September 17, 1832. Goods were being delivered and gold and silver was being accepted for the purchase of Exchange notes. A second office was opened in December. The scheme might have succeeded, had not Owen been exploited by an avaricious landlord, one William Bromley. He hiked the rent of the Gray's Inn premises beyond what Owen felt the Exchange could afford. The landlord took over the operation and it soon failed.

The failure of the Labour Exchange, a scheme to help workingmen but designed and put into effect by people with no experience of the hardships of a lower class life, was typical of upper class outreach to the laboring classes. Organizations were set up that presumed to speak for workers but those running them understood little of the workingman's problems or hopes. One, the Society for the Diffusion of Useful Knowledge, sent a lecturer to the Birmingham Mechanics' Institution on June 7, 1832.[3]

Alfred Fry's talk enraged the audience for its "loose and indefinite generalities." He endorsed the idea that a workingman could save enough from his wages to take a three-year holiday after nine years of labor. This was a "gratuitous and gross insult," declared a resolution passed at a later meeting. No savings were possible by workers who were paid "less wages than are necessary to procure a sufficient quantity of the coarsest food that is used by human beings." As for spreading useful knowledge, the Society's publications were "ill adapted" for the laboring classes who "have little time for reading elaborate treatises on the sciences, whilst themselves and families are surrounded by poverty and misery."

Many workers in early nineteenth century England could read and write, if only at a primitive level. Some in direst need were to able to get together paper and pen to write to their parish overseers requesting relief. Frances Soundy of Battersea penned the following: "I ham [sic] sorry to say my husband as left me a gain with 3 small children going the fortnight and will not give me one farthen to by them a bit of bred."[4]

Hoping to help workers and to encourage those like Frances Soundy's husband to be more responsible, Robert Owen chose Birmingham for his short-lived national labor union. Working class agitators had been setting up local labor guilds in many English cities, but there was no overall central body. Various laws hampered the formation of unions, particularly one banning the taking of oaths in secret. Unionists had no choice but to swear in secret to uphold their cause; if any word reached their employer they were immediately dismissed. When six Dorsetshire farm laborers later known as the Tolpuddle Martyrs were sentenced to eight years transportation for having their members swear fealty on a solemn oath, protest rallies were raised across the country.

In 1834, Owen stepped up to be Grand Master of a Grand National Consolidated Trades Union. Its formation "caused profound alarm amongst the propertied classes" and in a few weeks half a million members had joined.[5] Once again, the law against the taking of oaths was used to crush union activity. Police in Exeter arrested two Union officers caught carrying cutlasses and masks, and white robes used in the initiation of recruits. By August Union leaders were meeting in London, recording they had met "much more opposition from the employers of industry and from the wealthy portion of the public, as well as from the Government, than its promoters anticipated." They voted to abandon secrecy, become an association of industry and knowledge, and sought a Royal charter.

Robert Owen was a millennialist, believing in a second coming of Jesus Christ that would "make truth known to the many, and enable all to enjoy the endless benefits in practice, which it will assure to mankind."[6] Preparation for this event that Owen believed not far distant, was more important than any trade union activity. A new organization was needed. On May 1, 1835, at a meeting in Charlotte Street in London, with Owen in the chair, the Association of All Classes of All Nations came into being. Its ambitious aim was to "effect an entire change in the character and condition of the human race." It blended reformist Christianity with a radical dose of utopian socialism—a word that had been rarely heard in England. The press and the pulpit put their own name to it—devilism.

It was by chance that George Holyoake first heard Robert Owen extol the virtue of his cooperative communities and the falsity of organized religion. A classmate, John Hornblower, mentioned Robert Owen would be speaking one night in June 1836. George misheard the name, thinking the reference was to Robert Hall, the Nonconformist preacher. Holyoake wasn't disappointed in what he heard, although he was more interested in Owen's social ideas than in his knocks on religion. "His passion was the organization of labour, and to cover the land with self-supporting cities of industry," George wrote of Owen.[7] "Beyond any gentleman of his time, Mr. Owen cared for the friendless, regardless of himself." He found Owen's appeal fresh and compelling and in February 1838, Holyoake joined the All

3. In Which It Is Hard to Change the Mind of a Midlands Man

Nations movement. He had the pleasure of shaking hands and talking with his illustrious leader.

~~~

Birmingham seethed with fresh protests when the gains promised in the Great Reform Act of 1832 turned out to be very limited. The Birmingham Political Union, inactive since Thomas Attwood's election to Parliament, tried again to arouse the population. "Men of Birmingham," a letter from the BPU's new chairman, P.H. Mutz, declared, "we have been long and patiently silent." What had been the result of the Reform Act? "Merchants bankrupt, workmen unemployed, factories deserted; distress and dissatisfaction everywhere present."[8] Further insult had come in the Poor Laws amendment of 1834. It was an act of austerity, designed to reduce the costs of relief by limiting assistance to those willing to go into workhouses where families were separated and men labored at menial tasks. The Holyoakes would have shuddered at the thought of ever having to subject themselves to such humiliation.

A new challenge now arose from the Chartist movement—a People's Charter. It was the brainchild of six members of Parliament and six workingmen. They met in Attwood's office in 1836 and drew up the Charter with a long list of demands: the vote for every man, a secret ballot, payment of MPs, equal constituencies, and annual elections. There were more huge rallies, but Holyoake missed most of them. His job at the Eagle Foundry and his attendance at evening classes at the Mechanics' Institute, along with nights spent observing meteor showers followed by candle-lit studies until two or three o'clock in the morning, had exhausted him. Sleeplessness, nervous strain, and moments of sheer terror led him to a doctor. The diagnosis: Holyoake was having a nervous breakdown. He had to rescue himself from the clamor of the Foundry and the strain of his studies. He had to be alone.

There was only one cure for the contagion of nervous trembling and fearful tremors of mind that had taken hold of George Holyoake: his doctor recommended a long, restorative walking tour, an escape from the pressures of study, work, and the social rebellion raging across the land. In the late summer of 1838, his pocket stuffed with five carefully hoarded pounds, George set out. His destination, by a roundabout route that would take him five weeks, was the Isle of Man.

Holyoake was moving into uncharted territory. It represented both risk and reward in terms of personal experience. Did he worry if he was up to it? Who, beginning a lengthy walk in unfamiliar surroundings, in city or country, has not felt tinges of apprehension and adventure? At a time before railways crossed the land, travelers had the choice of riding coaches or rambling on foot. Armed with a 1780 road map, George followed a circuitous route to his island goal. "Columbus was not more enchanted at seeing new lands than I was at seeing new places."[9] He headed north into Derbyshire, bound for an inn in Matlock where he'd written ahead to engage a room. He was kept waiting until midnight and was offered not a room, but a bench to sleep on. He protested, left, and wandered into a public house "full of wake revelers and a young fiddler playing for dancers." He ended up sharing a bed with a young man but slept on the edge so as not to disturb him. He was pleased to trade some of his copies of *Penny Magazine* for use of the bed. This "left my limited purse undiminished."[10]

George lodged in cottages wherever he could, went without breakfasts, and puzzled over the fact that people often took him for a foreigner. He thought it might be due to his "peculiar voice" or his "freedom of manner and speech." He didn't realize how much his Birmingham accent set him apart from others in the Midlands. He reached Manchester on a Sunday, expressing "no little astonishment at its mills, its buildings, and its incessant streets." He went hunting for Bally, the plaster sculptor who had failed to deliver on his promise to do George's head. He didn't find Bally, but he did encounter Robert Owen, a meeting that reinforced George's commitment to the social ideals of the man he most admired.[11]

Holyoake had an eye for history here, as he did in every place he visited on his tour. He probably passed through St Peter's Field in central Manchester, site of the 1819 Peterloo massacre (named as a riff on the Battle of Waterloo a few years previous), and then but a stretch of land near the city center. What happened in Manchester on August 16, 1819, became legend to Holyoake in England's struggle for equal rights and a representative Parliament. Since childhood, he had heard stories of the fateful day when a peaceful gathering of fifty to sixty thousand people—large numbers of them women, some with their children—were ridden down by cavalry of the 15th Hussars Regiment. The mounted riders—yeomen all—wielded their swords indiscriminately, killing eighteen protesters including four women, and wounding several hundred. In contrast to the tolerance of Birmingham authorities, the Manchester magistrates read the Riot Act despite the absence of any violence. The radical speaker Henry Hunt was hauled from the speaker's podium, arrested, and spent two years in jail. The other great radical of the day, Richard Carlile—whom Holyoake hoped someday to meet—was on the speaker's platform but escaped arrest and made his way back to London. Carlile, who would be jailed seven years for publishing Thomas Paine's works, wrote a searing account of the atrocity in his own paper, *Sherwin's Political Register*. Just as outspoken was *The Morning Chronicle* of London. Its reporter wrote: "Hunt had addressed the multitude for a very short time and all was certainly perfectly peaceable, when a body of cavalry rode up through the crowd, brandishing their drawn swords …

3. In Which It Is Hard to Change the Mind of a Midlands Man   35

and seized Hunt and his associates. Manchester this day has witnessed a scene as few could have expected."[12]

From Manchester Holyoake took an early morning barge boat to Liverpool where he spent "enchanting days" before stepping aboard a small steamer going to the Isle of Man. The weather was bad, an old lady died of fright, and George met the editor of the Manx Herald who invited him to contribute a piece about the Birmingham Mechanics' Institute. "I was paid by a roast chicken and a pint bottle of port wine." It was his first literary sale.

Before going on his walking tour, George had met Eleanor Williams, a clerk in the Unitarian bookshop of James Belcher in Birmingham. Belcher's father had been imprisoned for selling radical political and religious works. Eleanor, or Helen as George called her, was much on his mind as he tramped the back roads of England. In a letter filled with affection, he wrote: "I am much better and I have seen most wondrous things. And my dear one, write to me if possible. Send me word how you have been and depend upon it I shall return to you in good health and spirit."[13] He had, George added, tasted "the famous ale of Burton, passed through Derby, and just now returned from walking and bathing in the splendid Crescent of Burton." Wandering through North Wales, George was asked to help lower a coffin by rope down a mountainside. He had seen where "Nature keeps an outlook on her dominions … hamlets sleeping in their morning beauty [and] the bewitching peace of the sea." It all convinced him that "not even ignorance could suppress the resilient diversity of humanity." One night, George smoked a cigar, his first in bed, hoping it would relax his nerves. He slept longer and better than ever before. He was back in Birmingham in time to resume his studies in the fall.

When George met his future wife at the Unitarian bookstore—he went there often to browse through the books, if not to buy them—he likely felt an instant attraction. He would have been under no compulsion, however, to rush into marriage. Men like George, intelligent, hardworking, and holding steady jobs, had many options—the military, emigration, leisure travel. Whatever they had the disposition or the means to pursue, and the class background to fit into, was out there for them. Helen's position as an unattached woman left her with much narrower choices. It was accepted across all strata of society that the Number One purpose of a woman in life was to get married, to look after a husband and to raise his children. Neither beauty, wealth, nor intelligence would set any young female apart from such expectation. Women needed to marry early, or be consigned to the ranks of spinsterhood, a "redundant woman" dependent for the rest of her life on the goodwill of brothers or uncles.

Even this unsatisfactory fate was not available to Helen, as she had no kin; her parents, farmers in the Kingwinsford district of the West Midlands, were dead, along with her sisters and brothers, if she had any. She must have viewed George as an especially suitable suitor. She lived at the home of Mr. Belcher and it was there George would visit her when he could free himself of his studies. It would have been a careful courtship and George would have made no improper overtures. He found Helen to be intelligent, alert, and with a good sense of humor. He was impressed that she subscribed to *Chambers' Journal*, a serious magazine of history, religion, and science. Christmas came and went and after knowing each other for most of a year, George proposed.

Holyoake was frank with Helen in telling her he was doubtful of the truths taught by organized religion, including the Unitarians, and that he was a member of Robert Owen's All Nations movement. He had, he said, no wish to be married in a church. For couples like he and Helen there was now an alternative to taking wedding vows in front of a minister. For years, the parishes of the Anglican Church had kept records of births, deaths, and marriages. With half the population now following other Protestant religions, their nonconformism left England without an accurate recording of its peoples' vital statistics. To correct this, a general registry office was set up in 1837 and the Birmingham posting went to William Pare, cabinet-maker and upholsterer, who had become a leading political figure in the city.[14]

George admired William Pare, considering him "one of the men of mark" in Birmingham. Pare had helped set up the Birmingham Mechanics' Institute and had been an organizer of the Birmingham Political Union. An Owenite leader, he was now a member of the Town council. It was in Pare's registry office in the handsome new Town Hall on Council House Square (now Victoria Square) that George Holyoake and Eleanor Williams, or Helen as we must remember George called her, were married on March 10, 1839. Pare officiated with "an assuring voice and a genius of enthusiasm" as Mr. Belcher gave away the bride. The newlyweds likely had a reception in an adjoining room, attended by George's family and their mutual friends. Holyoake was happy but he felt resentment that there was no "bright chamber hall or temple to give distinction to the ceremony, only the business office of a Registrar of Deaths, infusing funeral associations into a wedding."[15] He thought the ceremony had been made purposely dull in order to drive people back to the church.

Congratulations to the newlyweds were tempered by politeness. Messages that have survived are absent of romantic allusions. John Watts of Coventry wrote to George: "I see you seated beside your intellectual companion working a problem in mathematics, or giving or receiving after general instruction. Oh, what a delightful contemplation, the imagination may dwell upon it for hours, and the knowledge that such cases are very rare should make the prize more valuable."[16]

From what Holyoake has written of his marriage, it might be assumed he'd been a reader of *The Young Husband's Book*, published two years before his wedding. His views matched those of the author: he must be "industrious and frugal" and prepared to "sacrifice his personal pleasure to the future well-being of his wife and family." As to "matters of little comparative moment like what shall be for dinner" he could let his wife "have her way," but he must remember "she is too delicate and too sensitive of mind to make any decisions for herself at all." George would not have disagreed that in all important things—place of residence, education of children, the principles he is to adopt as to public matters, who he is to have as friends—the decision "must be left solely to the husband." Of sex, the *Young Husband's Book* had little to say. Women were not supposed to enjoy it, and men could conserve vital health by rationing its frequency. Compounding the emotional problems of sex, the appalling ignorance about fundamental sexual functions left couples unequipped to deal with this important aspect of their lives. Lacking birth control information, they relied on such techniques as coitus interruptus ("being careful"), or extended abstinence. Despite this, Victorians had large families and many couples would have led enjoyable sexual lives. Given George's emerging feminist leanings and his wife's relative sophistication, the Holyoakes probably experienced a comfortable intimate relationship.

George left Inge Street and Helen said goodbye to the Belcher household. They rented a cottage in the Sandpits district, an area of mined-out sandstone quarries. There would have been a tiny parlor, a kitchen with a hearth for heat and cooking, and probably only one bedroom. Helen cultivated a small bed of mustard and watercress under their bedroom window. These greens, served with bread, passed as a meal when food was short. Helen could always be counted on to see that every scrap of food was put to good use, having the ability to conjure up meals seemingly out of nothing but forgotten morsels in the pantry.

Holyoake proved himself a traditional husband. "At no time did I inquire of her opinions on theological subjects," but, he adds, "my own opinion was not concealed." He concedes that she had "a way of speaking and writing more compact than mine, by which I was instructed." He had no desire, apparently, to control or censor his wife's thoughts, and he freely admitted he could learn from her. Helen was clearly of a reformist bent of mind, which would have pleased George; he might not have asked his wife her opinion in public affairs, but she held strong views and did not hesitate to express them. Their discussion was at times heated but lacking in rancor. It is said George's mother had raised her children "in the strict puritan manner." It is not clear exactly what this meant. The vengeful spirit of raw Puritanism had long since burned itself out, exhausted after colonization of the New World. In the case of the Holyoakes, the puritan manner likely meant an embrace of piety, hard work, plain living, and an abhorrence of boastfulness. Such were the impressions gained by the time George was into his twenties. Although Holyoake would not always be faithful to these precepts, they would remain embedded in his Midlands mind all his life.

4

Is It Possible to Be Rational About Religion?

The cottage in the Sandpits glowed with candlelight at night, long after George Holyoake's return from work at the Eagle Foundry. He'd arrived home around seven o'clock and washed morosely from a pail set out beside the hearth before heaving himself into a chair at their supper table. Aside from their bed, the table was the most substantial piece of furniture they owned. His plate was seldom filled; perhaps on this occasion Eleanor had managed to obtain a rarely seen shank of lamb. George's duties were wearing him down, and the dirty, monotonous work that consumed his days left little energy to study and improve himself. If he was ever going to better himself, he had to get out of the Foundry. He gave notice he would be leaving in a week. He hoped, utilizing the learning he'd acquired at the Mechanics' Institute, to become a teacher. Freed from the Foundry, he took whatever part-time jobs he could find. He applied for the position of lodge-keeper at the Birmingham Botanical Garden but despite many letters of support, was turned down. His reputation as an independent thinking, somewhat troublesome young man had preceded him.

While Holyoake sought work to meet his daily expenses, he might have pondered what lessons he had learned from the Eagle Foundry and his life so far, and how he might apply them to his future. He would have concluded that workers needed each other. They would have to stand together, whether or not the law permitted it. Things absent in George's life also had their influence on him. There was no padre at the Eagle Foundry and little interest in churchgoing among the men. Not many workingmen were in the pews on Sunday mornings; they'd didn't have the proper dress, they couldn't afford the rental fee some churches charged for pews, and Sunday morning was the only time they could lie in, or recover from a Saturday night of binge drinking.

If Holyoake had been a reader of the *Birmingham Gazette*—and it is very like he was—he would have noted with a mixture of amusement and scorn a front page account on Monday, June 23, 1839, of a meeting of the Birmingham Missionary Society. As English cities again seethed with unrest that summer, the Rev. Richard Spooner was offering reassurance to his fellow clergy: "A man must be blind indeed if he did not see in the signs of the times, amidst much which alarmed and threatened, that great and glorious period which was approaching when all the world would be converted to the true faith of their God."

If there was to be any conversion, Holyoake would have insisted, it would be to Robert Owen's growing All Nations movement. It had celebrated a great Congress in May in Birmingham with a new name, the Universal Community Society of Rational Religionists. Holyoake had helped organize the meeting and he treasured the note from Owen expressing appreciation for the "excellent arrangements" that had been made.

The 1839 Congress directed that the Central Board of the Rational Religionists Society, and the Rational Friendly Society which it absorbed, be set up in Birmingham, along with the offices of its newspaper, *The New Moral World*. It proclaimed that Owen's "reign of truth had now commenced on earth, and would prevail for evermore." The new Rational Society, it was announced, had fifty-three branches operating across England.

The Bishop of Exeter, Dr. Henry Phillpotts, alarmed anew by what he was hearing of Owens's latest machinations, pushed back from his seat in the House of Lords. This High Anglican demanded various Owenites be charged with blasphemy. An inquiry was ordered and magistrates were directed "to make a diligent search for books of a blasphemous and seditious nature."[1] It surprised no one that Dr. Philpotts, who believed church leaders like himself deserved to live on a scale matching that of the nobility, was so insistent in harassing nonconformists like Owen.

Bishop Philpotts was born in Gloucester, where his brother was the local MP and his innkeeper father was a land agent to the Dean of Gloucester Cathedral. Educated at Oxford, he was consecrated Bishop of Exeter in 1831, thus gaining himself a seat in the House of Lords. He engaged in arcane arguments over Church of England baptismal procedures and violently attacked members of the Oxford Movement who were issuing tracts demanding the church return to more Roman ways. He was highly unpopular in his Diocese and knew it but didn't much care. In fact, he was a bigoted Protestant who railed against Catholics and all other ilk who didn't share his interpretation of Anglican doctrine. He was, of course, an

4. Is It Possible to Be Rational About Religion?

opponent of the 1832 Reform Bill and of virtually every progressive thought ever expressed in either House of Parliament.

While the Bishop pressed on the levers of power of church and state, the levers moved very little. The Prime Minister, Lord Melbourne, allowed Robert Owen to present a petition from the Society to young Queen Victoria on June 26. Owen's presence at the court was roundly denounced by the press. *The Worcester Journal* called it "one of the most humiliating events" of recent times, "the sin and shame of national degradation."[2]

Holyoake would have felt a greater shame belonged to Parliament for its refusal to heed a petition from Birmingham's Thomas Attwood, signed with more than a million and a quarter names. It repeated the Chartist demand for votes for all men. As the weather warmed into midsummer, incidents of civil disobedience became more frequent. In Birmingham on Monday, July 15, two men were arrested for carrying placards announcing a protest rally to be held that evening in the Bull Ring, the square adjacent to St. Martin's Church. Around eight o'clock, a band of armed men made their way to the Public Office, setting fire to houses and demolishing shop windows as they went. Holyoake was there to see it all, "if not an actor a sympathizer." He witnessed a soldier chop the nose off a neighbor who stood unarmed, watching the events unfold. George made it home safely, but he and Helen returned at four o'clock in the morning.

George Holyoake and his wife saw soldiers attack civilians in 1832 at the Birmingham Bull Ring protest (courtesy Birmingham Public Library, Department of Archives and Manuscripts).

> I went with my wife, who wished to see whether Mr. Belcher, whose house had been fired, needed aid in his household, as she had great respect for him. Although we alone crossed the Bull Ring, the soldiers rushed at us, and tried to cut me down. I did not like them. Until then I thought the duty of a policeman or soldier was to keep his head, protect the people, and keep the peace except in self-defence.[3]

As a young man of radical bent, Holyoake faced choices that would dictate the course of his life. He was asked to join a secret political society organized by David Urquhart, a Scottish politician who would later introduce the Turkish bath into England. Urquhart's so-called Foreign Affairs Committee, according to Holyoake, was dedicated to cutting off the head of Lord Palmerston, the British foreign minister in the 1830s. Many regarded Palmerston as having betrayed England to Russia. George agreed "somebody's head ought to be cut off" but he declined to sign up. The committee's secretary was a Chartist leader named Warden who instead of beheading Lord Palmerston, severed his own by cutting his throat.

That fall, an exhibition of machinery was organized at the Shakespeare Rooms in New Street. One of George's favorite instructors at the Mechanics' Institute, Daniel Wright, was invited to recommend a student to act as a guide and attendant. He chose George. Daniel Wright, in George's opinion, "was a man immovable in a cause he believed to be just."[4] Wright was a Unitarian and a loyal disciple of Robert Owen. "Mr. Wright gave me the first confidence in living that I ever received." Holyoake's new job paid just enough to put food on the table and gave him the chance to practice greeting high officials. Among the visitors he escorted were Prince Albert and Sir Robert Peel, Home Secretary and a future prime minister. One morning, Daniel Wright came to see how his student was getting on. George met him at the entrance. Wright was shaking hands with Captain Van Burl, the treasurer of the exhibition, as he dropped to the floor. He died on the spot. The student body petitioned that Holyoake be appointed in his place. "In our opinion," they wrote, "there is no individual so well qualified as G.J. Holyoake to succeed our revered and much lamented tutor. We think that he is the only person competent to fill the place."[5] Within months after quitting the Eagle Foundry George Holyoake had found what he wanted to do, and now he had the chance to do it.

Holyoake's thirst for knowledge was matched by his desire to dispense it to others. He understood instinctively how to organize information, synthesize it, and present its key components in easily digestible chunks. His ability at storytelling, honed while giving Sunday School lessons, served him well as he began his new job. His closest friend from the Institute, Frederick Hollick, addressed him in a December letter as "High and Mighty

Secretary of the Mech. Inst., Professor of Mathematics, Chirography, etc., etc." George might have looked at the letter with chagrin and uncertainty. Things were not going as smoothly as he had expected.

Many in the Owenite faction at the Mechanics' Institute, which included believing Christians as well as freethinkers, were not entirely comfortable with yet another radical, especially one as young and assertive as George Holyoake, taking over a prominent posting. George, attracted initially to Robert Owen's teachings of socialism, shared his mentor's criticism of the errors of organized religion. Christian Owenites had not forgotten that Robert Owen had insisted on the right of "all individuals to worship the Supreme Power of the Universe, according to their consciences." Holyoake may have had problems with the parents of some students, or with other teachers or the Board. Frequent flashes of arrogance and self-righteousness would have contributed to his difficulties. He had forgotten his mother's teachings of modesty and self-restraint. Holyoake says nothing of the circumstances of his leaving the Institute, but he was finished there by January 1840. Hollick, now an Owenite Social Missionary in Sheffield, sent his sympathies: "I am exceedingly sorry to hear of your leaving the [Institute], both on account of the treatment you have received and the loss they must have experienced."[6]

It was back to casual jobs. For three months Holyoake gave lessons in a private school, then worked part-time as a bookkeeper for a Venetian blind-maker, Mr. W.B. Pemberton, at a starvation level eight shillings a week plus two meals. He wrote advertisements for a manufacturer and concluded that "to tell the truth about their wares would be the greatest novelty." He tutored unlettered mechanics who had been hired to write technical manuals. Helen was in her first pregnancy and a daughter, Madeline, was born in May. Between jobs, George made himself available to the Birmingham branch of the Rational Religionists. He filled in for T.S. Mackintosh during the Birmingham social missionary's absence and helped in the opening of the socialist District Rational School on Allison Street. He arranged the lease for the Lawrence Street Chapel of the Rationalists and in July he joined the Birmingham District Central board. In August, he was elected president of the Birmingham branch. He applied to the Central Board for appointment as a social missionary when the 1840 Congress assembled in Leeds, but for all his efforts he was passed over for appointment.

Holyoake had thrown his lot in with the Owenites, and he was not to be denied. The Worcester branch, which had no local missionary, invited him to lecture there. His talks were well received, and he was encouraged to apply for the position. "They have in Worcester," he wrote to the Central Board, "an apology for a Mechanics' Institution. They want a real one;

which I think I could soon supply to them."⁷ He was referring to the single room, up a flight of outdoor stairs in Garden Street, that the Owenites had dedicated as their Hall of Science.

Holyoake had clearly won the confidence of the Owenites in Birmingham. Physically unimpressive and lacking a powerful speaking voice, he had nonetheless created a positive impression through his intelligence, honesty, and abundant sincerity. A glowing letter from L.G. Hornblower, secretary of the Birmingham District Board, supported his appointment: "His morals are known to be unimpeachable, while of his mental acquirements much, very much, might be said without doing adequate justice to him."⁸

James Plant, the head of the Worcester branch, sent news of Holyoake's appointment on September 15. "It is with pleasure that I perform my present duty of communicating to you the result of our Special General Meeting."⁹ There was unanimous agreement to hire him at sixteen shillings a week, although not all the required funds had yet been raised. "I thank you for your beautiful letters and for those clever lines." Holyoake was already demonstrating his capacity to communicate and convince, a trait he would employ to good effect throughout his life.

Holyoake left his wife and daughter Madeline in Birmingham and walked each week the twenty-six miles to Worcester. He began each trip confident in how he'd arranged "the order of my intended discourse" but as he walked on "my grasp of the subject seemed weaker."

The topics of George's two Sunday lectures at the "Hall of Science" in Worcester were seldom of a religious nature; astronomy, mathematics, natural science all became familiar subjects to his listeners. As well as lecturing, he ministered to a poverty-ridden assemblage of workers from the foundries and porcelain factories that had made the town famous for the high quality of its tableware.

In Holyoake's first lecture at Worcester, he made clear his support for the socialist cause and his disdain for Christianity's failure to ease the distress of the working class:

> They have toiled, but others have consumed; abundance of their creating surrounds them, and they are left to starve, with the choice only of the gloomy degrading Poor House or the premature grave. Is this right? … Is this Christianity? If the poor man asks for his Political rights, he is told he is too ignorant to have them. He is not too ignorant to toil and starve, but only to obtain redress. The praying of eighteen centuries has only left us without even the sign of a better state.¹⁰

By October, Holyoake's radical political views came to dominate his talks. In one lecture he took aim at "the utter inefficiency of all political reforms as effectual remedies for the evils under which we all labour." Another was titled "What the World Calls Socialism," a talk that he devoted to debunking the false charges of "devilism" aimed at its supporters.

4. Is It Possible to Be Rational About Religion?

Holyoake's sixteen shilling salary didn't go very far. "One advantage was that my family, though it consisted of only three persons, found themselves under favourable circumstances for acquiring the art of economy."[11] To supplement his meager stipend, he taught mathematics at a girls' school as "Mr. Jacobs."

~~~

Eleanor soon tired of George's absence and insisted on joining him in Worcester. Shortly before Christmas, Holyoake, Eleanor, and Madeline took the afternoon train of the Birmingham and Gloucester Railway from Worcester to Cheltenham, a larger and more prosperous West Country town. They rode in a third class carriage and their train skirted the escarpment of the Cotswold Hills where the snow was deep on the ground. They were at a hopeful age, he twenty-three, his face betraying no awareness of the injustices soon to be inflicted on him; she, two years younger, small and timid in appearance, holding a restless infant at her breast. They hunched uncomfortably on the wooden slats of their seat and tried, as far as possible, to wrap themselves in a blanket tired from years of use. It gave them little protection from the swirling snow and chill wind that blew in through the open windows—windows bereft of glass, as befitting the economy at which the railway had sold them passage, a few shillings for their thirty mile journey. He would never forget how "the intense cold wrapped around us like a cloak of ice."[12]

Holyoake was on his way to the spa town of Cheltenham in answer to an invitation to lecture there. His subject would be the merits of socialism and the need for workers to lift themselves, by education and cooperation, out of the dire poverty that gripped millions of Britons. Whether Holyoake realized it, in joining the Rational Religionists he had become part of a faction of emerging dissidents whose fierce loyalty and obedience might in modern times brand them a cult.

It was dark when the train stopped at the railway station a mile outside Cheltenham. With little Madeline wrapped in her mother's arms, George and Eleanor descended carefully from their coach and set out to walk to "a friend's house" where they would spend the night before moving on to their assigned lodgings. The candle-lit shop windows cast a red glare onto the snow-covered ground. Chilled to the bone, they stopped at a public house and "when at last we found a fire we had to wait to thaw before we could begin to speak."[13] Warmed, they trudged on to their destination, a grand house on the Promenade, one of many that in season served as guest houses for the visitors who traveled great distances to bathe in the mineral springs around Cheltenham.

George Holyoake was well aware the place had a reputation as "a fashionable town, a watering, visiting place, where everything is genteel and thin."[14] Its thirty thousand burghers enjoyed gas lights, piped water, sewers, and a dispensary that gave free medicines to the poor. George remarked to his wife that just as the parlors of some prudent housewives "are kept for show and not to sit in," so in Cheltenham "numerous houses are kept to be let, and not to live in."

It was in just such a house they found themselves, sitting on a bench by the kitchen fire from eight o'clock until after midnight without a morsel of food or a drop to drink. The baby was colicky and restless, and Helen was too exhausted to speak. George was sorry he had not followed her advice to procure some food before their arrival. "Buy food?" he'd asked, exasperated. "The people of this fine house will be outraged to see me bring in food." But finally, he spoke up to his host. "We have talked all night about social progress, and if you have no objection we will make some. And if eating be not an irregular thing in your house, we will take some supper."

"I am very sorry to say," his host replied, "we have nothing to offer you."

"Charge me bed and board while we are with you," George pleaded, "but let us have both. You have bread, I suppose?" There was rice bread, and it was toasted and George spread salt butter on it. Needing a drink stronger than "my good host's choice reserve of cold water," George put on his hat and went into the street looking for an all-night public-house. Wandering in the dark, he soon realized he was lost, "not knowing where I stood on the slippery ground, made so by frozen rain on a bedding of snow." He finally succeeded in his errand, but at a grog shop so disreputable as to be "the last place at which I should wish to be found."

These young people, unaware they were part of a generation bent on carrying Britain to its greatest height, would overcome barriers and change society in ways that would reverberate into the twenty-first century. Their legacy of freethought and the pluralism of the secular state, built on principles first expressed in Britain during the Enlightenment, belonged to the future and the future would embrace it.

When George and Eleanor moved on the next day to the home of their designated hosts, George and Harriet Adams, he took time to stock up on loaves and chocolates. Their stay with the Adamses was quite pleasant. George gave his lectures, but he was unsuccessful in collecting expense money. When he returned to Worcester he found himself out twelve shillings. "I felt the want of them for a long time afterwards."

The towns and villages in which George Jacob Holyoake spent the first twenty-five years of his life are clustered together, all reachable on foot within a few hours for a young man of his stamina and determination. Eighteen months on from this first visit to Cheltenham he would walk there to give another lecture. That it would lead to his arrest and trial for blasphemy, and of the upheaval in his life this would cause, he had no forewarning. Cheltenham was, he would write, "the last town I should have selected as the scene of such an occurrence as the one which I have to narrate."[15]

Part II

Dare to Be an Atheist

5

An Honest Answer to a Difficult Question

The Central Board of the Society of Rational Religionists, made up of the most faithful and dedicated followers of Robert Owen, chose Manchester for their 1841 annual meeting. Spring had once again been delayed by foul weather, and only now, well into May, were flowers and ornamental trees coming into bloom. After paying tribute to the workers and their women who died at the Peterloo Massacre in that industrial city, the Board set about its most important business—assigning social missionary contracts for the coming year. When the vacancy in the northern Midlands town of Sheffield came up, George Holyoake, after barely seven months in Worcester, was nominated to fill the post. His work had so impressed the Worcester delegation the Board felt it must agree to his promotion to the more important position.

George Holyoake welcomed the change and went with the praises of the Worcester branch for his strength of character and his persuasive presence: "It is to be hoped that the social, literary, and scientific lectures that have been delivered have done much to diffuse morality and intelligence."[1]

Holyoake's salary was raised to thirty shillings a week. Whether he collected it depended on the generosity of those attending his three Sunday lectures at the Hall of Science on Rockingham Street. He and Helen moved into a cottage at 179 Broomhall Street and he taught fifty children at the Rational Society's local day school. With a territory that stretched from Nottingham to Derby, he walked to nearby towns like Huddersfield to lecture, pocketing the allowance given him for a railway ticket.

Yet Holyoake was troubled by the direction the Rational Religionists were taking. William Galpin, secretary of the Central Board which was now back in London, wrote to Holyoake that that the day would come "when our Society will carry the world before it, or rather our Founder for he alone possesses the true knowledge." But George saw few practical steps being taken to hasten the reaching of that goal.²

A break in Holyoake's routine as teacher and social missionary came with the Sheffield Winter Fair on the last two days of November. He would not have missed the opportunity to mix with townspeople and perhaps gain new adherents. Helen, heavy with pregnancy, would have attended reluctantly if at all. "The pleasure fair had an unusually animating appearance," reported the *Sheffield Independent*, "some of the shows being of an interesting character."³

One of them turned out to be of special interest; George found himself portrayed in a Christmas pantomime as "Jack the Giant-killer." The show was not as interesting as the fair's Abyssinian giraffe, "an animal never seen here before." But it gave him a start to realize he had achieved notoriety as the public face of a small and not very significant faction of sometimes eccentric outcasts.

The Central Board, facing economic pressures due mainly to the costs of the Queenwood project, ordered a clampdown on local expenses. Instruction came from London that the affairs of local branches be controlled from the top; the Central Board called it a system of "elective paternal" management. George complied, but during the winter of 1841–42, his relations with the Rational Society grew fractious and unsettling. He differed with the Central Board on the movement's overall aims, advocating more emphasis on education and less on empty platitudes about socialism. He thought the Board was sacrificing principle to expediency. The Board's Walter Newall wrote to tell Holyoake that "in the peculiar circumstances of this Society, we cannot avoid differing with you in opinion."⁴ A note from Galpin acknowledged "the value of free discussion."⁵

As the winter days shortened, Holyoake taught school five days a week and prepared thoughtful commentaries for his Sunday lectures. His audience clung tightly to the town's traditions, bound by the reputation handed down from Sheffield's Company of Cutlers for the excellence of their knives, razors and axes. Holyoake might have read that an early visitor, Daniel Dafoe, had found "the streets narrow, and the houses dark and black, occasioned by the continued smoke of the forges, which are always at work."⁶ Holyoake would have thought things hadn't changed much over the intervening century.

Holyoake had to deal with quibbles over his salary when his Sunday lectures fell off to one from three, the turnout being insufficient for more than a single session. Helen did her best to make a pleasant home of their little cottage. Madeline was walking and talking, and George and Helen welcomed a sister for her, Eveline Ellen, on a cold morning in January 1842. A young Scottish convert, Thomas Paterson, stayed with the Holyoakes for nine months. George made him his assistant, calling him his "curate." Holyoake wrote pamphlets, one of them on *The Advantages and Disadvantages of Trade Unions.*

~~~

George Holyoake would likely have spent his life as a borderline agnostic if he had not received word of the arrest in Bristol of his friend and Owenite colleague, Charles Southwell. The charge was the most damning accusation the Church of England and civil authorities could level at their critics: blasphemy. Southwell, a Londoner of great wit and charm who had captivated Holyoake from their first meeting in Birmingham, had moved to Bristol and set up an atheist newspaper, the *Oracle of Reason.* It was one of a flurry of radical journals that helped stir revolt against the Christian social order of the nineteenth century.

Southwell had recruited Holyoake as one of a "defiant syndicate of four" in support of the project. A cutting from the *Bristol Times and Mirror* reveals Southwell had been arrested on November 27, 1841, in his shop at 16 Narrow Wine-Street.[7] He had since been "committed to prison for want of bail" on the testimony of one Samuel Rogers, an agent of the magistrates' office. Rogers testified that Southwell had sold him a copy of *The Oracle* and that "the contents of the book [sic] of which the wretched man took pride in announcing himself the author, was one of the most openly blasphemous description, some of the worst passages of which were exposed to view in his window." The reporter for the *Times and Mirror* added his own judgment of the case: "The treadmill is the only antagonist for such a person."

Charles Southwell, three years George's senior, was the youngest of thirty-three children of a London piano maker but the only child of his mother, Fanny, who protected him from the depredations of his siblings. He had been a soldier of fortune in Spain, an actor, the proprietor of a London bookshop catering to buyers of radical titles, and a teller of extravagant anecdotes that made him the center of attention. When his wife Mary died in 1835 Southwell fulfilled her last wish; that her heart be cut out by a surgeon to ensure she was really dead, and that it be used thereafter as an anatomical specimen.

Somehow, Southwell acquired the literary skills to write convincingly of his atheistic views. In his first issue of *The Oracle*, which sold six thousand copies, he promised "All opinions to be set forth in these columns will be anything but palatable to authority." The little sheet caught the attention of church officials and the police. When its fourth issue featured "The Jew Book," a piece that reflected "the coarse tone of which is indicted by its title," they pounced. They could hardly ignore its inflammatory challenge:

5. An Honest Answer to a Difficult Question

> That revoltingly odious Jew production, called BIBLE, has been for ages the idol of all sorts of blockheads, the glory of knaves, the disgust of wise men. It is a history of lust, sodomies, wholesale slaughtering, and horrible depravity; that the vilest parts of all other histories, collected into one monstrous book, could not parallel! Priests tell us that this concentration of abominations was written by a god; all the world believe priests, or they would have rather have thought it the outpourings of some devil![8]

The article attracted no denunciation for its anti-Semitism, widespread among most Christians. But by depicting the Bible as a dirty book, Southwell was striking at the pretensions to respectability of all devout Christians:

> Its heroines are strumpets, an account of whose debaucheries is fit only for the hell of human imagination. It is a book which contains passages so outrageously disgusting and scandalously indecent, that were it not called the word of a god, no modest woman would suffer to allow it to be read in her house.

There was much in the King James version of the Bible that Southwell could have pointed to as containing "horrible depravity." He refers to the Genesis account of "the old drunken Lot, before and after his incestuous intercourse with his own daughters." He could have added that Lot, to save two visiting male angels from homosexual assault, offered his Sodom townsmen his two virgin daughters with permission to "do ye to them as is good in your eyes." Southwell might have noted the Genesis telling of how Abraham, having tied up his son and placed him in burning brush, hovered over him with a knife until God, in a sudden decision, accepted that Abraham's love of the Lord had been sufficiently proven. No sacrifice was needed.

In the Book of Judges, Southwell would have read, the Israelite general Jephthah of Gilead is anxious to defeat a rival Ammonite tribe. He tells God that if he is given victory he will make a sacrifice of the first person he sees on his return home. He achieves the victory "with a very great slaughter" but the first person he encounters coming from his house is his only daughter, who has danced out in joy to greet her father. True to his promise to God, Jephthah—after allowing his daughter to spend two months in the mountains bewailing her virginity—sacrifices her as a "burnt offering."

There were other passages that gave Southwell doubts about the existence of a loving God. As from Deuteronomy: "…in the cities of the nations the Lord your God is giving you as an inheritance, do not leave alive anything that breathes." Or in Numbers: "Now kill all the boys. And kill every woman who has slept with a man, but save for yourselves every girl who has never slept with a man."

One could argue, as probably Southwell and Holyoake did, that the Bible is an entirely human document, reflecting the fears and follies of its writers for their times and the times before them, recording from observation and from fable events that they knew or imagined had taken place.

Holyoake was outraged that his friend had been denied the freedom to express his opinion about these Biblical fables. Distracted and depressed, he gave little thought to the approach of Christmas.[9] Nor did the new baby's arrival take him from work on a speech addressing "The Cruelty and Intolerance of Christianity." Holyoake delivered it on January 9, 1842, a few days before Southwell's trial. He didn't have to know its outcome—a year in jail and a fine of one hundred pounds—to realize his friend's detention had destroyed the last of his faith in Christianity. He began the lecture by reading from Southwell's article. Then he made his fateful declaration of atheism:

> I was born pious, and was nursed in orthodoxy; and have been, till within a very short period of this, a believer in the humanising tendency of Christianity; but the persecution of my friend has been, within these few weeks, the cradle of my doubts and the grave of my religion. My cherished confidence is gone, and my faith is no more.[10]

Holyoake's public assertion of atheism was not entirely well received by fellow Owenites. He alienated more of his flock when he took up editorship of *The Oracle*. His first article appeared in the February 12 issue. "The Great Lama never dies," it averred, "so with the priest of the *Oracle*; Lama succeeds Lama, until the god seems immortal, and as such is worshipped." Holyoake was honing his satirical skills, which would become deadly in future articles. "Read this and mark it well, ye gentlemen of the jury," Holyoake wrote of Southwell's trial, "enlightened and tolerant batch of free and independent Englishmen, whose fathers were stripped, pilloried, and hung up, like dogs, on the same pretence as that for which ye immured Charles Southwell—Look to it!"

Such outright derision led to Holyoake's usefulness being questioned by some of the Rational Religionists. Queenwood, the Owenite communal village in Hampshire needed propping up financially. Holyoake was disgusted when he heard the editor of the *New Moral World* warn: "If you offend people's prejudices, the capitalists will never lend us money." Resentments turned to crisis when complaints were made that the Owenite Halls of Science were passing the collection plate on Sundays, a privilege reserved by law to the nation's churches. Holyoake declined to go along with their claim of being a "congregation of Protestants called Rational Religionists" gathered for "religious worship." He refused to sign a public oath of adherence to the Protestant faith and wrote a pamphlet charging the Central Board with expediency over principle. Secretary Galpin wrote Holyoake to tell him he hadn't yet read it, but that if Holyoake's charges were true, "the executive should be dismissed at the Congress."[11] Instead, came a circular giving three months' notice of dismissal to all the missionaries, unless they were reappointed at the next Congress scheduled for May.

Distressed over Charles Southwell's jailing, firm in his newfound support for atheism, uncertain of much longer having a job, Holyoake decamped from Sheffield, early in May. He took his family to his sister Matilda's home in Birmingham and on May 22 he began the ninety-mile walk to visit Southwell in Bristol. He'd written to the Cheltenham branch of the Society to offer a lecture; he had hopes of replenishing his purse with donations collected at the talk.

When George Holyoake walked into Cheltenham, he noticed that placards had been put about the town, on posts and in shop windows, announcing his lecture on "Home Colonization as a Means of Superseding Poor Laws and Emigration." It offered an alternative to the perilous voyage to the colonies his countrymen were making to escape a life of poverty. He went straight to the terraced home of George and Harriet Adams on King Street, with whom he and Helen had stayed on their first visit in 1840. They welcomed him, fed him, and put him to bed in a spare room. When they went to the Mechanics' Institute on the evening of Tuesday, May 24, 1842, the three expected nothing more than the usual gathering of socialist-minded freethinkers, offering up a few precious hours to hear this interesting young man and his theories on how to make England a better place.

Holyoake scrutinized the faces of the hundred or so workingmen, an occasional woman among them, he found waiting for him. They were a lean and eager lot, mostly young, from the town's varied industries—brewery employees, tanners, shoemakers, and attendants at the numerous salt baths of Cheltenham Spa.[12]

Amid this sympathetic crowd, Holyoake harbored a disturbing sense of apprehension. The influential local Anglican cleric, the Rev. Francis Close, had made clear his indignation toward anyone ministering on behalf of Robert Owen and his Rational Religionists. The Reverend Close, following the example of the Bishop of Exeter, had railed against the Owenites as "blasphemous and ungodly," reminding his parishioners that blasphemy against the Lord, as Southwell had learned, was a serious crime under the laws of England.

It was nine o'clock when George Holyoake rose to speak. It was his intention to create no controversy nor cause upset of any kind. Still but twenty-six years of age, he neither looked nor sounded like the radical atheist he was rumored to be, bent on challenging the triumvirate of clergy, nobility, and manufacturers who saw it their duty to maintain an orderly society in Gloucestershire. Holyoake's face bore the pallor of the Birmingham foundry and his thick, dark hair, falling in a tangle almost to his shoulders, gave him the appearance of a character out of a Jane Austen novel.

His frail voice, high-pitched and barely discernible at the back of the room, seemed ill-fitted for the calling he had chosen. Holyoake might, it was feared, soon exhaust himself of breath even though the doors had been opened to allow fresh spring air to dilute the hall's odor of sweat and grime. For all that, he had an instinctive ability to connect with his audience. They laughed at his humorous asides and listened quietly when he scourged the country's ruling class for catering to landowners while neglecting the workers.

The time had come, Holyoake argued, for England to stop sloughing off to the colonies its excess of labor from farm and factory. Instead, the tired workers like those who sat astride the wooden benches of the Mechanics' Institute should join in building their own Socialist communities, in the fashion of New Harmony in America. Holyoake struggled on for more than an hour. He praised the flock building a Socialist community at Queenwood in the county of Hampshire. He jabbed at a Parliament that refused the vote to all workingmen. He said not a word about religion. When he took his last sip of water and sat down, the chairman of the meeting moved to the front of the stage. He invited those present to put to the speaker "relevant questions or offer what objections they consider useful."[13] By now, the hall was damp with sweat and the cool night air. For a long and lingering moment, the benches were silent. Finally, someone identified only as a Mr. Maitland, a "sort of local preacher" and a proud temperance worker, rose to his feet. A man of obviously stern demeanor, he likely thrust his jaw forward as he spoke, signaling exasperation at the need to challenge the speaker. He began not with a question but with a complaint: Although Holyoake had been careful to tell the audience of their duty to man, he had said nothing of their duty to God.

Did Mr. Holyoake, Maitland asked, not "believe we should have churches and chapels in our community?" The question, clearly loaded and most probably planted, left everyone on the benches tittering nervously, their faces a mix of perplexity and amusement. George Holyoake would have understood this might be the trap into which the Reverend Close would be pleased to see him stumble. The giving of an honest answer, he may have thought, could be dangerous. His problem was that he knew not what else to give.

Holyoake stood pondering the question. For his exact answer, we must rely on Holyoake's recollections and on the not entirely accurate reports that appeared in local papers. There is no doubt he went at it head-on:

> I do not desire to have religion mixed up with an economical subject, but as Mr. Maitland has introduced questions in reference to religion I will answer him frankly. Our national debt already hangs like a millstone round the poor man's neck, and our national church and general religious institutions cost us, upon accredited

computation, about twenty million [pounds] annually. Worship being thus expensive, I appeal to your heads and your pockets whether we are not too poor to have a God? If poor men cost the state as much, they would be put like [retired] officers upon half-pay, and while our distress lasts I think it would be wise to do the same thing with [the] deity. Thus far I object, as a matter of political economy, to build chapels in [our] communities. If others want them they have themselves to please, but I, not being religious, cannot propose them.[14]

George Holyoake knew he was by now beyond any hope of recovery but he had more to say:

Morality I regard, but I do not believe there is such a thing as a God. Religion in my opinion has ever poisoned the fountain-springs of morality. The pulpit says "Search the Scriptures," and they who are thus trepanned get imprisoned in Bristol jail, like my bosom friend Mr. Southwell. For myself, I shudder at the thought of religion. I flee the Bible as a viper, and revolt at the touch of a Christian.[15]

A smattering of applause, growing as more added their approval, spread through the crowd. According to George Holyoake's recollection, "Perhaps this reply was indecorous, but it was nothing more, and as it was delivered in a tone of conversational freedom, it produced only quiet amusement on the meeting." He would later have cause to reflect more soberly on what he had done. "This unforeseen incident brought consequences which affected all my future life," he admitted in a memoir. "Had I prohibited discussion, I should have saved myself a world of trouble. But I should have been dishonest to the hearer, and have known myself to be so. Free discussion has its penalties as well as its advantages."[16]

The few steps it took George Holyoake to reach the floor of the meeting hall gave him little time to catch his breath. A small crowd clustered around him while most of the audience drifted away into the spring night. A favorable comment, a pat on the back and George Adams and his wife took Holyoake back to their home. George was up at dawn to begin his long walk to Bristol. He was most likely clad in light trousers and wore sturdy walking boots, carrying a satchel and his jacket on his arm. A black slouch hat would have protected him from sun and rain. He probably experienced both. We have no knowledge of where he stopped overnight, but by Thursday afternoon he was in Bristol.

Over the next two days, Holyoake visited Southwell at the Bristol jail on Cumberland Road. They would have talked mostly about *The Oracle*, with Southwell expressing his satisfaction with George's articles. He doubtless warned George to be careful, a caution he repeated in a letter he sent later: "I am not without hope that the authorities will soon see the folly of meddling with the press, but you will do well to prepare for the worst."[17]

Holyoake would not have given a lot of thought to his stopover in Cheltenham; he preferred to forget the fuss about the question that ended the meeting. That changed when he read the latest issue of the *Cheltenham Chronicle* that he perhaps picked up from a newsagent. He discovered a short article headed ATHEISM AND BLASPHEMY:

> On Tuesday evening last a person named Holyoake from Manchester delivered a lecture on socialism (or, as it has been more appropriately named, devilism) at the Mechanics' Institution…. He impiously remarked that if there was [a God] he would have the deity served the same as the Government treated subalterns by placing him upon half-pay. With many similar blasphemous and awful remarks, which we cannot sully our columns by repeating, the poor misguided wretch continued to address the audience. To their lasting shame be it spoken that a considerable portion of the company applauded the miscreant during the time he was giving utterance to these profane opinions.[18]

The article went on to call Holyoake a "monster" and claimed the newspaper had three employees at the meeting who would testify to what he had said. Appended to it was an editor's note: "We therefore hope those in authority will not suffer the matter to rest here, but that some steps will immediately be taken to prevent any further publicity to such diabolical sentiments."

Holyoake immediately made up his mind to return to Cheltenham. He intended to hold another public meeting and justify himself to the town. "Foot-sore and weary—for the journey was more than thirty miles, and the day very hot—I reached Cheltenham on the 1st of June, and proceeded as privately as a 'monster' could to my friends the Adamses."[19] He had no doubt the Rev. Francis Close had his hand in all this. The *Cheltenham Chronicle* appeared ever ready to do his bidding, which included attacks on the Vicar's favorite targets—alcohol, tobacco, horse racing, and theatrical amusements.[20] When Holyoake told George Adams he wanted to speak again at the Mechanics' Institute, he learned the Chartist Society had already rented the hall. "I being a friend of theirs, they gave up their room to me. It was soon nosed about that I was actually speaking at a public meeting in the town."

Holyoake remembers he "slid like sleep into the meeting, lest the police should prevent me from addressing it." The police revealed themselves only after he'd been talking for nearly an hour. "Superintendent Russell came in with about a dozen men, who were arranged on each side of the door, and their glazed hats formed a brilliant, but a dubious background for a meeting on Free Discussion. I spoke an hour after they came in. So rare an audience was not to be thrown away, and I thought we might convert some of them."[21] That was not to be, and at the end of the meeting Holyoake was arrested and charged with blasphemy. He asked the arresting officer if he had a warrant and was told it wasn't necessary. Many from the audience joined the procession as Holyoake was led to the police station. He was

5. An Honest Answer to a Difficult Question

put in a small, filthy cell. "That night the plank bed in the cell was unpleasant," Holyoake would recall, "and more so the tipsy and turbulent inmates there."[22] It was all very well for Holyoake to make light of his confinement, but he knew that an enormous number of deaths occurred in England's prisons. Otherwise law-abiding citizens had been jailed for nothing more than their opinions. They suffered the consequences of disease, malnutrition, illnesses of body and mind, and early death.

A squad of three magistrates, two of them clergymen, awaited Holyoake's appearance the next morning. The Rev. Dr. Newell chaired the panel, supported by two lay magistrates, a Mr. R. Capper, Esq., and one J. Overbury, Esq. Neither had a legal background. Holyoake thought Newell at least "ought to have had the pride, if not the decency, to have kept away."[23] He protested his arrest without a warrant. Mr. Capper had a ready response: "We refuse to hold an argument with a man professing the abominable principle of denying the existence of a Supreme Being," The prosecutor, a Mr. Bubb, described by Holyoake as "a particularly gross, furious, squab-built, vulgar person," called two witnesses, both employees of the *Chronicle*.

The first, William Henry Pearce, could only say he'd heard Holyoake speak the same infamous words as were reported in the *Chronicle*. The second, James Bartram, a printer at the *Chronicle*, had nothing of consequence to add. The magistrates deemed the evidence sufficient to commit the prisoner for trial. Mr. Overlay thought him guilty: "Your attempt to propagate the infamous sentiment that there is no God, is calculated to produce disorder and confusion, and is a breach of the peace."[24] Such was justice, Cheltenham style.

Holyoake was offered release on his own recognizance at a surety of one hundred pounds, supported by two others who would each post to the value of fifty pounds. An excuse was found to reject one of the offers that were made, and Holyoake was taken in handcuffs back to his cell. He was put under the care of the police surgeon, a Mr. Pinching, who subjected him not to a medical examination, but to a religious quiz. "Did I believe in Jesus Christ," Pinching demanded to know. After a chorus of questions that Holyoake was given no chance to answer, he called for a halt. "Stop, stop, Sir! Unless you converse with me upon equal terms I shall not answer you." The police doctor dedicated to the health of his charges hurled a final insult: "I am only sorry the day is gone by when we could send you to the stake instead of to Gloucester gaol."[25]

The police had planned to make Holyoake walk the nine miles to the Gloucester prison to await trial at the Quarter Sessions. He would have made a fitting public spectacle, hampered by handcuffs and guarded by two policemen. But the day was unseasonably hot, Holyoake's handcuffs chafed his wrists, and he pleaded for a looser pair. His wish was granted. He was saved from the embarrassing trudge when two friends came forward to pay his train fare and that of his escorts. Holyoake rode to prison in the comfort of a railway coach, its passengers no doubt staring at him in wonderment. "I had ample time to think of all this as I sat on the edge of my cell bed during the first night in Gloucester Gaol. The lice I observed creeping about the blanket prevented me from lying down."[26]

6

The Lure of London and a Trial by Tyranny

The pursuit of disbelief in Cheltenham did not end with the arrest of George Holyoake. At a meeting called to protest the questionable procedures used in Holyoake's arrest, George Adams passed among the crowd selling copies of *The Oracle*. He'd sold only a few copies when he was arrested and taken to the police station. Harriet Adams went on with the sales, a baby slung on one hip as she waved copies of the paper. She was arrested and held overnight, while her four other children shifted for themselves at home. Neighbors were indignant when they found the children alone. The charge against Mrs. Adams was dropped, and George Adams was released on bail.

The protest meeting had some success. A petition was sent to the Home Secretary, Sir James Graham. He spoke in the House of Commons of "grave irregularities" surrounding Holyoake's arrest. A bill that had lain untended on the order paper for months was brought forward and promptly passed. It listed eighteen offenses, including those relating to "speculative opinion," that were to go to the Assizes rather than be heard by justices of the peace at the Quarterly Sessions. In Holyoake's case, this ensured he would not be tried by those who had already dealt summarily with him at the time of his arrest. It gave him at least a glimmer of hope that more impartial judges might recognize his right to free speech. Sixteen days dragged by before Holyoake obtained bail on June 18. He had orders to be back in Gloucester for the Assizes opening August 6. He returned to Birmingham for a brief family visit and then made his way to London,

Holyoake walked most of the way although his arrival on an early July Saturday evening by way of Woburn Place suggests he may have taken the train to Euston Station, opened only five years before as the terminus of the London and Birmingham Railway. He would have walked out under the large arch over the station entrance, and was looking forward to a few weeks of respite. It would give him time to ponder how he would defend himself when next he stood before the bar of British justice.

~~~

London in 1842 was the largest city in the world, populated by almost two million people. It was twice the size of Paris and almost seven times bigger than New York. Sprawling, dirty from the coal dust of thousands of hearths, smelly from the human waste and garbage that was everywhere spread about, its mass of humanity lived mean and mostly short lives. George Holyoake had time for hardly a glance toward those for whom he spoke with the greatest conviction—the abject poor who suffered violence and abuse in the slums of the east end and other foul parts of "darkest London." Having poured into London seeking work, most found themselves caught up in a grim and wretched existence.

Henry Mayhew, the journalist who would make a name for himself recording their deplorable circumstances, found children emptying buckets of waste into open sewers in the streets; in one district one in four infants died before their first birthday. Dozens of people were crowded into squalid rooms in large houses built on what had been Thames River swampland. Landlords ignored the decay of their buildings and houses often collapsed, killing their occupants.

Holyoake would have been aware that a privileged few, such as the fabulously rich Grosvenor family that lived for more than a century at Grosvenor House in Park Lane and the Cadogans who held title to ninety acres in Kensington and Chelsea, enjoyed the luxuries of wealth derived mainly from rent of their land. Their ninety-nine-year leases kept their properties within the family while yielding the revenues to sustain an opulent lifestyle.[1]

Holyoake had never before been to London and for all its filth and poverty, he thought it an "enchanted city." He was suddenly a celebrated figure among the freethinkers, most of them Owenites, and assorted other pursuers of radical causes. His mistreatment at the hands of the authorities had taken up much space in the radical press, especially the *Weekly Dispatch*.

Holyoake spent his first night in London in a Lambeth greenhouse with a friend, Malthus Q. Ryall. Together, they plotted the defense Holyoake would present when he went on trial in Gloucester. "Morning had long broken before we lay down on the benches to sleep." One of the first new acquaintances Holyoake made that day was Richard Carlile, the freethought publisher and writer whose many convictions made him, Holyoake thought, the most persecuted man in England. Holyoake's accounts of their meeting differ. In his biography of Carlile, *The Life and*

6. The Lure of London and a Trial by Tyranny

Character of Richard Carlile, Holyoake says he found an invitation to tea from Carlile when he stopped on his first night in London at the office of the *Oracle of Reason*. In *Sixty Years of an Agitator's Life*, Holyoake says he met Carlile on Sunday when a friend introduced him to this "short, thick gentleman with piercing eyes." They supposedly met up at Blackfriars Bridge, a poorly built stone span on the Thames River that seemed always under repair. However memory might have failed Holyoake, he thought of Carlile as an almost mythic figure. Each possessed an unquenchable thirst for freedom and Carlile, forty-two when they met, would become both a mentor and a hero to George.

Carlile's lifelong crusade for freedom of the press and universal suffrage had earned him almost ten years of imprisonment. The son of a shoemaker, he took up the tinsmith trade until being radicalized in 1816 when his wages were cut and he became a witness to England's widespread poverty. His first conviction for blasphemy came in 1819 when he was sentenced to three years for having published Tom Paine's *The Rights of Man* and the *Age of Reason* (which criticized the Anglican Church) in his own paper, *The Republican*. He helped distribute the radical weekly *Black Dwarf*, and narrowly escaped the Peterloo Massacre in Manchester when the 15th Hussars attacked the crowd as he was about to speak. He leaped from the speaker's platform, found a stage headed for London, and published the first account of the assault. "Horrid Massacres at Manchester," blared the headline in Carlisle's paper. Another of Carlile's offenses was to publish the first book on birth control in England, *Every Woman's Book*.

Carlile had spent most of his life wobbling between atheism and a suspicion that Christian morals were worthy of emulation. When Holyoake met Carlile he heard him express belief in "a power in nature superior to my comprehension." He invited Holyoake to hear him lecture that night on "a new scientific interpretation of the Scripture." Holyoake went, and took part in the discussion, having first warned Carlile that no argument would ever convince him that any "theologic, astronomic, or miraculous mode of proving Scriptural doctrine could ever be made ... intelligible."

Holyoake attended a session of the House of Commons and was captivated with the atmosphere of this hallowed place and the spectacle of England's leading men debating affairs of state from the benches of a crowded and noisy hall. He watched Sir Robert Peel, in his second term as prime minister, best his Whig opponents in debate, and receive congratulations for having taken steps to make London more law-abiding by establishment of a Metropolitan Police Service. He heard John Arthur Roebuck, the MP for Bath, speak in favor of the bill that would allow Holyoake to be tried at the Assizes. Holyoake spoke at the Rotunda on Blackfriars Road, where Carlile had converted several buildings into a meeting hall. Events there were said to have been "attended by all the public men of note out of parliament."[2]

Reluctantly, Holyoake hastened back to Birmingham in time to see his wife and children before his trial. He stayed only a few days before moving on to Gloucester, leaving Helen dependent on the ten shillings a week promised by the Anti-Persecution Union. "It was a bright summer afternoon when I set out alone … to proceed to the Gloucester Assizes. It was not in my power to leave any provision for those I left behind. My little daughter, Madeline, ran from her mother's knee to the door, when she found I had gone, and called after me down the street. Her sweet clear voice arrested me. I looked back and saw her dark eyes gleaming."[3]

Historic plaque remembering George Holyoake, unveiled by the National Secular Society in London, 2018 (courtesy Robert Forder).

The walk from Birmingham, a familiar route for Holyoake, led him up the Lickey Hills south of the city, and once through its scenic vales, down onto grasslands and meadows edged by stout hedgerows of oak and elm trees. He arrived in Gloucester on the second day of his walk, the day before of the opening of the Assizes. He took a room at the Ten Bells public house on Westgate Street, an establishment catering to the less privileged of travelers.

Holyoake was not alone in standing against the charge he faced. He had many supporters, locally and in London. "Mr. Carlile came down to Gloucester and remained all the ten days the Assizes lasted," Holyoake would remember. Another visitor was Knight Hunt, an experienced reporter hired by the Anti-Persecution Union to make a record of the trial. At times, his room became "as crowded as a convention."

A local sympathizer, Mrs. Chichester, sent Holyoake wine and birds—quail and songbirds of various species—delicacies familiar only to the English upper class. Holyoake had a habit of responding to good fortune and bad with the same lighthearted banter or exaggerated anecdotes. Tongue in check, he remembered how the delivery of these delicacies was

6. The Lure of London and a Trial by Tyranny

put in the hands of a Mr. Fry of Birmingham, editor of a protest sheet, the *Communist Apostle*. Fry, according to Holyoake, was "A practical man ... being as a teetotaller he drank all the wine himself, and being a vegetarian, he ate the birds."[4] The only item confirmed to reach its designated recipient was a bottle of raspberry vinegar sent by Mrs. Chichester to Holyoake on the morning of the trial. It was to quench his thirst while speaking, and he would need it before the day was done.

When the presiding judge, Mr. Justice Thomas Erskine, learned that Holyoake intended to defend himself, he moved the case to the bottom of the court calendar, causing the Summer Assizes to run into a second week. Holyoake delivered himself into the authority of the court on Monday morning, August 14, 1842. It was a short walk along Westgate Street to the Shire Hall, an opportunity to observe the handsome Greek portico that gave the building its commanding presence. He took note of the heavy traffic from the Birmingham and Gloucester Railway station and from ships tied up on the Severn River or the Gloucester Canal.[5]

Holyoake had paid close attention as the court worked its way through a docket of miscellaneous crimes during its first week: John Troughton, for theft of a silver spoon, transportation (shipment to Tasmania or elsewhere) for seven years; Sarah Gibbs, having stolen sixty yards of nets, transported for ten years; William Garroway, an illiterate laborer, charged with theft of coins and a head of mutton, transported for life to Norfolk island. Holyoake was stunned and disgusted when Garroway, trained in obeisance, could only answer, "Thankee, my Lord."

Holyoake had prepared diligently his defense against the charge of blasphemy. He'd studied accounts of the multitude of freethinkers, atheists, and assorted rebels who had been tried under a common law embedded in English jurisprudence since 1676. He examined recent cases: that of Charles Southwell; Edward Moxon's 1841 conviction for publishing Percy Bysshe Shelley's *Queen Mab*; Henry Heatherington's condemnation for a like offense; Richard Carlile's multiple convictions for such transgressions as publishing Thomas Paine's *The Rights of Man*. The common denominator in these blasphemy cases, Holyoake knew, was their offense to the Church of England, ergo their guilt by common law, a stark example of religious dictate of public practices.[6]

Holyoake arrived at the Shire Hall in the company of Richard Carlile. They had breakfasted on beaten eggs before setting out from the Ten Bells Inn. A porter followed them, lugging a stout chest that Holyoake had shipped from Birmingham. It held a trove of books, pamphlets, newspapers, notepads and other paraphernalia. Holyoake took a seat close to the prisoner's dock and by ten o'clock the courtroom was full. According to one observer, "Country gentry, ladies, and clergymen mingled with sobre groups of Chartist and Socialist workers, and sipped their wine and nibbled their cakes as the long hours passed."[7] Many were anxious to see the object of their derision dealt with in the manner he deserved by judge and jury.

~~~

The court had first to deal with George Adams, his charge of publishing a blasphemy—selling the *Oracle of Reason*—having been held over from Cheltenham. The barrister defending him, Mr. Thompson, called several character witnesses but Mr. Justice Erskine saw no merit in their testimony. Such evidence would count in a case of robbery but "in extenuation of a religious offence it was of no service." Pleading for a light sentence, Adams's lawyer said the accused felt "contrition" for what he'd done. Holyoake couldn't let that go by. He told Adams, in a voice loud enough to be heard by the court, "Don't permit him to do that unless you are really contrite."[8] Adams promptly refuted what Thompson had said, and Mr. Justice Erskine set his sentencing over to the end of Holyoake's trial.

When George Holyoake's name was called the turnkey in charge of prisoners, Mr. Ogden, directed him to the prisoner's dock. "Do not be in a hurry," George told him. "First, hand me my books." This was not the usual behavior of a prisoner at the bar. The turnkey looked at the chest resting on the floor. Holyoake describes him as stout, surly, imperious, and pock-marked. "You can't have that box here," he told George, "go to the bar and plead."[9] Holyoake insisted, and when Ogden hauled up the chest, George asked Mr. Justice Erskine for a table. He was told to use a ledge beside the dock. Twenty minutes later, having spread his papers and books as if he were in charge of "a young bookseller's stall," Holyoake turned and bowed to the court. A barrister described Holyoake as "a wretched-looking creature, scarcely emerging from boyhood, whose wiry and disheveled hair, a lip unconscious of the razor's edge, and dingy looks, gave him the appearance of a low German student."[10]

The clerk read the charge: On May 24, 1842, Holyoake, a laborer, being a "wicked, malicious and evil-disposed person," had told his audience he did not believe "in such a thing as a God," and that he would have the Deity "placed on half pay," such a statement being "to the high displeasure of Almighty God, to the great scandal and reproach of the Christian religion, in open violation of the laws of this kingdom..."[11]

Holyoake was more upset by being described as a laborer than being called wicked; he saw himself as a mathematics teacher. He pleaded not guilty and challenged several members of the jury, including farmers who he thought were not likely to understand the issues involved in the trial. The challenges were denied and the jury—seven farmers, and a shopkeeper, grocer, poulterer, maltster, and miller—took their seats.

6. The Lure of London and a Trial by Tyranny

The Crown prosecutor, Mr. Alexander, rose to speak. He had plotted his strategy carefully. Holyoake had made his blasphemous statement in answer to a question, and Alexander knew the jury might consider this a mitigating factor. He insinuated a different scenario: Holyoake had put about placards announcing a speech on Home Colonisation, Emigration, and the Poor Laws. "Had he given any hint of what was to take place, his end might have been defeated, and no audience attracted to listen to the blasphemous expressions you have heard. But he did obtain an audience, a numerous audience, and then declared that the people were too poor to have a religion—that he himself had no religion—that he did not believe in such a thing as a God, and—through it pains me to repeat this horrible blasphemy—that he would place the Deity upon half-pay." Having twisted the facts to suit his case Alexander suspected the jury might see through the veil he had thrown up. "It may be urged to you that these things were said in answer to a question," he conceded, but "such innuendos" should be disregarded.

The prosecutor called but one witness, James Bartram, the *Cheltenham Chronicle* printer who had testified at Holyoake's first hearing. He said he heard a man put a question to Holyoake: "The lecturer has been speaking of our duty to man but he said nothing as regards our duty towards God." Bartram confirmed that Holyoake's answer was as alleged in the indictment. "He was the length of the room off; I heard him distinctly; he spoke in a distinct voice."

Holyoake's cross-examination was brief but pointed. Why did Bartram think the words he had spoken were blasphemous? "Because they revile the majesty of heaven, and are calculated to subvert peace, law, and order; and are punishable by human law, because they attack human authority." This was a more articulate answer than anything heard from Bartram at the Cheltenham hearing. Holyoake asked, "Who has instructed you to define blasphemy?" Bartram said he had not been instructed, that he had given his own opinion. "In my opinion you spoke wickedly; I was sober, I deny on my oath I am given to drinking; I have been a preacher."

Mr. Alexander rose to tell the court the case for the prosecution was now complete. Holyoake had expected more witnesses to be called. "I am not a little surprised to hear that the case for the prosecution is closed," he said. "I have heard nothing, not one word, to prove the charge in the indictment."

"That is for the jury to decide," Mr. Justice Erskine said. Holyoake challenged his conclusion. "I thought, my Lord, as the evidence is so manifestly insufficient to prove malice you would have felt bound to direct my acquittal." Again, the stock response from the judge: "It is for the jury to say whether they are satisfied."

It was a quarter to twelve, and time for George Holyoake to begin his defense. He would be speaking himself, but he was not entirely alone. Richard Carlile beamed at him from his seat. Mr. and Mrs. Partridge, who gave him supper Sunday night, were there. George Adams and his wife Harriet watched silently from their seats. Other friends nodded their encouragement. Holyoake carried in his pocket a friendly letter from William Galpin, offering him encouragement and hinting that he still had a job with the Society of Rational Religionists. Holyoake may have taken a moment to think of his wife. He had written to warn her just the day before: "I am sure to have some imprisonment so do not be surprised should you hear this result, I do not expect much."[12]

Holyoake understood that not only was he on trial, but also his cause: the cause of freedom of speech and freethought, and the cause of atheism as an antidote to the superstitions and fantasies fostered by religion. His indictment for blasphemy had been intended to suppress and silence him, but he would use his trial to declare the truth of the nature of Christianity and the brutal consequences visited on the population as a result of the fraudulence and knavery of the church establishment.

The entire process of his arrest and trial had been improper, Holyoake began. He had been taken from a public meeting a week after the objectionable words had been spoken, arrested by a policeman at near midnight, "without a warrant, seized in the manner of the inquisition."

Holyoake argued that comments by Mr. Justice Erskine, published in the *Cheltenham Chronicle* at the time of his arrest, had led the public to prejudge his guilt. What was worse, according to the statement attributed to his Lordship in the *Chronicle*, was that Holyoake had spoken to people who lacked a sound religious education. If they had been properly educated, Mr. Justice Erskine had said, they would not have received Holyoake, as they did, "with cheers, but with disgust." Mr. Justice Erskine stared glumly from his dais. Holyoake added:

> I spoke openly, and you [of the jury] who usually have to punish dishonesty, are now called upon to punish honesty—for hypocrisy and lying would have saved me from this charge. I have infringed no law, injured no man's reputation, taken no man's property, attacked no man's person, broken no promise, violated no oath, encouraged no evil, taught no immorality—set only the example of telling the truth. I was asked a question and answered it openly.... What can we think of the morality of a law which requires secret inquiry, which prohibits the free publication of opinion?

~~~

George Holyoake had only begun to defend himself. Witnesses in the courtroom heard his voice, usually weak, grow stronger as he pressed his argument. He was erect, standing tall, his frail body coiled, his arms outstretched. Holyoake turned to the books and pamphlets in his chest and one after another, read passages from each of them. He quoted Socrates, Jean Jacques Rousseau, Thomas More, and Robert Owen; John A. Roebuck, the MP for Bath who raised his case in Parliament; the poet Kirk White; he quoted from his own articles in the *Oracle of Reason*; he read from Mosheim's *Ecclesiastical History*; and quoted the words of Dr. Cave, from his book *Primitive History* to show Christians were once considered atheists. "Cries of blasphemy," he said, "have always been rife when priests thought their power and privileges in danger." It was a tool applied to control freethought. Richard Carlile, sitting close by, handed George notes listing points he should be making.

Women in the courtroom cried as Holyoake retold the demand of the Rev. Mr. Moseley of St. Martin's for the Easter tithe, of how Holyoake's family had been suddenly reduced by virtue of a commercial panic, from "a state of comparative affluence to one of privation." When the summons to pay four pence came, and then a demand for another two shillings and six pence, "we gathered together all the money we had, which was being saved to purchase a little wine to moisten the parched lips of my dying sister, for at this time her end seemed approaching." When his mother returned from her six-hour wait at the church, the child was dead. "Gentlemen, will you wonder if, after this, I doubted a little the utility of church establishments?"

Christianity, Holyoake argued, had many faults; It is inconsistent and barbarous; capricious in its treatment of blasphemy; it disregards equal justice and debases religion into superstition. He spoke of the cost of religion to England. "I have lived all my life among those classes who suffer from the burden of poverty, and I find by a calculation that has never been disputed, that the English pay five times as much for their religion, in proportion to their numbers, than any other nation." He read figures asserting that England's twenty-one million Christians were paying their clergy more than £18,000,000 a year.

Holyoake had reached a crucial point in his defense, the point at which he could have won his case. "If you can convince the jury," Mr. Justice Erskine told him, "that your only meaning was that the incomes of the clergy ought to be reduced, and that you did not intend to insult God, I should tell the jury you ought not to be convicted."

By now, Holyoake had reconciled himself to going to prison. He would almost welcome it, having been hailed by the freethinkers of London and applauded for his courageous decision to stand by his principles. To get off now on the simple excuse of having merely meant to challenge the income of the clergy? He couldn't do that. He preferred martyrdom.

"I could have proved," Holyoake told the judge, "that the religion of Christians is a religion of mammon." Holding a Bible in each hand, he went on: "I now turn to the question, what is blasphemy." Holyoake was away on another long, convoluted, and to the jury, tiresome exposition on sin, Thomas Paine, Galileo and the Inquisition, and Lord Russell's views on petitions. It was four o'clock, the sun still high in the sky over the countryside, and Holyoake, sipping from his bottle of raspberry vinegar, had been speaking since noon. The jury asked for a break to refresh themselves. On their return, Holyoake resumed his defense, attacking points of law to argue he had committed no crime.

"There is no statute which punishes a man simply for denying the existence of God." Holyoake declared. "My firm conviction is that the common law doctrine which constitutes offences against religion is altogether based upon error." He took apart, detail by detail, the arguments for blasphemy made by Sir William Blackstone, the great interpreter of English law. He veered into a defense of socialism, and berated the church for its failure to defend the poor.

It was now ten minutes past nine o'clock, and darkness had descended on the West Country. Still the crowd filled most of the benches in the courtroom. "My Lord," Holyoake told Mr. Justice Erskine, "You do know that a great principle is involved in the decision now to be arrived at. The thinking portion of this country will estimate your Lordship's character by your conduct this day, and posterity will behold the glory or degradation of this nation in the decision to which your Lordship, the jury, and this court shall come."

Holyoake had delivered one of the great speeches ever to emanate from a non-legal mind in a British courtroom. But he had gone on too long. He had spoken for nine hours and fifteen minutes, he'd exhausted what patience the jury might have had, and he'd tired Mr. Justice Erskine, who sought now to bring the case to a close. His charge to the jury took only a few minutes. He sought to be scrupulously fair: "…it is important you [members of the jury] should notice that the words [leading to the blasphemy charge] were not the subject of the lecture, but uttered in answer to a question put to him. The question is whether these words were uttered with the intention of bringing God and the Christian religion into contempt. Any man who treats with contempt the Christian religion is guilty of an indictable misdemeanour. If you are convinced that he did it with that object you must find him guilty, despite all that has been addressed to you. If you entertain a reasonable doubt of his intention, you will give him the benefit of it."

There was little doubt in the minds of the jury. They were convinced that Holyoake, in answering the question he'd been asked, had spoken with contempt for God and Christianity. The jury deliberated for barely more than two minutes. The verdict: guilty. Before passing sentence on Holyoake,

6. The Lure of London and a Trial by Tyranny

Mr. Justice Erskine ordered that George Adams, found guilty of publishing a blasphemy by selling copies of *The Oracle of Reason*, be brought in for sentencing. A month in jail would do for him.

For George Holyoake, Mr. Justice Erskine observed, no such trifling sentence would suffice, his penalty must balance punishment with prudence. "Proceeding on the evidence that has been given, trusting that these words [of blasphemy] have been uttered in the heat of the moment, I shall think it sufficient to sentence you to be imprisoned in the Common Gaol for six calendar months."

"My Lord, am I to be classed with thieves and felons?"

"No, thieves and felons are sentenced to the Penitentiary—you to the Common Gaol."

In writing of his trial, Holyoake always took care to stress his respect for all laws but one. His conscience would have him make this single exception: "What is called the common law relating to blasphemy is mere caprice, an opinion interpreted by ignorance or sectarian prejudice, and enforced at the call of bigotry—malevolent to the humble while neutral toward the rich. Against this tyranny one is obliged to rebel."[13]

7

How a Prisoner Became the Watchmaker's Nemesis

The voice of the street crier was loud and clear, even in George Holyoake's narrow cell in the Gloucester jail, on the first morning of his six-month sentence as a "prisoner of blasphemy." He saw his status as distinct from those imprisoned for crime. "Howitt's correct list of all the cast, quit and condemned," the voice cried. "George Jacob Holyoake, for uttering certain blasphemous words against God," the shout went on.[1] The street crier was selling a list of those imprisoned in Gloucester jail, and was giving emphasis to Holyoake's name above that of two cases of willful murder. When George Holyoake asked a prison turnkey for a copy, he saw his name in bold type. He knew then that the sentence passed on him was true in fact, and that his trial had not been a nightmare conjured out of mindless fear.

After Mr. Justice Erskine's sentencing, Holyoake was taken to the cells below the courtroom where Captain Mason, the governor of Gloucester jail, awaited with two guards. "We have another prisoner to take down, one convicted of a felony, will you walk with him?" Mason asked. "No, I will not," Holyoake said. "I will go down with George Adams instead." Handcuffed, they were escorted along the road to Gloucester prison. Holyoake was exhausted, hungry, and thirsty, having had nothing all day but swallows of raspberry vinegar. It was now close to midnight. The only food offered him was "a very hard apple" and a cup of warm water. "The transition from the excitement of the court," Holyoake would remember, "to the darkness and coolness of the night cell, made me feel as if going into a well, and my supper not serving to compose me, I continued restless till the morning."

Holyoake's treatment would be harsh. Breakfast was a dish of gruel "which I had not the slightest disposition to eat." He was ordered to attend daily prayers, which he refused to do. Next came a demand that he change

7. How a Prisoner Became the Watchmaker's Nemesis

into prison clothes. That order, too, met resistance from the obstinate new inmate. In the eyes of his jailers, George Holyoake was a difficult prisoner. He represented a challenge to Captain Mason, to Mr. Ogden, the turnkey officer, to the Rev. Mr. Cooper, the prison chaplain, and to the local magistrates who pursued their prize catch not only through the courts, but into the cells of Gloucester Gaol. Holyoake was not a violent or profane prisoner, either of which the warders would have found it easy to deal with. Instead, he was psychologically immovable and impossibly stubborn, a prisoner the like of which they had not before encountered and had no idea how to handle.

One of the first visitors to Holyoake's cell was the prison chaplain and magistrate, Bransby Cooper, who had sat on the bench with Mr. Justice Erskine. "Why, Holyoake, I did not know you yesterday," he said. "You did not seem the same person you were before, when you were so gentle and submissive. But yesterday there was so much hauteur about you." It was true; like a butterfly emerging from its chrysalis, Holyoake had transformed himself into a forceful advocate, someone quite unlike the diffident, cautious and uncertain young man he had been. Now he would need all of his wit and guile to make it through the next six dreary months.

On his second day at the jail the weather had cooled, and Holyoake took up a seat before a small fire in the common room where prisoners were allowed to mingle. Suddenly a bell began to peal, and all the other prisoners marched out, single file. The voice of turnkey Ogden shouted through a grate in the ceiling. "Holyoake, did you not hear that bell?"

"Yes, what of it?"

"All the other prisoners have gone to prayers, and you must, too."

"Let the poor devils go if they like, I will not."

Holyoake stayed where he was, but after prayers he was summoned to the chapel of the Rev. Mr. Cooper. Why had not Holyoake come to prayers, the chaplain wanted to know?

Holyoake, feeling bruised by the pressure put on him to indulge in a ritual of the religion that had sent him to prison, was ready with a combative answer.

"You imprison me here on the grounds that I do not believe in a God, and then you would take me to chapel to pray to one? I cannot prevent your imprisoning me, but I can prevent your making me a hypocrite, and must," Holyoake said.[2] After long and acrimonious discussion, a compromise was reached. Holyoake would attend Mr. Cooper's Sunday sermon, but would take no part in daily prayers.

As we see often in Holyoake's accounts of unwelcome incidents, he did his best to make light of his circumstances. In addition to the prayer bell, he wrote in a memoir, "I enjoyed such a propinquity to dock bells, basin bells, cathedral bells, and gaol bells, that had I been inclined to *rebel*, it would have chimed in with the others."

Holyoake faced a further problem when he announced he would have nothing to do with the prison uniform he'd been ordered to wear. He insisted on his own clothes, which he saw as a symbol of his individuality. If they wanted him in prison garb, they would have to dress him every day. "To carry me to prayers or to dress me every morning was far more offensive and troublesome to them than breaking my head, so they left me alone."

Holyoake called it "passive resistance, in prison the only resistance possible, and often very effective." He was denied his mathematical instruments (he might use them on himself) and was ordered to douse his candle at six o'clock. Holyoake sent off an appeal to Sir James Graham, the Secretary of State, protesting his conditions. It won him the right to stay up until nine o'clock, a privilege afforded only to those in jail for debt. He suffered sores that he believed he obtained from the grasp of a filthy inmate, but nursed them himself rather than undergo the drastic cure of brimstone and pitch given to men suffering such contamination. Holyoake lost weight and grew weak on the prison fare of gruel, coarse bread, and potatoes. An extra food allowance, offered as a special privilege, consisted of rice of "a slimy look" and a slice of salt beef twice a week. He had not the money to buy anything better—the ten shillings a week from the Anti-Persecution Union went to Helen and was barely enough to feed her and the two girls. Friends sent Holyoake small sums and by depriving himself of extras, he was able to send a guinea home to Birmingham.

A letter from Richard Carlile brought Holyoake a sense of reassurance that he had been right to argue, cajole, and push back against his accusers. Carlile had been in the courtroom every day as the Assizes ground through its agenda. The argument Holyoake had put up in court, Carlile wrote, "was certainly the most splendid of the kind ever delivered in this country. I could scarcely restrain myself from jumping into the dock to embrace you..."[3]

One of the magistrates who forced himself most often on Holyoake was the Rev. Samuel Jones, insistent in his determination to win him back to Christianity. Jones may have been devout, but he was also deceitful. While Holyoake was awaiting trial, he claimed that Richard Carlile had died "a very horrible death" and with his last breath had recanted "his dreadful principles and denounced his infidel colleagues." Not long after, Carlile walked up to Holyoake's cell, "alive and well, to offer me his generous sympathy and advice to enable me to combat the old enemies of freethought and free speech."

Early in Holyoake's sentence, Jones arrived with a new translation of the Psalms of David. He summoned the inmates, lined them up twelve to eighteen by rows, and announced he had come to do a reading. After quoting the first verse of the Psalms with David's observation that "the fool hath said in his heart that there is no God," Jones paused and looked around. "Now, Holyoake, you complained that we called you a fool—you see David says you are a fool."[4]

Holyoake would not forget the encounter. "I gently but distinctly observed," he would recall, "I no more like rudeness in the mouth of David than in the mouth of a magistrate." Mr. Jones, a man of many years, "turned round, shut up his book, and walked away without saying a word, and I never saw him afterwards."

Holyoake's fellow prisoners were mostly illiterate, and he did what he could to teach them reading and arithmetic. "They were, with one exception, ignorant, and were there for acts of violence, or minor thefts, or frauds."[5] The exception, apparently, was a Mr. Wall, who had been the postmaster of Cheltenham. "He had opened letters and taken the money out." In one case, he stole the cash a servant girl was sending to her solider lover. When the girl received no answer, she thought him unfaithful and poisoned herself. The soldier, never hearing from the girl, thought she had deserted him and shot himself. Holyoake might have thought the incidents could have formed the plot of a romantic tragic novel. For all that, he found "this scoundrelly postmaster was pleasant-spoken, gentlemanly, and cultivated. He was entirely pious, and punctual at prayer, but a knave at heart."

Holyoake's incarceration was brightened occasionally by a kind gesture from outside. A woman until now unknown to him, Mrs. Price, brought him dinner every Sunday. The niece of the owner of the Ten Bells Inn where Holyoake had stayed took a liking to him and "frequently brought me refreshments." The connection blossomed in romance for the girl; she married Holyoake's friend William Chilton, the printer and part-owner of *The Oracle* newspaper.

~~~

Holyoake worried about his daughter Madeline when he heard she had fallen ill. He remembered she had sent him off with smiling eyes when he last left Birmingham. Helen had told him, "Do what it seems your duty to do, and I and the children will take care of ourselves as well as we can."[6] The guinea Holyoake had sent home, intending it to be used to buy Madeline a warm coat, was instead spent on another object—a coffin. A succession of colds, combined with malnutrition, had brought on a fatal infection. "My dada's coming to see me," were among Madeline's last words, uttered in "a cheerless, fireless room." A "morose turnkey—a fit messenger of misery"—handed him the letter that brought news of the child's death. Captain

Mason came to see him but Holyoake could find nothing to say, and turned away. He wandered into the exercise yard, where another prisoner put a coat on his shoulders.

Holyoake could not get it out of his mind that Madeline "had died the death of the poor; she had perished among the people who knew neither hope nor comfort." She was buried "without priest, or priestly ceremony." Having been taught like all proper Englishmen to cloak his emotions in silent acceptance, Holyoake turned to literature when he wrote to his wife. He quoted Plutarch of the man who was told it was "no use to weep for his daughter because that would not recall her." Plutarch has the man reply, "For that very reason I do weep."[7] Holyoake was denied leave to attend the funeral and his letter to his wife implored her to "remember Madeline's beauty and charms as a pleasing dream and together be glad that it continued so long, than grieve that its duration was so short."

A notice placed in the *Birmingham Post* recorded that "Madeline, the interesting and beloved daughter of George Jacob Holyoake," would be remembered for the fact that:

> Beauty and virtue crown'd thee!
> Death in thy youth hath found thee!

Holyoake had resisted Helen's wish to visit him in jail, but he relented after Madeline's death. Mr. Bransby Cooper, the first of the magistrates to send his condolences, arranged for Holyoake's use of the magistrates' committee room, "an elegant and cheerful apartment." When the time came, the magistrates had other uses for it and Holyoake was allowed to receive his wife, his little daughter Eveline and his sister Caroline, in the prison's Lodge. "No turnkey was sent in, and I was allowed to see my friends with an air of perfect freedom." Caroline brought him wine and cigars but as both were prohibited by the jail, he declined to touch them. He would remember the visit for Helen's aching confession of having slapped Madeline to quieten her when she cried for a bun she had seen in a shop window in Bull Street.

The dismal conditions of English jails were well known. Of his cell, Holyoake would write that "the floor was filthy, the bed was filthier, and the window was filthier still, for in the window was—what I sicken at while I write—a rag full of human excrement. And of the bed, a prisoner assured me that when he lay in it the lice crept up his throat off the corners of the blanket which covered him."[8]

After the death of a Chartist prisoner from malnutrition and disease, a commission of inquiry was ordered. When its members arrived at the Gloucester Gaol, Holyoake let it be known he had no complaint to make.

Quizzed by the chief commissioner, Dr. Blisset Hawkins, he said he could not give evidence "before these gentlemen," nodding toward Captain Mason and his deputy. Holyoake said the captain behaved "with courtesy and humanity," but a prisoner, fearing retaliation, could not speak freely in his presence. Only when the officials left the room did Holyoake complain of filthy cells with beds alive with vermin. The prison doctor, Holyoake added, was fearful of retaliation by the local board of magistrates if he criticized jail conditions. Holyoake got a mutton-chop in his broth the next day. The inquiry report, when it came down, found the Gloucester jail to be low and unhealthy, and recommended its closing. Nothing happened.

There was little spirit of Christmas in Gloucester as the last days of 1842 sank over the prison. Word spread that a penniless workman had committed a crime so that, being in jail at Christmas, he would be fed a Christmas pudding. Hearing this, the board of magistrates, mostly church ministers, canceled the pudding. "Thus these clergymen," thought Holyoake, "taught the prisoners to rejoice in the 'glad tidings of great joy' brought by Christ."

George Holyoake did what prison inmates call "hard time." For as long as he was held in Gloucester, jail officials worked to devise ways to overcome his obstinate behavior. Captain Mason ordered that all his letters be detained, and refused him the privilege of writing to his family. "The reason assigned by the governor for this was the enforcement of new rules, but I know that they were enforced without proper authority, and I believe applied only to me."[9]

~~~

Amid the importuning of clergymen and magistrates and the cancellation of his mail, Holyoake was surprised one day to receive a neatly wrapped package bearing the return address of the Hon. (and Rev.) Andrew Sayer, another of the local magistrates. Inside Holyoake found a book, *Natural Theology or Evidences of the Existence and Attributes of the Deity*. Its author was Dr. William Paley, and the book had attracted great attention in educated circles since its publication in 1802.[10] Even Charles Darwin, it was said, had studied it carefully and given it high regard.

As Holyoake leafed through Natural Theology, paying particular attention to the case it made that an ordered universe could only have been created by a superior being, he was struck by what he saw as it contradictions, faulty logic, and far-fetched conclusions. Paley, a well-informed man for his time, ranged over the whole of biology and natural science as they were then understood. He wrote, in elegant nineteenth century style, of the capabilities of birds and fishes; of a newborn child lifting up its eyelids; of topics as varied as the mechanisms of the body's muscles and the function of an eye compared to a telescope. His central argument would come to be known as the watchmaker theory; the proposition that as a watch must have a maker, so the universe must have a creator, it being God:

> In crossing a heath, suppose I pitched my foot against a stone, and were asked how the stone came to be there.... I might possibly answer it had lain there for ever. But suppose I had found a watch upon the ground ... we perceive—what we could not discover in the stone—that its several parts are framed and put together for a purpose ... the inference we think is inevitable, that the watch must have had a maker.[11]

Pressing his argument, Dr. Paley arrives at the "invincible conclusion" that the watch could not have reproduced itself, but that it had "an artificer who understood its mechanism and designed its use." To believe a watch might reproduce itself is as foolish as to believe that every manifestation of design that existed in the watch, also exists in the work of nature. "This," he proclaims, "is atheism."

To Holyoake, Paley's arguments defied reason. It was a false analogy to argue that because the universe is complex as is a watch, the universe must also have had a watchmaker. All watchmakers have fathers, so who is the father of God? And to argue that everything God does is good—that even pain is good because of the pleasure that ensues when it goes away—was ridiculous, Holyoake thought. In a pamphlet he was working on, Holyoake summarized Paley's foundational belief and then promptly set about undermining it:

> Paley contends that natural objects manifest marks of design, and from this he reasons that they must have had a designer, that this designer is a person, and that this person is God.... Most decidedly I believe that the present order of nature is insufficient to prove the existence of an intelligent creator, and that no imaginable order—that no contrivance, however mechanical, precise, or clear would be sufficient to prove it. Paley seems to insinuate that no person can be of "sound mind" who sees reason to arrive at a conclusion different than his own.[12]

It was Holyoake's view that Christianity was baseless on multiple grounds. Its teachings were inconsistent, barbarous, and capricious; it disregarded social justice, and it debased religion. "Any account of religion.... which implicates it with hope of reward, or fear of punishment, is low and injurious, and debases religion into superstition."

Holyoake was at work at the small table in his cell when he was interrupted by the arrival of the man who had sent him William Paley's *Natural Theology*. The Rev. Andrew Sayer had come to ask what conclusions Holyoake had reached from reading it. Holyoake felt his most private thoughts were being violated. "Sir, I am surprised at your asking me this question. Does it become you, a clergyman and a magistrate, to ask me to commit crime?"

"What do you mean?" Sayer asked.

"Having punished my expression of opinion as a crime, by bringing me here, it does not become you to put religious inquiries to me again." Punishing any expression of dissenting opinion, Holyoake said, disqualified Christians from seeking the state of a man's thoughts on religion. The conversation was short and when it was over, Holyoake applied himself once more to his pamphlet. He called it *Paley's Natural Theology Refuted in His Own Words*. He was sure it would demolish all of Paley's arguments.

"My opinion is that Dr. Paley, in his well-known work on Natural Theology, meddles with a subject which exceeds human comprehension," Holyoake wrote. "The existence of Deity is a question upon which research has been employed to no purpose, and learning has been expended in vain. Ingenuity has not been able to show more than that nothing can be known." He pointed to Paley's lack of originality; arguments like the watchmaker theory had been known since the days of Socrates "but he who first develops an idea is not so much the originator of it as he who so loudly and perseveringly proclaims it."[13]

If God were the watchmaker, Holyoake was making of himself the watchmaker's nemesis.[14] He was writing seventeen years before Charles Darwin would publish *On the Origin of Species,* and Holyoake could draw on little hard science to counter Paley's belief that the universe was divinely made. There was support for the idea of "gradation"—the development of the human species through gradual steps—but it was backed up by no scientific rationale. Nevertheless, the gradation of the human species had become a popular subject for radical papers like the *Oracle of Reason*. One of the chief exponents of gradation, Charles White, had written a tract that in a later age would be considered both racist and sexist:

> Ascending the line of gradation we come at last to the white European, who being most removed from the brute creation, may, on that account, be considered as the most beautiful of the human race. No one will doubt his superiority in intellectual power; and I believe it will be found that his capacity is naturally superior also to that of every other man. Where shall we find, unless in the European, that nobly arched head.... Where, except on the bosom of the European woman, two such plump and snowy white hemispheres, tipt [*sic*] with vermilion?[15]

Holyoake said nothing of gradation in his rebuttal of Paley but his pamphlet stands as one of the first salvos fired in an argument that runs to the present day. Twenty-first century creationists defend what is now called "Intelligent Design," using Paley's reasoning to argue against authors such as Richard Dawkins and his book, *The Blind Watchmaker*.

When Holyoake's pamphlet was published, sales were slow and the freethought press gave it little notice. Holyoake's biographer, Joseph McCabe, thought it "rather pretentious, but fairly acute and informed." Sylvia Dobson Collet, an early feminist who Holyoake would meet at the South Place Ethical Chapel in London, wrote of his Paley pamphlet in a radical newspaper, the *Free Inquirer*, and in a biography of Holyoake she published in 1855. She thought the pamphlet had a sarcastic style "too frequent in his early writings," but that it showed "decided intellectual power in its conception and arrangement."[16] Becoming a lifelong supporter of Holyoake, Collet remained a member of the Unitarian church. She published several books in which she condemned Biblical oppression of women and lamented their inferior role in Christian doctrine.

On a day that was wintry and cheerless to all but George Jacob Holyoake, the main door of the Gloucester jail swung open and its most notorious prisoner was freed to the world. Holyoake left the prison on Monday, 6 February 1843, a week shy of completing his full six-month term. His thoughts were on an audacious and perhaps unachievable goal: to lift the heavy hand of religion from English civil life, even at the cost of whatever trouble "might befall a wilful person—imprisonment, darkness, privation, cold, and insult."[17] Holyoake refused to accept a parole, proffered in return for a recanting of his views. He rejected the assistance of the prison chaplain, the Rev. Mr. Cooper, who promised to secure Holyoake a teaching appointment at a girls' school where his wife could serve as the mistress, if only he would agree to "desist from the advocacy on which I had embarked." He was sure his wife would resent it if he were to abandon his life's greatest purpose solely on her account. "So when I was free I took the warpath again."[18]

8

The Light of Freedom Shines on a Liberated Blasphemer

George Holyoake's warpath led him from the Gloucester jail to reunions with friends in Worcester and Cheltenham where he stayed a night with George and Harriet Adams. He'd paid a "certain price" for free speech, and having paid it, he felt he had purchased the right to speak his mind. Only by staying true to his beliefs, he was convinced, could he earn recompense for his six months of imprisonment.[1] Buoyed by the encouragement of his friends, Holyoake turned his feet in the direction of Birmingham. Three days later, he arrived home to be welcomed by Helen, who he thought looked thinner than ever, and baby Eveline, apparently healthy and beginning to walk at thirteen months. George Holyoake had rejoined what he called "the remains" of his family.

Helen and the surviving child, and Madeline before her death, suffered privation as a result of George's imprisonment. Holyoake writes touchingly in his memoir, *The History of the Last Trial by Jury for Atheism*, of the suffering of his family. "Cold succeeded cold, when want of more means caused them all to go to live in a house ill ventilated, and where several were ill of fever, which soon attacked Madeline." Helen found friends and neighbors shunned her: "One or two friends whose professions had before been profuse were cold, or to her they seemed so. She thought they feared a continued acquaintance might lay them under some tax to contribute to her support. This she could never bear. Offering her hand to one who did not take it, she went home, and nothing induced her to subject herself to such suspicion anymore."[2]

Holyoake fails to explain why his wife and children went hungry and homeless while his parents and his eleven siblings were close at hand in Birmingham. His father still worked at the Eagle Foundry and half a dozen of his siblings, older than sixteen, would have had jobs. His parents still lived in the house in Inge Street and his well-to-do aunts resided in comfort in

Selly Oak. Any one of them could have taken in his wife and the children. Instead, Eleanor was forced to find refuge in a drafty and uncomfortable house whose occupants were both poor and ill.

Holyoake's public pronouncements of his atheism and his conviction for blasphemy, topics of much gossip in his hometown, would have brought his family shame and embarrassment. His mother had to withstand the disapproval of her fellow parishioners at the Wesleyan church she attended in Carr's Lane. "The church forgets no offence against it, and rarely forgives it," Holyoake would write. The shame of George's religious irreverence and his headstrong denunciations of Christianity would have made the Holyoakes virtual outcasts in respectable Birmingham society. Reputation was everything; more important than what you thought you were, was what others thought of you. It is likely the Holyoakes' inability to endure such social opprobrium triggered a schism within the family, an estrangement that would lead to hunger and deprivation for Helen and the children. Other than a reference to George returning home ten years later to smoke a pipe with his dying father as lay in his deathbed, only George's brother Austin, who worked with him on Fleet Street, receives any mention of note in Holyoake's memoirs.

The estrangement of Holyoake from his parents would eventually soften, but George would not forget that the success of his siblings stemmed in good part from the support and encouragement of their parents: Austin, who brought accounting skills to George's future publishing business; William, who became an artist of some note with one of his paintings hanging in the House of Lords; Horatio, who operated a bookstore in Melbourne; and Walter, who did well as a London photographer. George had an affectionate relationship with Caroline, the sister who brought Helen to see him in prison, but was distanced from Selina, who married and moved to America.

Holyoake says little of his reunion with his wife and his child. His mind was on his mission, and he was trying to work out how to return to London and find employment. First, he had letters to write. He had barely begun when a note arrived telling him of the sudden death of Richard Carlile. He'd long suffered with bronchitis and an attack came on when Carlile, searching for a son who wandered away while they were unpacking at a new residence in London, returned home and fell into a fit of coughing. He died February 10, 1843, apparently of cholera, only four days after George's release from jail. After a lifetime of struggle he'd seen the light of freedom but dying at the age of forty-three, he had not long enjoyed its glow.

While mourning Carlile's death, George got off a fresh article for *The Oracle*, where William Chilton was carrying on in his absence. He poured into it all his grievances from his time in prison. "It is now six months since

8. The Light of Freedom Shines on a Liberated Blasphemer

cut and hacked, I fell, not merely in the language of the parable, but literally, among thieves." Of his treatment, he wrote in *The Oracle* of February 18:

> The prison diet was bread, gruel, and potatoes. On two days of each week boiled rice was substituted for potatoes; and after I had been in prison nine weeks I was, by the rules, allowed a small portion of salt beef on Thursdays and Sundays. As this fare is considered in Gloucestershire a famous specific for the cure of atheism, it may not be out of place to explain its virtues. The whole of the food could be taken by a ploughman's appetite, and only be digested by a navigator's stomach.³

Most of the article consisted of Holyoake's usual critique of Christianity. "The conviction should be permanent that Christianity is a fearful thing. But bad men may laud it … a system which tramples upon the feelings of humanity and the principles of liberty." He echoed his bitterness at his confinement in a letter to the *Cheltenham Free Press*. That paper, unlike the *Cheltenham Chronicle*, had covered his trial with fairness, reporting on the irregularities of his arrest. Offering "a little recent experience" of prison life, Holyoake credited his survival not to the care given by the jail or its warders, but to "my friends, who supplied me with such food as my constitution required, for had I been compelled to subsist on the diet of the prison, my health, by this time, would have been quite broken."

To be able again to express himself was highly satisfying, but Holyoake needed to reach out to the public if he was to win converts and pave the way for profitable employment. He still considered himself an Owenite and it was under sponsorship of the Society of Rational Religionists that he struck out on a lecture tour. Now notorious for his conviction and audacious in his attacks on religion, he gave four lectures in Leicester, beginning on Sunday, February 26. The posters announcing his appearance screamed of his blasphemous reputation.

COME AND HEAR THE LIBERATED
BLASPHEMER!
MR. G.J. HOLYOAKE
Who has just been liberated from six months' imprisonment in Gloucester Gaol
for the alleged offence of BLASPHEMY, will deliver a course of
FOUR LECTURES

The four-night series had a lighter moment when a ball was held on Tuesday (Shrove Tuesday evening) at which Holyoake gave a short talk amid the dances and quaffing of beer. His share of the one pence admission would have been slim, and it is likely he received donations from friends. From Leicester he lectured in Northampton and Coventry before settling in for several weeks with socialist friends in Worcester. Holyoake was insistent on returning to Cheltenham where a large and enthusiastic audience greeted him. He repeated the statements that had led to his arrest but the authorities were nowhere to be seen. They had learned from the criticism of the House of Commons that Holyoake was a man not to be harassed or interfered with.

His speeches were warm-ups for London. He arrived there on May 7. He was penniless, having given Helen what little cash he had earned from his lectures. "If I starve in a garret I follow illustrious precedents," he wrote in his diary. He was determined to make it in London, having turned down an offer to become the headmaster at the communal settlement of Ham Common, a vestige of Owenism still functioning in Surrey under the name of Concordium. "The Concordists wish to form a school there and are desirous to meet with a competent educator.... Neither milk, butter, cheese, eggs, nor any species of flesh meat, nor animal flesh; neither tea, coffee, nor any of those artificial stimulants do the Concordists partake of.... The working members receive no wages but are supplied with lodging, food, clothing, washing, baths, and whatever is needful for their giving their service to the Concordium."[4]

Holyoake didn't remain penniless for long. On May 26, John Firmin wrote from 3 Blackfriars Road to invite him to take a position with Branch 53 of the Rational Religionists. It was one of a dwindling number of Owenite outposts in London. Firmin wrote that as Holyoake was "without any permanent employment and convinced that your services to the cause of Rational Reform have been highly valuable ... we do earnestly hope that you will permit yourself to be put in nomination for the office of Secretary."[5] The pay was only ten shillings a week, but it would be all right if Holyoake gave "one or two" lectures a week, from which he could presumably keep the proceeds of the collection plate.

Holyoake took the job, giving talks at the Rotunda in Blackfriars Road, a favorite gathering place of radicals, atheists, and other freethinkers. He picked up extra change by conducting classes on "the study of literary composition, logic, and oral investigation" for the London Theological Association, whose name belied the fact it was actually a group of freethinkers who met at Bailey's Coffee House in Soho. His teaching fee of six pence per week was largely drained off in work he was doing for the Anti-Persecution Union. He also arranged with the radical publisher Henry Hetherington, who had been jailed for printing blasphemous books, to bring out *Paley Refuted in His Own Words*. At last Holyoake could count on an income, however irregular, and he sent for Helen and Eveline to join him.

As George Holyoake struggled to establish himself in London, the early 1840s held few prospects for improvement in the lives of most Englishmen. The Industrial Revolution had reached its second stage of

8. The Light of Freedom Shines on a Liberated Blasphemer

centralized, coordinated production and distribution, facilitated by the construction of canals and railways. The new wealth created by the mines and mills brought little benefit to the bulk of workers, giving rise to fresh fears that a rebellious population might one day turn against its masters. The Whig government of prime minister William Lamb, the 2nd Viscount Melbourne, hoping to ease the outcry over the indiscriminate use of child labor, appointed a commission to inquire into their treatment. Lamb had just survived a sex scandal, brought on when the husband of society beauty Caroline Norton attempted to blackmail him for carrying on an affair with her. The establishment shrugged off the scandal and in typically British fashion, political business went forward normally.

The child labor report, when it came out in 1842, shocked the country. Thousands of pages of oral testimony, some from children as young as five, revealed the hellish conditions they were condemned to endure. Especially shocking was the revelation that girls as young as six, "with a girdle bound round their waists," were forced to drag loads of coal underground. The report led to the banishment of underground women workers, and outlawed the employment in the mines of boys under ten. Elsewhere, old habits, such as public hangings, were hard to break. A hanging in Derby in 1843 of two men who had murdered a woman attracted a crowd of forty thousand.

Charles Southwell, now a freelance lecturer following the decision of the Rational Religionists to abandon its missionary network, returned to London from Bristol, refusing to have anything further to do with *The Oracle*. He went on tour and in Manchester drew crowds in the thousands. He took turns traveling with an acting troupe before taking over the Charlotte Institution in London from a band of Owenites. Southwell converted it into the Paragon Hall and Coffee House and started his own radical sheet, *The Investigator*.

In the face of troubles at home, activist Victorians were ever ready to take up the cause of persecuted foreigners. Ill feelings swelled over the treatment of Protestants on the Portuguese island of Madeira when a woman was hanged for "denying the divinity of the consecrated wafer." A Scotch Protestant missionary, Dr. Robert Kalley, was arrested in 1843 for distributing Protestant Bibles and holding Bible classes that had become popular among peasants and day laborers. When Holyoake heard of Kalley's arrest he offered the resources of the Anti-Persecution Union. "Your alleged offence," he wrote to Kalley, "is against the Mother of God. Mother or father, it makes no difference to the Anti-Persecution Union."[6] Dr. Kalley, recognizing such aid would be a provocation that might harm his case, declined the offer. Among those present at a protest meeting in Edinburgh were Charles Southwell and Thomas Paterson, Holyoake's Sheffield "curate." Both had been campaigning for freethought in Scotland and were eager to use the Kalley case as an opportunity to attack Christianity.

The government shortly after negotiated the release of Dr. Kalley. Paterson, became involved on the Scottish Anti-Persecution Union and set up a bookshop in Edinburgh, provocatively naming it The Blasphemy Depot. Following the arrests of two local booksellers, Henry Jeffery and William Budge, Paterson was taken into custody on blasphemy charges on August 5, 1843. His trial was held at the High Court of Scotland on November 8. He treated the jurors to a four-hour speech, reeling off attacks on Christianity and the Bible, but saying little about the crime of which he was accused. The jury took forty-five minutes to find Paterson guilty, since "his sole end and object were to asperse, ridicule, vilify, and bring into contempt the Christian religion and the Holy Scriptures." He was sentenced to fifteen months in Perth penitentiary, from which he is said to have emerged laughing. The two other booksellers were jailed for shorter terms. A woman, Matilda Rolfe, then opened her own bookshop, was soon raided, and jailed for sixty days.

Freethinkers were a fractious lot, and after Southwell's departure from the *Oracle*, Paterson had taken over the editor's chair, with Malthus Questell Ryall, one of the "defiant four" behind the sheet during its heyday in Bristol, running the business side. Paterson had "the bluster of Southwell but not his ability and the quality and circulation of the *Oracle* declined rapidly." When Paterson was jailed, the printer William Chilton took up the editorial chair. Reputable news agents would not handle *The Oracle* and its last issue appeared in December 1843.

George Holyoake saw an opening and together with Malthus Ryall, a firebrand of Victorian infidelism, launched *The Movement*, a paper with a mission to "Maximize morals, minimize religion." Like the *Oracle*, it played up its atheist outlook from its first issue on December 16, 1843, attempting to appeal to the freethinking audience that supported its predecessor. Ryall's contributions reflected the same "fisticuffs style" as Southwell had bragged of, but Holyoake's pieces were cast in a more moderate tone.

Holyoake makes no mention in his memoirs of how he and his family observed Christmas. It was growing in popularity as both a religious observance and a holiday occasion; the first commercial Christmas cards were published the year Holyoake regained his freedom and *A Christmas Carol* by Charles Dickens had come out on December 12, 1843, its first edition selling out by Christmas Eve. We are left to speculate that it was Holyoake's rejection of religion that led him to ignore Christmas, although his wife and children may have insisted on a family exchange of presents and a Christmas dinner with the traditional roast goose.

Within a month of the launch of *The Movement*, Holyoake had another mouth to feed. A son, Manfred Gryffyn, was born to Helen at their home near Finsbury Square, in the St. Luke's district of London, in January 1844. Added to the satisfaction of fatherhood, Holyoake saw two of his educational pamphlets published by Henry Hetherington. A rebel against grammatical convention as well as religion, Holyoake wrote *Practical Grammar* with a view it should be just that. He banished *thou* and illustrated his examples through amusing anecdotes. A review in *The Spectator* thought it the work of "an ultra-radical setting the world to rights." His more prosaic *Handbook of Graduated Grammatical Exercises* followed in 1846.

Holyoake needed the royalties they earned because Branch 53, a last stand of the Rational Religionists in London, was suffering from low attendance and even lower revenue. Holyoake got word in early spring that he would no longer be paid his secretarial salary, forcing him to subsist on what he could earn by tutoring, no more than a pound a week and what compensation he could draw from *The Movement*. The solution was a lecture tour, and Holyoake set out for the provinces, using the Manchester Hall of Science as his headquarters. Admission fees and the collection plate would, he hoped, restore his treasury. His tour through the Midlands was largely successful. At Rochdale, he made a notable speech to a group of farmers and merchants. His remarks on how they could work together for their mutual benefit helped spark the launch of the co-operative movement in England.

Itinerant lecturers of Holyoake's type were straggling down English roads and byways, each bringing their own brand of religious or supernatural tales that entertained people whose only diversions were the local public house or the racetrack. Living a Romany-like existence, Holyoake was usually able to obtain lodging from Religionists or their friends but sometimes he had to resort to an inn or a rooming house, not always with satisfying results.

> Once in Windsor I selected an inn with a white portico, having an air of pastoral cleanliness. The four-poster in my room, with its white curtains was a further assurance of response. The Boers were not more skilful in attack and retreat than the enemies I found in the field. Lighted candles did not drive them from the kopje pillow where they fought. In Sheffield I asked the landlady for an uninhabited room. A cleaner looking, white-washed chamber never greeted my eyes. But I soon found that a whole battalion of red-coated cannibals were stationed there, on active service. Wooden bedsteads were the fortress of the enemy, which then possessed the land. Iron bedsteads have ended this, and given to the workman two hours more sleep at night than was possible before that merciful invention.[7]

Holyoake's audiences were not always appreciative or understanding of his remarks. He soon learned there were "various classes of hearers" some with a capacity and thirst for new ideas, others who had "only room for one idea at a time in their heads and if by chance they get a new one, it puts out the one they had." He also had to contend with newspaper reporters whom he thought of as "petrified publicists" with "mere Esquimaux minds, all blubber and bearskin."

～～～

As Holyoake struggled to feed and clothe his family, the Religionists Society was falling into crisis. Its main problem was the ambitious Queenwood settlement that Robert Owen saw as a reaffirmation of his belief in the virtues of a collectivist community. Its success would make up for the failure of his socialist experiment, New Harmony, in America. Members of the Central Board invested in the project but much greater amounts had been collected, a few shillings at a time, from workmen throughout the country. Now it was in trouble. Great sums had been invested in building an ornate Harmony Hall and the community was running a serious deficit. The Board rebelled, and Owen was ejected from the presidency. He returned to America soon after.

Despite all the differences George Holyoake had with the Central Board and the direction of the Owenite movement, he still considered himself a loyal follower. But he had doubts about Queenwood as a viable home colonization project and on October 14, 1844, he set out to visit the colony on behalf of a group of shareholders. He would see for himself what was happening and report what he found in *The Movement*. Holyoake began his trip by paying the pedestrian toll to cross the Thames on the Vauxhall Bridge. Once on the south bank, he turned left and made his way along Nine Elms Road to the London and South Western Railway station. He kept an eye out for pickpockets, knowing he was in a dicey district. At Nine Elms Station he asked for a ticket to Nine Mile Water, Harmony Hall, and was told he would have to travel to Farnborough as "that's the station."

Riding in an uncovered carriage during a pelting rainstorm, he alighted in due time at Farnborough and thought, "Well, after all, Harmony Hall is not so far off as people said." When he asked directions to Harmony Hall the station superintendent told him, "There was a gentleman once before came here asking for that place. It is forty or fifty miles below, you had better take the next train to Winchester and then inquire again."[8] As he waited, Holyoake watched the station become crowded with people, including many police and certain characters he took to be security officers. He recognized one he had seen at Gloucester Gaol, and realized he was being surrounded by the A Division of Police from Scotland Yard.

8. The Light of Freedom Shines on a Liberated Blasphemer   89

There were not there for him, he realized with relief, but to protect Queen Victoria and Prince Albert, who were arriving to see off the king of France, Louis Philippe and his queen, who had been their guests at Windsor Castle. "Many a Frenchman would envy me," Holyoake thought. "Louis Philippe I could have shot half a dozen times." He saw nothing inviting about the king; "His cheeks hung like collapsed pudding bags." Prince Albert, when he saw him, "had a right princely appearance" and the Queen, whom he had not seen since glimpsing her in Birmingham when she was only eleven, "had become a graceful young woman."[9]

The train for Winchester set out at three o'clock and reached that town by four-thirty, with Stockbridge, his destination, still nine miles off. He was soaked and cold, but with the rain abating, he walked the distance. His travesty of a trip had come to an end. "There I found a pretty, kind creature of a landlady. And by half-past seven I was engaged with toast and tea."[10] As he ate, he listened to the song of a farm laborer coming from the saloon.

The next morning, with rain still pelting down, Holyoake set off for Harmony Hall. After being misdirected several times he finally arrived at "an entirely respectable-looking building, half red, half blue, a compound of brick and skate, with two spires in front, and two glass chimneys, apparently to let people see the smoke come up."

While admiring the building that had been used for schooling, Holyoake surveyed the ground before him. He saw that the flinty soil would make for poor farming, "intended by nature not for a colony of socialists, but for a colony of gunsmiths who, before percussion caps came up, might have made their fortune there." A second handsome building, in a part of the estate called Rosewood, had been put up by Joseph Hansom, the inventor of the Hansom cab. Holyoake found it served as a dining hall and noted it "had hardly a rival in London." After the expenditure of £30,000 on such projects, there was little money for farm improvement. The Owenite leaders who had invested most heavily would be the hardest hit by Queenwood's failure. William Galpin, the Central Board secretary, had put in £8,000 and William Pare, the Birmingham registrar who'd married George and Helen, £5,000, while a Frederick Bate had given an entire fortune bequeathed to him, £14,000. More troubling to Holyoake were the "noble sacrifices" made by hundreds of working men, "ungrudgingly and unrepiningly, although all their savings of a lifetime were put into it."[11]

All of these facts and impressions Holyoake reported in *The Movement*. He drew attention to the extravagance of Queenwood's fine structures—"richly finished ceilings" and walls of the dining room "covered in fine art." He charged there had been poor bookkeeping and that the location had been poorly chosen, miles from any convenient market for farmstuffs. His articles drew some praise but mostly bitter criticisms from the

Owenites, yet another episode in Holyoake's uneasy relationship. The controversy threw the future of *The Movement* into doubt; if it lost its Owenite subscriber basis, it might not long survive.

George Holyoake had other projects in his mind. An early exponent of women's rights, he was excited by the return to Britain of the Scottish woman, Frances Wright, who had started a women's movement in America and had married a French physician, Guillaume D'Arusmont. He tried to get her to come to London, without success: "I thank you from my heart ... all my sympathies are with you."[12] George Holyoake had enjoyed the light of freedom since his release from Gloucester; he was determined it should shine on all. This, especially, must include the half of the population that because of their sex, enjoyed few rights or privileges in mid–1800s Britain.

Part III

Discovering Secularism

9

Fleet Street Ink and the Fight for an Unstamped Press

George Holyoake's first run as an editor of the radical press in London was both short and unnoticed. His first newspaper, *The Movement*, took on both church and capitalism, as well as Owen mismanagement of the Queenwood colony. "The errors of the priests are not less dangerous than the mistakes of the capitalists," Holyoake declared in its first issue of December 16, 1843. It was a great achievement to have launched his own newspaper only ten months after his release from prison but it lasted, beset by debts and a dwindling subscription list, only until April 1845. Holyoake managed to pay off its £25 of debt that included salary due Malthus Q. Ryall, his partner. Nothing more would be heard of Holyoake's vision of an "Atheon," a scheme he'd advanced in *The Movement*. His Atheon was to have been a great institution modeled after the Pantheon, the former temple in Rome dedicated to the many gods, and now a Roman Catholic church. Serving no god, Holyoake's Atheon would have been both a museum and a center for the dissemination of "fraternal intelligence." Holyoake put his scheme aside and sadly, Malthus Ryall died shortly after, in penury.

Early in 1845, Holyoake received an invitation to go to Glasgow as a social missionary for the Rational Religionists Society. Scotland at this time was "an unknown world" to Holyoake. He realized that taking the posting would mean the interruption of his newfound role as a London journalist. Perhaps it didn't matter; the year had not started auspiciously for Holyoake. To add to Holyoake's disappointments and setbacks, he had fallen ill, having to return to London after a month's lecturing in Leicester. Too poor to summon a doctor, he recovered only when friends gave him money for medical treatment. A "little lecturing and a little journalism" earned Holyoake a pound or two a week, but it was the offer from Glasgow's Owenites that lifted him from weeks of indecision and self-doubt.

Holyoake, his wife and two small children, Eveline and Manfred, traveled by train from London to Liverpool, from where they would complete the journey to Glasgow by boat. "We arrived late one evening at a temperance hotel in Liverpool, near to the dock," Holyoke would remember. "Temperance hotels were then penal settlements of teetotalism. A rasher of bacon (which had grown black by exposure, and dry as a slice of mummy cat), an old teapot, a chipped cup and cracked saucer lying in a dusty window," greeted them as they checked in.[1]

Liverpool was bustling with emigrants bound for America. Some of Holyoake's poorest and least educated countrymen were converts to the new American religion of Mormonism, the result of much proselytizing carried out by the missionaries of Joseph Smith. Holyoake may have met some at their hotel, a likely stopping-place for the outbound faithful, having foresworn not just alcohol but also coffee and stimulants of any kind. He would have been keen to hear what they might tell him of their religion, but was disbelieving of their fanciful stories of scripture written on golden tablets found in the wilderness of New York State. Little would have been said of the Mormon practice of polygamy; only after the emigrants were securely on board New York–bound ships would many of the converts' wives learn of this sanctified behavior.

The vessel the Holyoakes boarded the next day took them north through the Irish Sea, docking at Greenock, a Firth of Clyde port serving the Glasgow district. They quickly learned that Greenock's Gaelic meaning of "a sunny knoll" was not a description that could always be taken literally. In Glasgow, Holyoake found one of the longest-lasting outposts of Owenism reduced to little more than a corporal's guard. Meetings were held in "a pleasant little chapel" in Great Hamilton Street, near Glasgow Green. His Sunday lectures "in a quaint old hall up a wynd in Candleriggs" (we would call it a narrow lane) earned him some notoriety. It was not the words he had spoken, but the way he had the hall cleaned up that caught the attention of his flock. He gave a woman half a crown to sweep and wash the stairs and the passage leading from the street "so that the entrance to the hall should be clean and sweet." Holyoake says she told a neighbor, "Mr. Holyoake's views were wrang [*sic*] but he seemed to have clean principles."[2]

∽∼∽

The response to Holyoake's Glasgow lectures was not always positive; the Owenite faithful demanded slashing, vigorous lectures like those delivered by Charles Southwell rather than Holyoake's more moderate tone. The abuse that had fallen on Holyoake after publishing his Queenwood expose in *The Movement* turned into reluctant admiration when newspapers across Britain reported the final failure of Robert Owen's great cooperative effort. The article in the *Leeds Times* was typical: "The Socialist experiment had proved a failure, immense sums of money has been thrown away upon it, and after some four or five years' efforts to keep it afloat, aided by large subscriptions from the working classes throughout the country, the end is bankruptcy."[3] Holyoake had recognized the problems of Queenwood and had anticipated its failure. He still hoped ways would be found to bring workers and their colleagues into fruitful cooperation and mutual prosperity.

~~~

As a social missionary with responsibility for outreach to the public, George Holyoake was anxious to make a role for himself in the life of Glasgow. Holyoake found himself in new company when he joined Glasgow's Robert Burns Lodge 1882 of the Manchester Unity branch of the Independent Order of Oddfellows. It was a "friendly society" set up in Manchester in 1810, its purpose being to lend money to members in need and otherwise assist them during hardships. The Order skirted the bounds of British law by having its members swear to a secret oath. Panic ensued at the Order's annual meeting in Hull in 1834 when word was received of six farm laborers—later known as the Tolpuddle Martyrs—being transported to Australia as penalty for using oaths borrowed from the Oddfellows.

Holyoake made friends quickly and was elected Grand Master of the Glasgow Lodge. The Order's governing body, the Annual Moveable Committee, met in Glasgow in May of 1845, and Holyoake was introduced to a newly elected Grand Master. John Dickinson was fifteen years' Holyoake's senior, but the two found they had much in common. Dickinson was a bookbinder who had started his own business in Manchester. He loved literature and knew many authors. He was, declared an Oddfellow magazine, as ready to "help a good fellow out of a ditch as kick a bad one into it."

The Glasgow meeting was a critical one for the British Oddfellows. After the Tolpuddle case, the Oddfellows abandoned secret oaths and watered down the lectures used in rituals where members received their degrees. The upheaval led to a breakaway by American members who formed their own Independent Order. Even worse, the secretary of the Manchester Lodge had stolen £4,000 of Order funds but charges against him were dismissed on the grounds that the Oddfellows were not a legal organization and could, in Holyoake's words, "be robbed with impunity."[4]

In his speech at the 1845 meeting, Dickinson referred to events that had threatened "the very existence of the mightiest organization of working men the world had yet witnessed." He conceded "a great secession had taken place," leading to "differences where unanimity and good feeling had hitherto existed." A particular sore point was the Lodge's Degree Lectures that many thought did a poor job of expressing Oddfellow principles. It was time for new lectures, and Dickinson announced a competition for essays that would be used in future ceremonies. There would be a £10 prize for the best essay on each of five subjects: Charity, Truth, Knowledge, Science, and Progression.

Holyoake submitted entries in all five categories. He prepared his scripts carefully, titling each paragraph in red ink and beginning the first sentence of each in capitals. Each essay went into a separate colored folder and he put his name on every one, knowing that each would be judged anonymously. It would not be helpful to his chances if adjudicators knew they were reading the works of one George Holyoake, atheist. He waited anxiously to hear if he had won, his mind filled with thoughts of how a ten-pound bonanza would set him up nicely in London when he took his family back to the capital. By the end of the year, having heard nothing, Holyoake assumed he was out of the running. He also came to the conclusion he was a burden on the small Glasgow branch of the Rational Religionists. He made the decision to resign early in 1846 after the birth of his second son, whom he duly named Malthus Questell in honor of his old friend and partner in *The Movement*.

Glasgow had by now received disturbing reports about the potato crop, both locally and in Ireland. As indications of a crop failure mounted, the *Glasgow Herald* was declaring, "We still hear conflicting accounts of the state of the potato crop." On December 5, the *Herald* quoted the *Ulster Conservative* for its opinion that "we may now say, with confidence, not only that the plague has been arrested, but that the loss sustained by it is by no means so extensive as was originally anticipated." Thus reassured, Glaswegians returned to their daily routines, unaware that a massive famine was mounting across the Irish Sea. Before the potato blight would run its course, landlords (mostly English) would evict thousands of Irish farmers from their small acreages. Starvation and disease would claim more than a million lives, with another million forced to emigrate to America.

Holyoake's wife urged him to ask the Owenites to send aid to Ireland. Later, when the extent of the devastation to crops and human lives became more widely known, she wrote to George's sister, Caroline:

> As to the famine, on account of which a fast is ordered, I am disposed to think that by the time it reaches Her Majesty, there will be other means resorted to for its removal than praying. I question whether the famine much affects the landowners. Why not allow the land to be cultivated for the support of poor wretches who are suffering rather than idly praying? I fear the fast is only a deceitful way of pacifying hunger, fearing that hunger may induce the hungry to eat food where they find it. I cannot think that any humane being would inflict more misery on the poor than they already suffer.[5]

During the long, cold Scottish winter, Holyoake exchanged letters with his London publisher James Watson, who wrote from his office in Paternoster Row, hard by St. Paul's Cathedral, in a street filled with booksellers.[6] Watson, friend of radical and freethought writers, had issued George's first pamphlet on grammar, as well as his pamphlet *Rationalism: A Treatise for the Times*. Watson preferred a neighborhood that was home to booksellers over Fleet Street, further to the west. That street had housed the city's newspapers ever since the *Courant*, the capital's first daily, had set up on the bank of the River Fleet back in 1702. It was then a fetid stream that took the sewage, dead dogs, and suicide victims of central London.

The letters between the two friends overflowed with ambitious plans for a new newspaper that would fill the void left by the demise of the Owenite journal, *The New Moral World*. The only other topic broached in Watson's letters came in an expression of sympathy for Helen Holyoake's prolonged illness after she gave birth to Malthus. "I am glad Mrs. H. is over her troubles, and that she and the infant are going on so well. I hope it will continue."[7]

Watson, who saw himself as publisher of the new paper, thought "a leading point in such a periodical ought to be the enforcement of the principles of morality as a question quite separate and distinct from religion or creed of any kind." It would be a bulwark against ignorance, drunkenness and idleness, all characteristics of the present-day society that responsible freethinking could eradicate. The paper should include literary pieces and scientific articles as well as essays on social issues that would help reunite Socialists in a common cause.

None of Holyoake's responses survive but we can infer from Watson's letters that he would have sought assurance of editorial freedom. "I mean you to have the editorship most certainly," Watson wrote Holyoake. "And to have the entire management, and also the proceeds ... as Editor your power is absolute." Holyoake also would be responsible for finding and working with a printer. After Holyoake's return to London, they talked over coffee and cigars in Watson's office. The only problem was neither had the funds to launch a new, national freethought paper. Watson saw the need to be "just to all partners," suggesting they would recruit freethinking friends to put up the needed capital.[8]

~~~

One day that spring, his mind perhaps occupied with how to raise money, Holyoake answered a knock at the door of his London flat. His visitor was John Dickinson, the Oddfellows Grand Master he had met in Glasgow. He had come from the Oddfellows 1846 convention in Bristol held on June 1, and he carried an envelope with him. He handed it to Holyoake. It contained five £10 notes. Holyoake's essays had been chosen over the work of seventy-nine entrants; he had won all five prizes.[9] "I remember I was much surprised, for I had never even seen so much money before," Holyoake would record. "It was with this money that I set up *The Reasoner*."[10]

In his ambition to start a newspaper targeting working class and freethinking audiences, George Holyoake faced challenges that would have spread his limited financial resources very thinly. He had to think of printing costs, finding and paying contributors, lining up news agents to sell the paper and subscribers to take it, and an office to publish it from, while hoping to have something left over to pay himself a stipend, no matter how small. All of this would have taken weeks—or months—to organize.

Holyoake moved into Watson's offices at 3 Queen's Head Passage, Paternoster Row, and from there issued the first edition of *The Reasoner*, dated June 3, 1846.[11] The timing suggests Holyoake had been organizing its launch well before Dickinson's visit. Winning the essay contest was a stroke of luck but Holyoake appears to have overstated its importance in saying he used the money to "set up" the newspaper.

In his opening editorial, Holyoake declared that *The Reasoner* would be "Communistic in Social Economy—Utilitarian in Morals—Republican in Politics—and Anti-Theological in Religion." A more daring onslaught on the status quo could hardly have been imagined. Along with Holyoake's attacks on religion in general came articles espousing various Socialist causes, inserted on the insistence of James Watson. At Watson's urging, the moribund *Herald of Progress*, the Owenite paper since the demise of *The New Moral World*, was incorporated into the new tabloid-sized sheet. *The Reasoner* sold for 2d and consisted of articles in small type with few illustrations. It was altogether not an easy read, especially by the workingmen whom Holyoake thought of as his main audience. It did, however, receive some good press; *The Leeds Times* allowed that "the essays and articles which it contains are written with considerable skill and power."

Holyoake calculated he would need a circulation of three thousand to break even. It appears *The Reasoner* sold no more than half that number. After thirteen weeks Holyoake calculated a loss of £37. He took no salary, the paper was cut to eight pages and its price was reduced to 1½d. Friends chipped in to keep *The Reasoner* going and a "shilling fund" was launched that gained three hundred contributors who donated nearly £100. In this manner, the paper would lurch on until 1861 as the only national voice of British freethought, and in the 1850s, his chief trumpet for Secularism. Holyoake proudly declared that "indirectly, covertly, insidiously, many papers attack religion, but only *The Reasoner* assails it openly and avowedly."

~~~

Holyoake had launched *The Reasoner* at a time when the notorious Stamp Tax—the hated "tax on knowledge"—stood at one penny per copy, reduced from four pence by the 1836 Reform Act. The tax went all the way back to Queen Anne, who proclaimed it as a "war tax" in 1712. It was only one of three taxes that burdened newspapers in Holyoake's time, the others being a tax on paper (newsprint) and a 1s 6d tax on advertisements. Together, the taxes brought in a million pounds a year but many observers of all classes saw them as primarily aimed at pricing newspapers out of the hands of working men. The tax rate varied over the years but was often boosted during times of rebellion—such as after the Peterloo Massacre—when ruling circles felt a need to suppress radical ideas.

In 1851, George Holyoake became a passionate member and fund raiser for a newly formed Newspaper Stamp Abolition Committee. He would remember: "A greater array of eminent men took part in this work than in any other agitation of that time."

The first blow against the knowledge taxes came the next year when a jury ignored the Stamp Act and acquitted Charles Dickens of putting out an unstamped newspaper, the *Household Narrative of Current Events*.[12] The Anti-Stamp committee cheered and Holyoake stepped up his fund raising. The committee's agitation led the Chancellor of the Exchequer, William Gladstone, to present a bill in 1853 to drop the advertisement tax to 6d. When the government was caught at an evening session with not enough MPs present to pass the bill, an alert Opposition member, E.H.J. Crawford, moved that the tax be set at 0d. His motion was carried.

The Crimean War of 1853–56 created a great demand for news of the conflict. With daily newspapers too costly for most readers, Holyoake took part in a brilliant, if devious, scheme to circumvent the Stamp Tax. Because the tax did not apply to monthlies, he undertook to publish four different papers, each called the *War Chronicle* in the name of a different editor, on successive weeks. Every Saturday, the public was able to buy a new *War Chronicle* recording that week's news of the war. In a further act of defiance, Holyoake also issued a weekly wartime *Fly Sheet* and put up a large sign in the window of his new office in Fleet Street House bearing the heading: "Sham War Against the Unstamped Press."

Holyoake had no intention of paying the Stamp Tax and he never did. The Attorney General issued orders that Holyoake pay fines of £20 on each copy for having printed them on "unstamped paper." He ignored these and other summons. In triumph, he claimed he had owed the Crown £600,000

9. Fleet Street Ink and the Fight for an Unstamped Press

and offered to pay a shilling a week. Embarrassment mounted for the government, forcing it to finally abolish the Stamp Act on June 15, 1855. The duty on newsprint was the last to go, being lifted in 1861. "News was no longer criminal," Holyoake would write.[13]

With *The Reasoner* barely afloat on loans of friends and donations by subscribers, there was no money to pay Holyoake a salary. Leaving the paper in the hands of William Chilton, a former partner and editor of *The Oracle of Reason*, Holyoake took to the lecture circuit. He spoke in all the favored Owenite towns—Sheffield, Manchester, Birmingham—but the fees he extracted from admission charges and the donation plate were slim. He faced constant difficulty in finding halls to speak in and rooms to sleep in. At Northampton, the landlord of the hotel where a room had been booked for a lecture refused to allow it to be used for so nefarious a purpose as preaching atheism. The Temperance Hall also turned him down. When he finally found a willing landlord, he was forced to pay four times the normal rate for an evening's use.

Holyoake had by now climbed the ladder of the crumbling Owenite edifice and was a member of its Central Board. His stay was a short one and after a few months he was replaced in a shake-up. With the future of Queenwood in legal dispute, the Rational Society lost its handsome Hall of Science in London. Holyoake had

George Holyoake lectured widely after coining the term secularism but was denied access to halls in many English cities (courtesy Bishopsgate Institute).

lectured there frequently and taught grammar and logic at the Mechanics' Institute in Gould Square. He wrote for the *People's Press*, a monthly published from the Isle of Man, from where it successfully evaded the stamp law.

A lighter moment came when Sophia Collet, Sarah Lewin, and Elizabeth Burgess, all friends attracted to the freethought movement, noticed that Holyoake wrote his copy seated on an ancient chair behind a rickety table. In faux legalese, they wrote to him with the gift of a new desk:

> Having learned with regret that the said G.J. Holyoake is accustomed to pen his erudite and doubtless world-convincing compositions from a writing-desk whose antiquated and ruin-like conditions must excite in the spectator's mind mournful reflections on the degenerate state of things, besides affording no protection against the predatory incursions of minikin marauders .,, The undersigned therefore hereby request the said G.J. Holyoake's acceptance of the accompanying writing-desk, with the wish that he may never pen from it a single sentence that he is not prepared to vindicate to all mankind.[14]

By 1850, Holyoake had written and published at least twenty-five pamphlets. He had written a life of Richard Carlile, an instruction book on public speaking, a primer on logic and reasoning, and an explanation of mathematics—*Mathematics no Mystery, or, the Beauties and Uses of Euclid*. His next work was a book on his trial, *History of the Last Trial by Jury for Atheism in England*, much of which he had written while in jail. James Watson priced it at 1s 6d, and for a time it sold briskly. Holyoake was writing for many newspapers, including the most successful Chartist outlet, *The Northern Star* of Leeds. He wrote frequently for the *Newcastle Star*, owned by his friend James Cowen, Sr., the Liberal MP for Newcastle. Holyoake's family was steadily increasing; Eleanor bore a third son, Malkes, in 1847 and a fourth, Maximillian Robespierre, in 1848.

After taking a job as parliamentary secretary to Cowen, Holyoake also sat in the press gallery as a correspondent. No thought was given, apparently, to the conflict of interest in which this placed Holyoake. It would have been comparable to a U.S. senator's chief of staff being a member of the White House Correspondents' Association. Throughout his life, Holyoake called himself a publicist, a team whose meaning would change and would come to represent not a journalist, but a press agent or a public relations representative acting for a paying client.

~~~

In 1853, with a £250 purse presented to him by supporters, Holyoake finally reached Fleet Street. The radical journalist found himself among the ink-stained wretches of the popular press when he purchased the lease to a building at 147 Fleet Street, dubbing the property Fleet Street House. It was close to where Richard Carlile had once put out his seditious tracts, and Holyoake felt the spirit of his mentor was with him as he settled into his new headquarters. Holyoake's younger brother Austin came with him as secretary and general assistant. The business was organized in three departments—publishing under Frederick Farrah, printing under John Watts, and a news agency, charged with distributing *The Reasoner* and other papers to dealers throughout England, under Thomas Wilks.

Holyoake, as Director of Fleet Street House, ruled over his domain with an understanding of his colleagues' problems, but also an insistence that the work be done promptly and carefully. "The shop was made bright, and, by removal of partitions, spacious. All new books of progress were on sale, and advertised without cost to the authors," Holyoake set a half dozen goals, the first three being to promote the solution of public questions, obtain civil rights for all, and influence public affairs. His salary never exceeded £200 per year.

Before Holyoake's publishing business could reach that level, he faced a myriad of family and health problems. His relations with his parents continued to be strained, as can be seen in a letter from his mother a few months after his return to London in 1846. "I have been very unkind in not answering your letter before but I hope you and Helen will forgive me for it. I have no good news to tell you.... Henry is very unwell indeed I fear he is going like poor Frederick did."[15] Holyoke's estrangement with his parents eased over the next few years. On April 12, 1853, Catherine wrote: "Dear George I have not forgotten that today is your Birth Day and all will join with me in wishing you many very happy returns of the Day. I have inclosed [sic] a small note [money] in token of my sincere love to you my Dear Son and Helen."[16]

Holyoake was much taken with the exploits of the French Revolutionary figure Maximilien Robespierre who had died under the guillotine, and he named his youngest son Max after him. With daughter Eveline, now six years old, Holyoake had five children and a wife to support, a not inconsiderable responsibility. Feeling middle-aged, he began to grow a beard, leading Eveline to say, "Poor dada, we have made his whiskers grow stronger at last." Holyoake, in fact, was an early adopter of the Victorian beard that became popular with the Crimean War. British soldiers grew beards to protect their faces from the cold. Later, lacking either razors or soap, they let them grow.[17]

Restless and seeking new causes to promote, Holyoake became a member of the Anti-Corn Law League that sought to overturn the restrictions that since 1815 had been imposed on the import of grain. The law had been enacted when the aristocrat-dominated House of Commons bowed to the demands of landowners to suppress the competition of foreign wheat.

Designed to protect poor as well as wealthy farmers, the law caused great bitterness among British workers, downtrodden and miserable in the face of low wages, incessant taxes, and costly food. Half the population was illiterate and most workers lived in stench-filled quarters, lacking plumbing and without sufficient fuel—coal or wood—to heat their decrepit cottages and flats.

The price of bread, a staple of working class diet, rose while the laws crippled Lancashire mill owners in their pursuit of foreign markets. Opposition to the Corn Laws was no mere populist protest; the League was supported by wealthy manufacturers who wanted relief from workers' demands for higher wages. If the cost of food could be lowered, they reasoned, there would be less pressure to raise salaries. The argument against the Corn Laws gained intellectual rigor and upper class elan when the Scottish hat manufacture James Wilson launched his *Economist* newspaper in 1843.[18] An advocate of free trade and classical liberalism, he helped convince "the higher circles of the landed and monied interests" that abolition would even out the ups and downs of supply and demand, creating new opportunities for the manufacturing class.

In a nationwide crusade led by Richard Cobden, cloth manufacturer and liberal party campaigner, and John Bright, a Rochdale cotton spinner, the Anti-Corn Law League played an important role in Conservative Prime Minister Sir Robert Peel's repeal of the Act in 1846. The League was Britain's first great organized pressure group, sending lecturers around the country while distributing millions of pamphlets and posters. It gathered six million signatures and petitioned Parliament on 16,000 separate occasions.

The consequences of repeal were not all that was hoped for. Millers and merchants manipulated the price of bread, keeping prices close to their historic levels. Small farmers suffered from the drop in grain prices as grain imports grew. In Gloucestershire, an area George Holyoake was familiar with, a combination of weather damage and crop disease left farmers with small yields from the thin, exposed soils of the Cotswolds. When prices dropped, relations between tenant farmers and their landlords turned bitter. "For the tenant farmer and his labourer [repeal] dealt a severe blow which lasted several decades," according to a local history.[19] Farm laborers struggled on a salary of six shillings a week and tenant farmers were often turned out by landlords seeking more profitable uses for their land.

~~~

To George Holyoake, education meant everything. His abbreviated schooling at the Birmingham Mechanics' Institute taught him methods of study and composition, while his alert mind sent him on a search for knowledge wherever he could find it. Like his idol Robert Owen, he had

9. Fleet Street Ink and the Fight for an Unstamped Press 103

the capacity to attract support from older and better established men. A London lawyer, William Henry Ashurst, had been Owen's chief legal advisor.[20] Ashurst was impressed with Holyoake when he met him in 1842 while Holyoake was in the capital awaiting his blasphemy trial in Gloucester. Ashurst's "friendship then and afterwards was of the greatest advantage to me," Holyoake would remember.[21] A man of liberal views, Ashurst never adopted Holyoake's atheism, but advised him on his legal defense at his Gloucester trial, becoming a reliable friend and supporter.

In 1847, Ashurst loaned Holyoake £50 to cover his fees to attend lectures at the Gower Street branch of the University of London. Holyoake toyed with the idea of becoming a lawyer but he realized it was not practical for him to pursue a degree; he would never assent to taking the oath, which was required of a lawyer. He repaid the loan but had to sell his wife's watch and some of his clothes to save his brother from the bailiff. An outbreak of cholera saw Holyoake whitewashing his apartment, noting in his diary: "If this epidemic takes me suddenly I shall be obliged to apologize to my readers and friends for my abrupt and unceremonious departure."[22]

Holyoake's friendship with Ashurst deepened after the lawyer's unwise financial decision to purchase a moribund newspaper, *The Spirit of the Age*. It had been launched to advance the Chartist cause and after his purchase Ashurst engaged Holyoake as part-time editor. Holyoake recommended that Ashurst dismiss the two founders who had been kept on after the purchase, causing the pair to become his bitter enemies. Holyoake kept careful track of costs, presenting Ashurst every Saturday with a "slip of paper on which appeared the number printed, the number sold, the sum received for papers, the sum received for advertisements, cost of paper, weekly average of rent, taxes and office expenses, the amount paid for salaries and contributions; total outlay and total loss or gain."[23] After several weeks Holyoake advised Ashurst to put no more money into the project and to consider the £600 already spent "as wholly lost." The paper was closed.

In 1850, Holyoake and Ashurst attended a meeting at the Whittington Club called by the Liberal activist Thornton Hunt and the writer, George Henry Lewes. They were planning a new political weekly, *The Leader*. Ashurst told the meeting that he understood Holyoake was to be its manager. He explained Holyoake had held a similar appointment and had saved him a thousand pounds by his advice, "when it was to his interest that he (Mr. Ashurst) should go on expending the money." Ashurst agreed to invest in the new paper. Holyoake hardly knew what to make of such praise. "The speech took me very much by surprise. I was confused and said nothing."[24] When his third and last daughter was born in 1861, she was named Emilie Ashurst Holyoake.

George Holyoake would go on to report for leading newspapers in

America as well as Britain. He covered meetings of the British Association for the Advancement of Science for Horace Greely's *New York Tribune* and witnessed a hanging in 1864 for the *Morning Star*: "No reprieve has come, no horseman rushes up to the throng; no shout of pardon is heard; no possible rescue, which always lingers in the minds of the doomed, occurs."[25] He would struggle through the 1840s against the resistance to atheism that he found wherever he went and would set his mind to finding a more acceptable alternative to identify his beliefs. But first there would be revolutions to support and victims to shelter.

10

Throwing Bombs in the "Springtime of the Peoples"

The first revolution to set Europe afire in 1848 came in February with the French revolt against the Orléanist monarchy and King Louis Philippe. George Holyoake, remembering the time he'd seen the king on the railway platform at Farnborough, gave the rebels his enthusiastic support. It was the beginning of what historians would call "the Springtime of the Peoples."[1] Holyoake was in the audience at the Literary and Scientific Institution in London to hear the report of their delegation to Paris. Disturbances there and in other French cities had brought down the government, given birth to a Second Republic, and forced the abdication of Louis Philippe. London's *Morning Chronicle*, by means of "an extraordinary express," had broken the news on Friday, February 25. Special editions were run off, with one account noting that events were moving "as rapidly as the rolling waves of the ocean."[2] The delegates reporting to the London meeting spoke of print shops of Paris filled with caricatures of the deposed king, and of the surrender of Royalist troops at the fortress of Mont-Valérien, the last of the fortifications to give up the fight against the provisional government.

The grandly named Literary and Scientific Institution, familiarly known as the John Street Institution for its location at 23 John Street, a short block between Fitzroy Square and Tottenham Court Road, was a gathering place for disaffected, discontented and sometimes seditious subjects of the British Crown. Handy for hansom cabs as well as on foot, the building was within hailing distance of Euston Station, where George Holyoake had alighted in 1842 for his first view of London. Friends of Holyoake might have thought his life was unfolding as it should. In the passage of six years the convicted blasphemer had gathered a wife and children, made a name for himself on the lecture circuit, and established a reputation as the leading exponent of freethought through his weekly journal. *The Reasoner*. Holyoake and the paper, as its masthead proclaimed, were "Utilitarian, Republican & Communist."[3]

Holyoake, however, was far from content with presiding over a chronically money-losing paper that struggled to meet its bills and find contributors willing to have their words published without payment. He had refused to pay the Stamp Tax that was applied to newspapers, arguing *The Reasoner* contained no news, only opinion. This was largely true. Its content consisted chiefly of attacks on religion and the churches, reprints of articles expressing similar views, and letters, many of them lengthy, setting out opinions on the issues of the day. "*The Reasoner*," one contributor wrote, "from the nature of its position, is inevitably occupied mostly with antagonistic criticism: but it is pleasing to see that it is equally ready to receive and spread such elements of affirmative thought or imaginative beauty as harmonise with freedom." Speeches by Holyoake and others were printed verbatim, filling many columns.

Holyoake's ambition was writ large, and it encompassed two main goals: to change society, but also to harmonize its discordant parts. He was still four years away from articulating what he would call Secularism, but he was resigned to the fact that most people would never accept atheism as an alternative to Christianity. Without God, one was sure to engage in immoral and indecent behavior. How could one be good without the fear of everlasting punishment for acting otherwise?

Holyoake watched from *The Reasoner's* cubicle in Paternoster Row as the old order appeared to be crumbling across Europe. The industrialization of the continent had brought millions of peasants to the cities, only to be impressed into twelve-hour days at starvation wages. The bourgeoisie was as discontented as the laboring classes. The Vienna Treaty that since 1815 had laid out the bounds of empire among European states was coming apart. Troubles in France, Hungary, Italy, the Papal States, the German States, Denmark, and throughout the Austrian Empire—the largest territory on the European Continent under a single monarchy, the Hapsburgs—brought together workers and middle classes in short-lived coalitions.

In all of Europe, only Great Britain escaped the turmoil and violence of this super-charged spring. This didn't surprise Holyoake, for three reasons that he outlined in a talk to "some friends of action" in London: The populace "are unused to arms," England has "an equality of towns," and the conflicting interests of the country's commercial class and the people make "political compromise the only ground on which society in England can exist." Holyoake argued that one could conquer Paris by revolution and France is conquered, but conquer London and you would still have Birmingham, Manchester, Glasgow, Edinburgh "to subdue." The British "do not want one [a revolution]" he added, citing a proverb that "they handle these things better in France."⁴

∼∼∼

The troubles on the Continent had begun with a little-noticed uprising in Sicily, where a revolt against the Bourbon kingdom of the Two Sicilies (the island and southern Italy) led to formation of an independent republic. In the thirty-nine states of the German Confederation, demonstrations led by students and intellectuals demanded a unified Germany, with a democratic parliament and a free press. Riots in all the old countries of central Europe threatened entrenched authority. The Austrian Empire shook with rebellion from March to August. Emperor Ferdinand was forced to accept the demands of patriots in Hungary for a constitutional government and a separate Hungarian parliament. Protest movements in Denmark and Switzerland achieved their goals: Denmark was transformed into a constitutional monarchy while Switzerland's independent cantons were absorbed into a democratic, federal state.

The French Second Republic roiled with unrest among the unemployed amid widespread discontent in the countryside. Louis Blanc, historian of the 1793 French revolution, joined the republican government and advocated worker cooperatives that would guarantee jobs for the urban poor. His scheme of National Workshops absorbed one hundred thousand of the unemployed but the shops were poorly managed and by midsummer were closed down. Blanc fled, becoming the first influential revolutionary figure to reach London. Holyoake knew him "from the beginning to the end" of his twenty years' exile. Holyoake writes that Blanc showed him "records of the great French Revolution, amid which were letters stained with the blood of those who had written them."⁵

In December 1848 the nephew of Napoleon Bonaparte, Charles-Louis, was elected president of the Second Republic. By 1851, he had usurped the powers of the national assembly, become Emperor Napoleon III, and head of the Second Empire. He would soon become preoccupied with the rebuilding of Paris by his prefect, Baron Haussmann.

In Hungary, a new government led by Louis Kossuth, a revered writer and lawyer from a noble Lutheran family, declared independence. The revolt was crushed with the arrival of three hundred thousand Russian troops, sent by Tsar Nicholas I to support the Hapsburg crown. Kossuth and his prime minister, Francis Pulsky, joined the exodus of revolutionaries to London. Holyoake dined often at Pulsky's house at Highgate. He remembered the Hungarian showing him his country's crown jewels that he kept in a half dozen chests in an upstairs room. Kossuth he saw frequently, often bumping into him as the two walked in Euston Square.

Falling like dominoes, bids for independence by Slovenes, Croats and Poles all failed. The Bourbon rulers of the two Sicilies—the Kingdom of Naples—were restored to their thrones. On the mainland, a new Roman republic took power, headed by a triumvirate that included Giuseppe Mazzini, a Genoa revolutionary who had gained fame as a "poor man's lawyer." Attacked by a French army sent by Napoleon III to support Pope Pius IX, the rebellious forces of Giuseppe Garibaldi held out for a month before surrendering. Covered in blood, he appeared before the Roman Assembly to urge continuation of resistance from the Apennine Mountains. "Wherever we go, that will be Rome."

Holyoake welcomed the Continent's political refugees as they arrived in London over the ensuing decade. Among them, the undercover activities of three Italians—Felice Orsini, Giuseppe Marzini, and Giuseppe Garibaldi—would lead to Holyoake's participation in revolutionary conspiracies that would culminate, if judged by twenty-first century standards, in acts of terrorism.

~~~

Like many Italian youths of devout Catholic families, Felice Orsini was encouraged by his parents to enter the priesthood. When young Orsini heard villagers discussing a new political society that promised them better prices for their crops, he dropped all ideas of a sacred life and joined the *Giovani Italia* of Giuseppe Mazzini. It was a radical reform movement and Orsini launched himself onto a series of revolutionary adventures. Arrested, he was sentenced to life imprisonment but was freed by Pope Pius IX in time to join the 1848 uprising against the papacy. Orsini served as a member of the short-lived Roman Republic's Constituent Assembly where he became one of Mazzini's most trusted lieutenants. Sent on a secret mission to Hungary, he was arrested, only to escape from his Austrian jail by sawing through the bars of his window and clambering to the ground on a rope of bedsheets. Orsini, according to George Holyoake, had dark hair, bronzed features, but most notably a "glance of fire." He arrived at 147 Fleet Street with a manuscript under his arm, and wanted Holyoake to publish it. It was an account of his imprisonment in Austria and his daring escape. Holyoake sent Orsini to another publisher, who gave him a £50 advance.

Orsini never forgot it was Napoleon III who sent troops to crush the Ronan Republic, and in England he cultivated French contacts who were dedicated to bringing down the Emperor. One of them, Dr. Simon Bernard, invited Holyoake to dinner in the coffee-shop of Ginger's Hotel. The purpose of their meeting became clear when Dr. Bernard drew from a package the unassembled portions of two bombs. He wanted Holyoake's opinion of

10. Throwing Bombs in the "Springtime of the Peoples" 109

their construction. "Understanding machine work, I could judge whether they were well devised for their purpose, which was my reason for being there." The bombs had been finely crafted in Birmingham by the gunsmith Joseph Taylor. Holyoake assumed they were to be used by insurgents in military warfare in Italy. "I had small conception of what I had undertaken in consenting to test them."[6]

Holtyoake writes of this episode as if he were scripting a comic opera or a modern day *Dr. Strangelove*, a laugh a line. The bombs Holyoake carried home that night were fitted with percussion caps that, "like porcupine quills, stuck out all round them." He was afraid they might detonate at any time and in order that they not give him "premature trouble," he put one in each of the side pockets of his coat. As he walked to his house Holyoake was careful not to fall down "as I might not be found when I wanted to get up." At home, he transferred the bombs to a "harmless-looking black bag" and Eleanor found a place to keep them safely overnight. The next morning, bound by train for Sheffield where he was to lecture, Holyoake put the bombs again in his coat pockets. He was fearful that if the bombs were left in his bag someone might bump into it, causing a blast that would "suddenly disperse the travelers themselves."

In Sheffield, Holyoake kept the bombs close by him, his watchfulness keeping him "a prisoner in the house" where he had booked a room. He carried the bag with its bombs with him to the two lectures he gave Sunday, "an entirely troublesome day with my percussioned companions, because I had to carry the bag [with me] and place it upon a table before me while I spoke." On Monday he headed out, one bomb left in his mattress and the other carried with him. He walked all morning in various directions without finding a suitable testing place. He tried again Tuesday and finally settled on an abandoned quarry not far from the center of town.

"There were several villas within sight of it, with gardens that came near to the verge of it." Holyoake hoped the noise of an explosion would pass unnoticed "among other commotions to which Sheffield was subject." He threw the bomb into the quarry and ducked behind a bush. "The sound was very great, and reverberated around." He rose quickly and sauntered away, encountering a man who asked him if he had heard a "great noise?" Holyoake checked later to see if any fragments had been left about but nothing was to be seen. He sent off a note to Dr. Bernard: "My two companions behaved as well as could be expected. One has said nothing; perhaps through not having an opportunity. The other ... went off in high dudgeon. He was heard of immediately after, but has not since been seen."

Holyoake took the remaining bomb back to London and a few days later headed to an isolated patch of Devon to test it and a third that had been given him. The train ticket cost thirty-two shillings and this was "the only expense to which I put the projectors of these wandering experiments." His object was "to ascertain whether the new grenades would really explode, when thrown as high as a man could throw them, and falling on an ordinary road." Holyoake shared his mission with a Devon friend who stood lookout at "a field which had a stone fence, where, after throwing the bomb into the air, I could at once lie down and be protected while the fierce fragments flew around." He tossed it as far as he could, but no explosion followed. Holyoake carefully retrieved it, and finding another location, successfully exploded both missiles. "Every fragment flew unto untraceable space." He concluded the bombs could only be set off by being thrown onto a hard surface like a paved road or a flagstone walk. "They would not answer for ordinary military operations."

Felice Orsini drifted out of Holyoake's circle shortly after the bomb tests. On the evening of January 14, 1858, three bombs were thrown at the carriage of Napoleon III who was on his way with Empress Eugenie to the Paris Opera. The bombs landed on and around the carriage, killing eight people and injuring more than one hundred bystanders. Napoleon and the Empress escaped injury but Orsini, who was with the bomb throwers, was stunned by a fragment that hit him on the right temple. He managed to make it home but was arrested the next day, put on trial, and sentenced to the guillotine. Dr. Bernard was implicated in the plot but Britain refused to extradite him, causing a brief crisis in Anglo-French affairs. Holyoake wrote of the last night of Orsini's life, March 14, 1858. Giuseppe Mazzini "and a small group of the friends both of Orsini and himself, of which I was one, kept vigil until the morning, at which hour the axe in La Roquette would fall."[7]

Holyoake was certain that the bombs thrown in Paris were not those that had passed through his hands, but there is little doubt that bombs he tested were prototypes for those thrown at Napoleon. His participation in the conspiracy—willingly or unwillingly—has to be connected to a £1,000 donation Holyoake later received for the Garibaldi Fund he was raising to support the Italian uprising. It came from a Mr. Hodge, described as a republican politician, who asks in his letter accompanying the check that the money be noted as coming from "a member of the old firm of January 14"—the date of the attempt on Emperor Napoleon's life.

Holyoake's willingness to aid his revolutionary friends was tested a second time when a young Italian stabbed four foreigners—spies in the pay of Napoleon—in a restaurant in Panton Street, Haymarket. The assailant escaped and Holyoake was asked if he would provide him a safe hiding place. "I readily agreed to do so." Holyoake was of the opinion the young man would not be taken alive "and a desperate encounter would have caused alarm in my family." He wanted no such scene in his home, and arrangements were made to hide the attacker elsewhere. "I lost the pleasure of succouring so alert and brave a man." The would-be assassin was never apprehended.

~~~

George Holyoake was willing to assist revolutionaries in carrying out violent actions, but he never publicly advocated violence against the state. His efforts to aid them were directed mainly to raising money to finance underground activities. German, Polish, Hungarian, Italian and French conspirators all met in London, constituting, in the eyes of European monarchs, "a huge anarchist club." Giuseppe Mazzini, the second of the trio of Italian rebels aided by Holyoake, had found refuge in the British capital in 1837 after being tried in absentia and sentenced to death for fomenting an uprising in Tuscany. He lived first at the Sabloniere Hotel in Leicester Square and always dressed in black, in mourning for his country. He organized an Italian co-operative and founded an Italian school before returning to Italy in 1848 to take a leading role in the new Roman Republic.

When the republic was crushed by Napoleon's troops Mazzini fled again, reaching London via Switzerland. To Holyoake, Mazzini was a great conspirator who "made war by secrecy—open war being impossible to him—but never by treachery." He was a faithful Catholic whose motto for his revolutionary movements was "God and the People." Holyoake once encountered Mazzini at a crowded party in Fulham where he found him arguing that an atheist could not have a sense of duty. Garibaldi, who was present, asked, "What do you say to me? I am an atheist." Mazzini's answer was cleverly diplomatic. "Ah," he said, "you imbibed duty with your mother's milk." Holyoake remembered that "All around smiled at the quick-witted evasion."[8]

Mazzini's religious bent was combined with a strong anti-socialist sentiment, but neither affected Holyoake's admiration and support of him. Holyoake had met Mazzini in September 1849, on the Italian's return to London. "Mazzini was not merely the great devisor of action on behalf of liberty, but the inspirer of public passion which made Italian Unity possible."[9] Holyoake described Mazzini as "a tall, slender man, with high forehead, and large black eyes flashing on you unexpectedly."[10]

Mazzini and some friends organized a Friends of Italy committee and when its name was changed to the People's International League, Holyoake took a seat on its board. At Mazzini's request he launched a shilling fund in *The Reasoner*. Workmen around the country responded and in a few months contributed 9,000 shillings, or £450. Holyoake published letters and articles by Mazzini that caused controversy among English freethinkers, both for the Italian's insistence on the rule of faith and for his opposition to socialism.

Looking for every means of promoting the revolutionary movements, Holyoake hired émigré artists to paint pictures and make busts of their leaders. He turned the second floor of Fleet Street House into an office of "Political Exchange" where revolutionary exiles plotted intrigues, betrayals, and sinister plans of revolt.

Of all the Italian revolutionaries to turn to London for support, Giuseppe Garibaldi made the most indelible mark on history. His great cause was the unification of Italy, but in fourteen years spent in exile in South America—after escaping a death sentence for participation in an uprising in Piedmont—he led military campaigns for independence in Brazil and Uruguay. Returning to Italy in 1848, he was made a general of the Roman Republic and won a major battle against the French. But Napoleon's numbers were too great to resist, and when they entered Rome on July 3, 1849. Garibaldi and his army fled to the north. His epic march to San Marino ended with a force of only two hundred and fifty troops still at his side. Garibaldi managed to find his way to Tangier. A wealthy friend bought a merchant ship that Garibaldi sailed to the United States where he spent a year before moving on to South America. Now an accomplished mariner, he was given command of another merchant ship that he sailed to China and back to the United States via Cape Horn. He returned to Britain in 1854 in command of yet another merchant vessel. Holyoake met Garibaldi at a dinner at Stansfeld's restaurant that year. He became Secretary of the Garibaldi Fund Committee and over the next several years would channel an unknown amount of money—possibly thousands of pounds—to Garibaldi's operations in southern Italy.

With Holyoake's encouragement, Britain sent more than money to fight for Garibaldi. It sent men also, in direct violation of the Foreign Enlistment Act. A recruiting drive was disguised as a tourist venture and Holyoake wrote leaflets that were scattered about London, inviting young men to join in the excitement:

> A select party of English Excursionists intends to visit South Italy. As the country is somewhat unsettled, the Excursionists will be furnished with means of self-defence, and, with a view of recognizing each other, will be attired in a picturesque and uniform costume. General Garibaldi has liberally granted the Excursionists a free passage to Sicily and Italy. And they will be supplied with refreshments and attire suitable for the climate.[11]

By now, 147 Fleet had become engulfed in the comings and goings of volunteers and Holyoake rented a house on nearby Salisbury Street to serve as a headquarters for the Excursionists. Many would-be volunteers were turned away but about one thousand were chosen for the expedition. Mysterious figures appeared to lead the regiment, including a self-styled Captain (later Major) Styles, and a Captain de Rohan, supposedly the General's naval-aide-de-camp. Funds disappeared, delays were encountered, and nearly half the recruits gave up waiting and joined the British Army or found other employment.

Holyoake witnessed the departure from Shoreditch on September 30, 1860, of *The Emperor,* carrying 550 remaining volunteers. It reached Naples on October 16, a month after Garibaldi had taken the city. Their one and only engagement came the next day when they marched to Capua and engaged a Neapolitan brigade intent on hurling the foreigners into the sea. Whether due to guts or greater firepower, the Excursionists forced the Neapolitans to give up the south bank of the Volturno River in a five-hour battle. Garibaldi expressed his appreciation in a letter to W.H. Ashurst, treasurer of the Garibaldi Fund committee:

> They came late. But they made ample amends for this defect, not their own, by the brilliant courage they displayed in the slight engagements they shared with us near the Volturno, which enabled me to judge how precious an assistance they would have rendered had the war of liberation remained longer in my hands. In every way the English volunteers were proof of the goodwill borne by your noble nation towards the liberty and independence of Italy.[12]

The battle of Volturno River was the only one the Excursionists fought, as the Second Italian War of Independence was winding down. Garibaldi agreed to turn over power to the Piedmontese monarch, Victor Emmanuel, in order that progress could be made toward the unification of Italy. In doing so, Garibaldi abandoned the republican Mazzini, who argued, unsuccessfully, for a restoration of the Roman Republic. Garibaldi would have other battles before Victor Emmanuel would reign over a united Italy but the main task facing the English Excursionists was to find their way home. They lost their clothes in switching steamers, ninety of the men were stranded at Gibraltar, and the main body landed in London on January 14, 1861, penniless and hungry. Some funds arrived from Italy but it took a personal visit by Holyoake to a certain banker in a certain English town to obtain the final £400 that had been collected by local workingmen for the Garibaldi fund.

George Holyoake never hesitated to lend aid to those who sought refuge from oppression. What was it that compelled him to support these desperate men? A foolhardy admiration for their daring? Doing good for his fellow man, an ethic that would become a fundamental aspect of the Secularism that was now thrashing about in his mind? Or a sense of obligation to any who were struggling to obtain the rights most Englishmen had enjoyed for generations? It is likely all these emotions played a part in shaping Holyoake's reaction to the crushing of the 1848 uprisings across Europe. Whatever his motives, his actions demonstrated a willingness to defy the law and lend secret assistance to assassins, risking his own fate in the process. Since his days as a Social Missionary for Robert Owen's Religious Rationalists, Holyoake had shown a principled commitment to his own particular ideas of public morality, social order, and responsibility to his fellow citizens. Atheism, anarchism, socialism—they all had their place in George Holyoake's complex and highly personalized view of the world. Strains of all these ideas were coming together as he launched onto the great work of his life—the invention of Secularism and its formula for the rational ordering of human affairs.

11

How the Idea of Secularism Came Into Being

> Greater than the tread of mighty armies is an idea whose time has come.—Victor Hugo

> **Secularism.** 1. The doctrine that morality should be based solely on regard to the well-being of mankind in the present life, to the exclusion of all considerations drawn from belief in God or in a future state.
>   a. As the name of a definitely professed system of belief, promulgated by G.J. Holyoake (1817–1906).
> 2. The view that education, or the education provided at the public cost, should be purely secular.
> —Oxford English Dictionary

When George Jacob Holyoake devised the word Secularism in 1851, he gave name to a movement that would affect the life experience of millions around the world. Holyoake's Secularism was founded on the idea that the duties of a life lived on earth should rank above preparation for an imagined life after death. Public morality—compassion, altruism, social enlightenment—need not depend on religious foundations. This idea, as old as the democracies of the Greek city states and as new as the radical theories of the freethinkers—Thomas Paine, Richard Carlile, Robert Owen, and others—would seep slowly into Britain's national life, changing forever the country's social and political landscape. Freed of religious impediments blocking entry of the irreligious to higher education, the professions, and positions of influence in public life, people could get on with the business of improving their lives. Where theology regarded life as a sinful necessity, Secularism saw life as a cause for rejoicing. It led George Holyoake to set out a new purpose for living:

> Leave religious dreamers to wait on supernatural aid—let us but look to what man can do for man.... Let pulpits rave, and, if such unhappily is still their wont, bigots scold in their erring zeal; but let no man fear to serve humanity—the end of that man will be peace. He who knows how to live will know how to die.[1]

While Holyoake saw Secularism as an alternative to Christianity, he realized it would never sweep away all the remnants of a Christian age. The two could co-exist, with religion remaining a freely chosen option for private life, but the state—education, science, government, the economy—devoid of religious dictates. Over the coming century, the United Kingdom embraced the substance of Secularism while retaining the formality of an established church and a monarch who serves as "defender of the faith." The appointment of Church of England bishops to the House of Lords and Parliament's role in the passage of church legislation, along with religious teaching in many state-sponsored schools, would remain accepted fixtures of national life.

European colonialism would spread variations of Secularism to much of the world, notably India, while America and France continued the pursuit of their own historic visions. The United States decreed in its Constitution that "Congress shall make no law respecting an establishment of religion," although the wall of separation would never be as impenetrable in America as in France or in the Canadian province of Quebec. The anti-clericalism of the French Revolution would hound the Roman Catholic Church until the Republic finally seized control of the nation's schools in 1905.

George Holyoake found himself leading multiple lives, any one of which would have challenged a less determined person. He was the exponent of the new concept of Secularism; the editor of a newspaper of anti-religious views; a sympathizer and supporter of political refugees exiled from their homelands; a lecturer of radical opinions; a teacher of grammar and mathematics; an author of political pamphlets and political tracts; and a husband and a father of four children with whom he spent very little time. Whatever his task of the moment, one issue would have shifted in and out of his thoughts: how to organize society so as to improve the material welfare of humanity and give everyone the right to live their lives without religious interference. He no longer held to the robust atheism of his youth and he had no wish to impose on the religious views of others. Holyoake wanted everyone—not only himself but *everyone*—to be subject to just rule, and to see it as their duty to apply a portion of their time and energy to the service of others.

Holyoake reflected on the combat that was raging between the churches and advocates of freethought when he became a social missionary ten years ago. Magistrates raised in the dogma of religion sent people like him to jail because of their opinions. The combat, he knew, had been going on for centuries and any independent, uncontrolled opinion had always been regarded as dangerous. Holyoake would sum up all that had gone before: "When the priest is master, inquiry is sharply reduced."[2] He believed it was time to end the mastery of priests. While monitoring the reverses suffered by the revolutionaries of 1848, he was pondering the principles that would become basic to Secularism.

~~~

There is no record of how or when George Jacob Holyoake struck on the word Secularism as the defining expression of public life free of religion. He must have discussed his ideas with his good friend and mentor, William H. Ashurst and with a newfound ally, the author George Henry Lewes. One can picture it: Holyoake up late in his rooms in Tavistock Square, London, stabbing with his pen at the sheet of paper in front of him. At his desk for hours on this midsummer night, he searches for the word to describe a single transfixing idea, one that would hasten the day when the public would enjoy a society shorn of religious regulation over every aspect of life. His table cluttered with Latin texts, French volumes, and London newspapers, Holyoake reaches for Dr. Samuel Johnson's dictionary, still the final authority on Her Majesty's English. He finds secular: "Not spiritual; relating to affairs of the present world; not holy; worldly" With a flash of insight and a scratch of his pen, Holyoake creates a new English noun, Secularism.

Unlike today when the language is filled with *isms*, using that suffix to create a new word, Secular-*ism*, was an act of rare creativity in George Holyoake's time. Google Secularism and you get 1,270,000 hits, an indication of the universal importance of the word in modern usage. Holyoake had been accustomed to using the term secular to indicate the absence of religious instruction in public education. In his autobiography, *Sixty Years of an Agitator's Life*, his first use of the word comes when he describes his designation as the teacher of a "secular school." It was to have been set up in the 1830s in Birmingham, financed by a £12,000 bequest in the will of George Russell, a publisher of "catnatch songs." The will was challenged and the bequest set aside, leading Holyoake to observe, "secular teaching was held to be hostile to Christianity."[3]

Great numbers of people were now interested in learning about Secularism. By the 1840s two-thirds of men and one half of the women in England were literate, each becoming a prospective convert. Since the establishment of the University College London (UCL) in 1837, students of all religions—or none—could enroll in their first avowedly secular institution of higher learning. Holyoake had briefly attended classes in Gower

Street in 1847, but he later implied that the university was not entirely free of religious influence.

On March 21, 1849, Holyoake noted in his diary: "Issued the first 'Secular' number of *The Reasoner*." The average reader would not have noticed much difference in the paper. In a speech on September 29, 1851, Holyoake made clear his support of secular education, describing three classes of persons as opposed to Christianity: the dissolute, the indifferent, and the intellectually independent. The latter, he declared, "avoid it [Christianity] as opposed to freedom, morality, and progress." He worked throughout October on articles and speeches on secular issues and in *The Reasoner* of November 9, set out the objects of the newspaper under a front page heading, *Truths to Tell*. One of these was: "To teach men to see that the sum of all knowledge and duty is secular—that it pertains to this world alone."

In December came the declarations that would bring the new word Secularism into public view. There was no grand launch, no great public meeting, no stirring speech, not even a pamphlet setting out Holyoake's thinking on his bold new concept. Instead, a series of brief announcements in *The Reasoner* hinted at what was to come. That month, Holyoake used the word secularist for the first time to describe a new way of thinking: "… we should certainly use the word secularist as best indicating that province of human duty which belongs to this life."[4]

A week later, Secularism appeared for the first time in public print. It was hardly a celebratory launching of his invented word; it appeared almost an after-thought in *The Reasoner's* announcement of a series of Free Discussion Festivals at the Hall of Science in City Road: "Mr. G.J. Holyoake, editor of *The Reasoner*, will lay before the meeting, on the 29th, a statement of the present position of Secularism in the provinces."[5]

It was a tea party as well as an evening of speeches. Tea was served at half past six. Austin Holyoake's wife played the piano and sang "Praise to The Martyrs." Holyoake repeated much of his September talk on Christianity and was careful to distinguish between thoughtful freethinkers and the "dissolute and the ignorant classes." To make himself clear, he added: "Freethinkers who *do* think should be distinguished from those who *do not* think, and this can be done only by announcing a principle, defining aims, and creating an organization to attain those aims." Its chief principle should be to uphold "the recognition of the secular sphere as the province of man." He invited his audience to join a newly formed Secular Society. It would have an air of exclusivity. "We do not need everybody to join in this work. A selection of earnest men will suffice for us." The lesson of Secularism, Holyoake reaffirmed, is that "all man's work and devotion ought to be directed towards the things of this world and towards humanity."[6]

Holyoake has been criticized for a lack of organizational skill, a charge that gains support from the fact Secularism received so few mentions in *The Reasoner* through 1852. He was still thinking out the nature of his creation. Should Secularism stand as an ethical creed of moral guidance or should it be offered up as a philosophical alternative to Christianity? Should there be an attempt to become a mass movement, or was it best to confine discussion of Secularism to the few thousand *Reasoner* readers and their freethinking compatriots?

It was the opinion of one reader of *The Reasoner*, Charles Frederick Nicholls, that an emotional appeal would help the spread of Secularism. "If Rationalists have any mission it is to secularize the world, that they may moralize it. A strong moral impulse must be given to the secular army." His letter, appearing under the heading "The Future of Secularism," was a feature of the February 4, 1852, edition. "What I want is—not that we should ignore the intellect in the slightest—that we should not overlook the poetical in human nature, the sympathetic, the emotional. Our exertions may lead to a new epoch, if we do not fail to speak to both sides of human nature, the intellectual and the emotional."

Holyoake took Secularism on the road in April. He spoke on three successive nights in Sheffield. *The Sheffield Free Press* sniffed, "Mr. Holyoake does not deny the existence of a God, but merely says he cannot see sufficient reason to believe that such a being exists. He calls himself a Secular." Always pressed for funds, Holyoake wrote to Eleanor from Sheffield to promise "I shall send you 10s to make up your £2–10–0 weekly" allowance.[7]

～～～

The circulation of *The Reasoner* rose and fell, but it was mainly through lectures and debates that Holyoake publicized the advent of his new social order. Holyoke enjoyed debating and he needed a strong Christian opponent who would put up a stiff defense of Christianity. He was sure his secularist logic would win out over simple faith. Holyoake found his rival in the Rev. Brewin Grant, a fast-talking, self-assured exponent of Biblical truths. Beginning on January 20, 1853, they went at it every Thursday night for six weeks in the Cowper Street School Rooms in London.

The debates were as elaborately prepared as duels, with Holyoake and Grant each having their own chairman. The contests were organized by the Holyoake family's old pastor, the Rev. John Angell James of Birmingham. The topic was: "What advantages would accrue to mankind generally and the working classes in particular by the removal of Christianity and the substitution of Secularism in its place." Holyoake always maintained that the reference to Christianity's removal came at Grant's insistence, not his. The fact Holyoake agreed to debate on these terms suggests he was convinced the conflict of Secularism and Christianity would only be ended by the withdrawal of church influence from the public arena. Christians and other deists would be free to practice their religion in private life. No longer would religion impose duties and burdens on an unwilling public.

Grant, a dissenting preacher, was loud, sometimes vulgar, and boasted that he could speak three times faster than any other man. Holyoake usually showed respect to Christian ministers, but he was not impressed with Grant's bearings or his superior airs. Grant "had manifest courage, pertinacity, and ceaseless fertility in objection, but the scrupulousness which commands respect was not so conspicuous." Holyoake thought him "the nimblest opponent I ever met … but his general epithets were below the level of street-corner coarseness."[8] Holyoake argued again that the "duties of this life which we know should take precedence over those of another which we do not know." Forty-five thousand copies of a report on the debate were sold at a half crown each.

The influential *Westminster Review* thought "Mr. Holyoake takes rank among the ablest expounders of the life according to nature," while the Reverend Grant "holds to the opinion that any amount of personal abuse is allowable." *The Review* saw Secularism as "the theory of doing without religion," but that "it may yet become religious."[9] There was still little understanding of how Secularism might evolve and George Holyoake was as uncertain as anyone else.

There were other debates, most notably a second round with Grant in Glasgow before a crowd of three thousand. "A Glasgow paper said the casual visitor would take Holyoake to be the Christian and Grant the infidel."[10] A further duel pitted Holyoake against the Rev. J.H. Rutherford in Newcastle. Both held firmly to their views but the next morning Holyoake and Rutherford enjoyed a leisurely breakfast together. It was characteristic of Holyoake to seldom speak negatively of his critics; over a lifetime this would earn him a reputation for kindness and respect.

~~~

While Holyoake was struggling to distill his thoughts on Secularism into a clear visionary statement, he berated himself for "crowding too many subjects on the canvas of my speeches."[11] He tried to correct this when he went on tours in 1851 to the main towns of the Midlands and northern England. He drew large crowds; people had few diversions and many held a consuming thirst for knowledge. His earnings from admission fees of a penny per person were a meager supplement to the salary he drew from *The Reasoner*.

On free evenings, Holyoake wrote lengthy dispatches for the paper. In a March issue he reported on three lectures he had given in Nottingham. His topics were Christianity, Catholicism, and an explanation of why the clergy avoided discussion of certain issues. Each night, the Rev. Mr. Collison, a parson of local notoriety, stepped forward to challenge Holyoake. "There was a certain classic repose about [his] speeches which made them very agreeable to hear." Much heckling took place and Holyoake warned he would regard anyone "who interrupted [the minister] in any manner, or on any pretext whatsoever, as my personal enemy."[12]

It was not like George Holyoake to refuse any request for help. The burden it might place on him or the distance he would have to travel did not matter. When the Workingman's Reading Club of Carlisle, the county town of Cumbria in northwest England, accepted an offer of a plot of land for its own building, it was on condition that the club stock no irreligious books, Tom Paine's *Age of Reason* among them. The decision split the club, and opponents of the deal invited George Holyoake to Carlisle to speak in their support. It was raucous event, and Holyoake had to stand on a chair to make himself seen. From the report of his speech in the *Carlisle Journal* describing a "densely crowded" meeting hall filled by three to four hundred people, we can imagine the smell as well as feel the heat of the occasion:

> The dissentients were instrumental in engaging Mr. G.J. Holyoake, of London, editor of a sceptical publication called the "*Reasoner*," to deliver a lecture upon the subject, on Tuesday night last. The Athenaeum could not be obtained, and the long room of the Blue Bell inn, Scotch-street, was therefore engaged for the purpose. The room, being imperfectly ventilated, even with the windows open, was insufferably hot and redolent of what Jack Falstaff would have termed a villainous compound of bad smells. The interest evinced was intense, and the satisfaction expressed with the views propounded by the lecturer unmistakable.[13]

Another time, Holyoake went to Whitehaven, a coastal town near Carlisle, to speak in support of James Hughan, a Unitarian street-lecturer who had been assaulted after talking about "Progression," a pre–Darwinian theory on how man developed from the lower orders. When the case against Hughan's assailant reached court, the magistrate, a minister, dismissed the charge and censured Hughan for having "incited" his attacker by his talk. Holyoake was warned his appearance would cause a riot and the sergeant of police told his men to stay away from the lecture hall so they would not get "their heads broken."

Holyoake was keenly attuned to class differences and he understood the behavior of aroused Englishmen. He'd been given the gift of a white silk top hat, and happened also to have recently acquired a new coat. "In this attire I walked out to inspect the foe. The local mob made way for me, and those who would have knocked me down had I worn a 'seedy' aspect, stepped involuntarily out of the way." His lecture went off with only minor interruptions. The audience was "astonished at not being outraged."[14]

Finding a platform from which Holyoake could talk about Secularism was never an easy task. He was often denied use of public halls, as a report in *The Reasoner* of June 15, 1853, made scandalously clear. In Bury, a suburb of Manchester, Holyoake arrived to find a notice on the door of the Phonetic Institute, signed by the local Vicar, denying him use of the room he had reserved for his lecture. "A member of the Institute, indignant at the conduct pursued, forced open the door, with the consent of many of his fellow-members, and let in the audience." Reluctant to be part of an illegal break-in, Holyoake refused to enter the hall. He had a placard posted the next morning: "The reverend rector who has prevented us being heard has forgotten the great injunction of his Master—to do to others as he would wish to be done unto himself." Holyoake finally found space at the People's Institute in Manchester and spoke twice there the following Sunday.

Holyoake further spelled out the goals of Secularism in a *Reasoner* article in August 1853. One aim was "to obtain the repeal of all Acts of Parliament which interfere with secular practice." He would later add: "This is exactly the attitude Secularism takes with regard to the Bible and to Christianity. It rejects such parts of the Scriptures, or of Christianism, or Acts of Parliament, which conflict with or obstruct ethical truth." A long battle would lie ahead to obtain for atheists the right to testify in court or accept public office with a simple affirmation they would speak the truth, instead of swearing the traditional Biblical oath. Secularism's roots were taking hold in the soil of a changing England.

~~~

George Holyoake was on tour when the 1851 census of England and Wales took place. Instructions were sent to every household to record on their census forms, on the evening of Sunday, March 30, all those present and sleeping in the house that night.[15] Eleanor Holyoake, in George's absence, spread the document in front of her, possibly on the kitchen table after the children had been put to bed. The address, 1 Woburn Buildings, Tavistock Square, in the parliamentary borough of Marylebone. London, had been written in by the census enumerator. Eleanor would have entered her own name and her relationship to the head of the family—wife. Then came the children, Ellen, Manfred, Malthus, and Maximillian, in order of their birth. Eleanor recorded two other occupants of the flat—a boarder, Henry Merritt, a picture restorer; and a cousin, Anne Porter, age nineteen, a "general servant." Satisfied she had done her civic duty, Eleanor folded and placed the sheet in the envelope left by the enumerator, and went to bed. The form was collected the next day, along with several million others that when totaled at the office of the Registrar General, would show England and Wales to have a population of 15.9 million.

Eleanor's enumerator, as it would turn out, erred when he copied her

11. How the Idea of Secularism Came Into Being   123

file into the account book that would serve as the official record for his district. He showed Eleanor as a widow, presumably because he had noted the absence of a husband, and had put down her occupation as an "annuitant." He also listed her as Head of the household, a status Eleanor would never have claimed. George was not himself accounted for in the 1851 census; one of many itinerants or travelers who were missed when the enumerators made their rounds. Holyoake never knew of the errors. It was likely not until census records were posted online and the Holyoake entry was examined in research for this book, that the errors were found.[16]

That summer, the Great Exhibition under the Royal sponsorship of Queen Victoria and Prince Albert held all of London and much of England, in thrall. It all came together in seventeen months. It was held in Hyde Park, a 350-acre expanse of green and water, one of four adjacent parks that provide the "lungs" of central London. The Exhibition opened May 1 and ran until October, attracting six million visitors. Everyone was impressed: Even Queen Victoria noted in her diary that "The Park presented a wonderful spectacle, crowds streaming through it, carriages and troops passing, quite like the Coronation day."

The Exhibition was put forward as a chance to show Britain as a world leader in industry, but it also had its critics. Karl Marx saw it as an emblem of capitalist exploitation while some conservatives expressed fear it would bring on outbursts by revolutionary mobs. Holyoake would have laughed at both extremes; he was no lover of capitalism but neither did he see any danger of rebellious gatherings. He wrote a pamphlet about the Exhibition, lamenting the fact it was the "unseen misery" of the workers that lay behind the pompous splendor of the Fair. "A belief arose that international commerce would increase," Holyoake wrote, but England saw little growth in foreign trade. By the time autumn leaves fell, the Great Exhibition of the Works of Industry of All Nations had passed quietly into history.[17]

~~~

As part of the 1851 census, a count was conducted of the 34,467 churches and chapels of England and Wales—fourteen thousand of them being of the "Established Church." *The Report of Religious Worship* determined there was room for ten million worshippers (fifty-eight percent of the population) on any given Sunday. In fact, based on tallies taken March 30, only half the pews were filled. The figures lead to the inescapable fact that barely more than a quarter of the population were regularly attending a place of worship. The census found that twenty-seven homegrown and nine foreign religions were active in the country. Aside from making a good case for the indifference of so many people, the census took no notice of avowed atheists or Jews; neither presence was acknowledged. But by the time the report was issued in 1854, Secularism had come to the attention of the Registrar General's office. *The Report of Religious Worship* noted:

> There is a sect, originated recently, adherents to a system called "Secularism," the principal tenet being that as the fact of a future life is (in their view) at all events susceptible of some degree of doubt, while the fact and necessities of a present life are matters of direct sensation, it is therefore prudent to attend exclusively to the concerns of that existence.... This [Secularism] is the creed which probably with most exactness indicates the faith which virtually through not professedly, is entertained by the masses of our working population; by the skilled and unskilled labourers alike—by hosts of minor shopkeepers and Sunday traders—and by miserable denizens of courts and crowded alleys. They are unconscious Secularists.[18]

The idea that Secularism was a new religion would not go away easily. To the Anglican historian W.N. Molesworth, "Secularism is, in fact, the religion of doubt. It does not necessarily clash with other religions." Holyoake's reaction? "There are tens of thousands of persons in most European countries who are without the pale of Christianity. They reject it, they disprove it, they dislike it."[19] He would never accept that Secularism and religion were in any way synonymous.

~~~

As immersed as Holyoake was in his formulation of secularist ideas, he maintained a lively interest in revolutionary activity on the Continent. His hero of the French Revolution was Maximilien Robespierre, the notorious figure who was largely responsible for the Reign of Terror that ended with his own execution. Holyoake would have us believe he admired Robespierre not for his bloodthirsty treatment of those he saw as traitors to the Revolution, but for the care the Frenchman took in preparing his speeches: "...he used one sized paper, and wrote out himself all his speeches in a large and careful hand. No one can do that without detecting verbiage, irrelevance, and limpness of expression."[20]

Holyoake had named his youngest son after Maximilien Robespierre, clear evidence of his admiration for this controversial figure. Holyoake was a guest at a tea party honoring Robespierre at the National Hall in Holborn on April 13, 1852. Handbills put about London to announce the meeting hailed "The Incorruptible Robespierre." The names of Holyoake, his friend Louis Blanc, the French political refugee, and Louis Kossuth, the Hungarian exile, were listed as among the invited.

Along with good family times, the 1850s were not free of personal disappointment and grief for George Holyoake. In 1853 he was summoned back to Birmingham; his father was dying. He found his father in bed, a long Turkish pipe at his side, its bowl resting on a chair. They shared the pipe until his father died on May 9. Holyoake's right hand man at *The Reasoner*, William

Chilton, was next, dying on May 28, 1855. Holyoake was ill, stricken with almost total blindness, and lay near comatose in a darkened bedroom. On July 8 his son Maximillian, only eight, fell under the hooves of a horse pulling a hansom cab in Tavistock Square. He died ten days later.

> A gentleman whose name I never knew carried him tenderly to University College Hospital. His own clothes were spoiled by the blood. I could never learn who he was to thank him for all that kindness. At the inquest I was allowed to make a statement as to the recklessness of the cabman who killed him, but was told that I could not give evidence against him, as I was unable to take the oath.[21]

It is likely that the congestion of London's streets, with horses and carriages fighting for space, was as much a cause of the boy's death as any inattention by the hansom driver. At Max's burial in Highgate cemetery, a secularist hymn written by the author Harriet Martineau was sung by Holyoake's friend, C.D. Collet. George and Eleanor returned home grieving the second loss of a child. Maximillian's death plunged Holyoake into such despair that alarmed friends raised a bequest to send him on a vacation in the south of France. He needed it, if he was to continue the radical life.

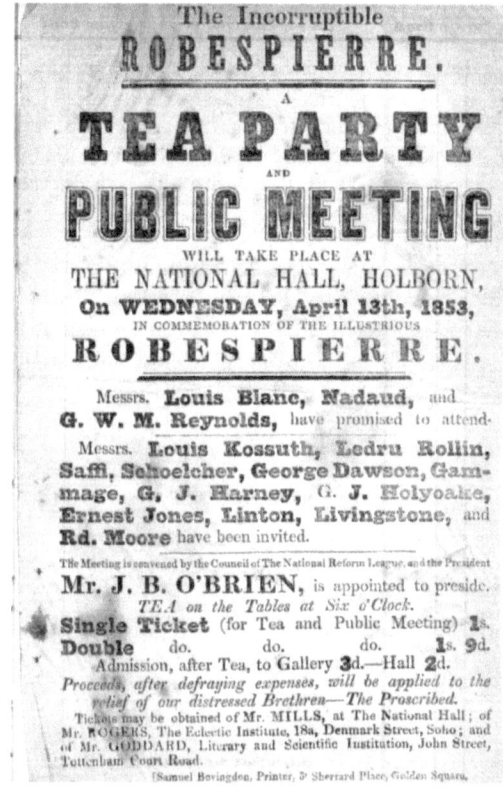

George Holyoake admired French Revolutionary figure Maximilien Robespierre (courtesy Bishopsgate Institute).

Holyoake came back from France determined to build *The Reasoner* into a more influential paper, and to gain broad public support for Secularism. He saw Secularism not as merely a movement, but as a philosophy for living that would replace the old shibboleths of religion with more humane ideals and values. This theme ran through his first pamphlet on his new ideology, *Secularism: The Practical Philosophy of the People*. He published it in 1854, and aimed his opening passage at the unjust society which religion seemed helpless to correct:

> In a state of society in which every inch of land, every blade of grass, every spray of water, every bird and flower has an owner, what has the poor man to do with orthodox religion which begins by proclaiming him a miserable sinner, and ends by leaving him a miserable slave, as far as unrequited toil goes? The poor man finds himself in an *armed* world where might is God, and poverty is fettered. Abroad the hired soldier blocks up the path of freedom, and the priest the path of progress. Every penniless man, woman and child is virtually the property of the capitalist, no less in England than is the slave in New Orleans.[22]

George Holyoake's idea of Secularism was that of a new moral force that would bring about an improvement in the material conditions of life, especially for the English workingman. The removal of religion from public life had become an almost incidental factor; but first there had to be a new feeling of goodwill in the hearts of men.

Part IV

A Respectable Man

12

Finding Yourself in Company of the Famous

Long before the "Four Freedoms" of Winston Churchill and Franklin Delano Roosevelt were ever heard of, George Holyoake spelled out the "four rights" to which Secularism was dedicated. These were, he wrote in his 1859 book, *Principles of Secularism Illustrated*, the right to Think for one's self; the right to Differ; the right to Assert difference of opinion; and the right to Debate "all vital opinion." Not unexpectedly, he added that these rights would hardly be guaranteed by any religion. "It is of no use that the Protestant concedes the right to think unless he concedes the right to differ. We may as well be Catholic unless we are free to dissent."

Throughout his life Holyoake would demonstrate that he practiced what he preached. In 1857 Thomas Pooley, a Cornish well driller who was not of entirely sound mind, was alleged to have scrawled a certain blasphemous phrase on a gate. He was represented at trial by no counsel and was sentenced to twenty-one months in jail. A clergyman swore he had seen the words on the gate but a second witness, a carpenter, denied such words had ever been put there. London secularists asked Holyoake to go down to Cornwall to investigate. His report in *The Reasoner*, and an editorial in the *Spectator* that censured the judge for "treating stark folly with a tragic retribution," caused what passed for a public outcry. Holyoake was of the view that Pooley had the right to express himself in whatever way he saw fit. But he turned up evidence that Pooley was of unsound mind and did not understand what he was doing. He was freed shortly after in an act of compassion by Sir John Coleridge, the trial judge. "Had what I learned of Pooley's life been known to the counsel and judge, their trial of Pooley would have ended differently."[1]

As interest in Secularism grew, so did George Holyoake's reputation,

12. Finding Yourself in Company of the Famous

with many admirers overlooking his days of repugnant atheism. He was older, calmer, more measured in his speeches and writing. The most important things in his life, next to family, were his friends and his books. Yet, he still felt alone. He needed support from the ranks above the working class and gaining it would become as important to Holyoake as the idea of Secularism itself.

~~~

The narrow circle of working class radicals and other freethinkers, mostly atheists, who took to Secularism gave George Holyoake his first sounding board for "the promotion of human improvement by material means." These early supporters came from all levels of the working class—skilled artisans whose ability with tools and machines made them an elite among workers, and the factory hands whose monotonous, unending toil laid the foundation for a new mechanical age. All were accustomed to the deprivations of industrial life and inured to the prejudice and disapproval of town elites and country masters.

Many of the working class—probably a majority—saw the church as a barrier to their betterment. Its removal from their daily lives would free them from social subjugation and give them hope for economic liberation. Their backing alone, Holyoake knew, would not be enough to move the establishment to embrace secular thinking. It would take the influence of the opinion leaders of nineteenth century England—intellectuals, scientists, writers, and other distinguished Britons—to "seek [in Secularism] that good which is intended by nature, which is attainable by material means, and which is of immediate service to humanity."[2] It was these thinkers—men and women occupying stations in life far above Holyoake—whose hearts and minds he set out to change.

Since founding *The Reasoner* in 1846, George Holyoake had realized he would achieve little social or intellectual standing as the obscure editor of a minor radical weekly. He had to prove himself worthy of literary recognition. His chance came when George Henry Lewes published his biography of Holyoake's hero of the French revolution, *The Life of Maximilien Robespierre*. Lewes was one of England's leading authors, having established his reputation with the scholarly *Biographical History of Philosophy*. In a bid for popular following, he wrote two novels that attracted wide if only short-lived attention. Charlotte Brontë, who had just published *Jane Eyre*, liked one of them, *Ranthorpe*, and wrote to Lewes to say "It is very different to any of the popular works of fiction; it fills the mind with fresh knowledge."[3]

Holyoake's review ran in two issues of *The Reasoner* in July 1849. He welcomed the attempt to rehabilitate Robespierre's reputation, but expressed doubt whether Lewes had "any distinct idea of his own of the hero of whom he writes." Holyoake saw Robespierre as a man whose reputation "has survived calumny unequalled in universality and hatred, unparalleled in intensity." Despite his reservations of Lewes's *Robespierre*, "we desire to keep prominently before the reader the gratitude we feel for what he has generously and ably done."[4]

Holyoake knew his review was no paean of praise, but he sent it off to Lewes's home at 26 Bedford Place in Kensington, then as now one of London's most prestigious neighborhoods. He was surprised with the warmth of the response that came three weeks later. Lewes had been to "the country" and had found the papers awaiting him on his return:

> Your review of my "Robespierre" gratified me exceedingly by its tone & talent, however I may dissent from most of your conclusions, & I should be happy to talk over this and other subjects with you, if you will smoke a cigar with me on Monday evening next. I fix the evening because Mr. Thornton Hunt who is now with me is desirous of making your acquaintance & that is the only evening on which he is at liberty.[5]

When Holyoake arrived at Lewes's three-story brick townhouse on the evening of August 8, he was likely taken to the library where he found his host and Hunt awaiting him. The three men would have examined each other from chairs set a few feet apart. Lewes and Holyoake were of identical age, Lewes having been born one day after Holyoake, in admittedly more favorable circumstances. Lewes looked elegant, as usual, his long hair falling in curls to his collar, his face uncommonly handsome, indeed almost beautiful, a term not usually applied to men. Holyoake was aware that Hunt, who was the son of the well-known poet Leigh Hunt, was making his mark as a journalist and novelist. Seven years the elder of Holyoake and Lewes, Hunt was known among his friends for his radical views on marriage and sexuality.

Holyoake was unsure of his grounds and would have allowed his host to carry the conversation. Lewes's wife Agnes Jervis Lewes, a lady noted for her beauty, might have served tea. Lewes would have opened his cigar box, withdrawn three of possibly Cuban but more likely Turkish or Egyptian tobacco, clipped off their ends, and handed one to each of his guests. Their conversation covered unrecorded subjects, but the three became friends notwithstanding their often sharply differing views. It is unlikely Holyoake would have learned, in this first meeting, that Lewes and his wife had an open marriage, an arrangement that would bring considerable complication to their lives.

The meeting with Lewes and Hunt proved a turning point in Holyoake's life. He was pleased to be accepted by members of the literary elite, no mean achievement for the son of a foundry worker. Lewes found Holyoake's forthright atheism accorded with his own views. Lewes and Hunt had plans for a new paper of advanced liberal opinion, which is likely why the meeting had been set for an evening when Hunt could attend. When Holyoake was asked to be the paper's business manager—probably some weeks after their cigar session—he agreed, while emphasizing he would continue to put out *The Reasoner*. Hunt was taken by Holyoake's fresh ideas and invited him to join his "Confidential Combination" of literary figures, made up of poets, writers, and other radical thinkers. He explained its purpose in a letter: "The tyranny which keeps down the expression of opinion in our time, though less dangerous than it has been in times past, is more domesticated, more searching, and more constraining."[6] As a result, good ideas were being lost. Hunt's new circle would bring independent thinkers "together without exposing them to the action of that social tyranny."

In a prospectus outlining the aims of the proposed new paper, to be known as *The Leader*, Lewes included Holyoake's name in its list of writers. This was the first time Holyoake had been given such recognition. Until then, he wrote in a memoir, "I had only an outcast name, both in law and literature."[7] There were mutterings from those who thought the writings of an atheist had no place in *The Leader*, but Lewes's and Hunt's support for Holyoake never wavered.

The first issue of *The Leader* appeared on March 30, 1850. It pronounced itself secular in education, liberal in religion, and in favor of church reform and free trade. Holyoake wrote under the name of "Ion" in order not to dilute his radical reputation as editor of *The Reasoner*.

George Henry Lewes, who was *The Leader's* literary editor, came by his writing ability and his considerable talent for acting quite naturally. He was the illegitimate son of the poet John Lee Lewes and the grandson of comic actor Charles Lee Lewes. His mother married a retired sea captain and George was educated at a variety of schools where he picked up local customs and dialects. His big interest as a young man was philosophy, and he visited Germany where he met leading figures in the field. The experience figured greatly in his writing of *History of Philosophy* and his later, more notable, *Life of Goethe*. Lewes dabbled in playwriting, went on the stage, wrote several more books on philosophy, and entered London's literary life where he met Thornton Hunt and rubbed shoulders with figures such as John Stuart Mill, the great liberal advocate and writer. He thought Mill "a teacher of the people" and often sent his writings to him, sometimes before publication. When Mill was an MP, Holyoake accompanied him to an illegal meeting of the Reform League. "He went to justify the right of public meeting by his presence."[8] With men such as Mill writing for *The Leader*, Holyoake observed, it was read by "the intellectual leaders of society."

George Lewes and his wife Agnes, whom he called Rose, were still faithful in their marriage when Holyoake met them, but their fidelity would soon lapse. Agnes found herself strongly attracted to Thornton Hunt and they began a lifelong liaison that produced four children, all of whom Lewes would accept in his household. He tried for divorce, but because he had signed as the eldest child's father and had thus condoned his wife's adultery, he was denied legal release. Holyoake, raised in an atmosphere of sexual repression, would never accept such promiscuity. Still, he admired Lewes. He had few rivals as a conversationalist, and Holyoake wrote of him as "intellectually the bravest man I have known."

It was Hunt, however, and his "Confidential Combination" that opened up the circle of London intellectuals to Holyoake. He described Hunt as "a fragile-looking man" with "piercing eyes and a singular precision of speech." Hunt had begun work on the *Spectator*, a weekly digest of news from the daily papers. Holyoake admired Hunt for his passionate dedication to political freedom, social movement, and liberty of opinion. Hunt was a workaholic and Holyoake warned him many times to slow down. "When I urged him to rest and travel, he would say it was impossible; he could not give the time." Holyoake told him there was one thing he would have to make time for: "Time to die. I generally observe that has to be attended to, and causes lengthened interruption in fulfilling engagements."[9]

The circle that Hunt drew about him and to which Holyoake was now given entry, included some whom Holyoake already knew—such as W.H. Ashurst, his lawyer and mentor—but many more he had never met. A favored location for meetings was the Whittington Club at the Crown and Anchor public house in The Strand. The anonymity of the gatherings made it possible for literary, political, and scientific luminaries to express their views on such suspect subjects as morality, socialism, and philosophical radicalism, including the new idea of Secularism that Holyoake would advance in 1852. He talked to Francis Newman, the brother of Cardinal Newman, the Anglican intellectual who had turned Catholic; Francis Place, social reformer and critic; Herbert Spencer,[10] biologist, classical liberal theorist, and former sub-editor of *The Economist* who was writing for *The Leader*; Louis Blanc, whom Holyoake already knew; and assorted literary figures including Savage Landor and William J. Linton. Holyoake respected Spencer for his intellectual achievements but disagreed with his laissez-faire social views. It was Spencer, after all, who had applied the phrase "survival of the fittest" to society in general after reading Darwin. More happily, Holyoake made the acquaintance of Harriet Martineau who committed early to Secularism and whose books on economics and social issues made her one of England's most popular writers.

Many of Hunt's group also met at 142 Strand, the combination home and office of John Chapman, publisher of the crusading *Westminster*

Review. It was here that Holyoake met Mary Ann Evans, a young woman from a village near Coventry who was struggling with her growing religious skepticism and her ambition to achieve success as a writer. Her mother had died young and Mary Ann, allowed by an indulgent father to buy whatever books she liked, found herself unable to reconcile Genesis with geology. On January 2, 1842, she refused to go to church with him. A well off mill owner, he died in May of 1849, leaving Mary Ann a trust of £2,000. She promptly headed to Switzerland in the company of the neighboring Bray family who held freethinking views. Evans had met John Chapman in Coventry and when she returned to England she went straight to London, moved into Chapman's house, and started work as assistant editor of the *Review*. Evans either wrote, or at least edited, the report on Holyoke's debate with the Reverend Grant that the paper ran in 1853.

Evans was romantically involved for a time with another member of the Hunt-Chapman circle, Herbert Spencer. He ditched her, but shortly after she met George Lewes and the two began an affair. When Holyoake organized working dinners at *The Leader* office she "sometimes came in and joined us at table." George Lewes was often there, sometimes in the company of his wife Agnes, who "had a singularly bright complexion." As ideas and opinions flew across the table, the affair between Lewes and Evans blossomed into a full-fledged romance. Evans would become Lewes's lifelong companion and achieve literary fame under the pen name of George Eliot. Her novel, *Middlemarch*, chronicling the lives of people in a small town affected by the political crisis of the 1832 Reform Bill, would be her greatest success.[11]

Holyoake also met Thomas Huxley, who after 1859, when Charles Darwin published his *Origin of the Species,* would become known as "Darwin's Bulldog" for his fierce defense of Darwin's findings and the theory of evolution. Ten years later, Holyoake would welcome Huxley's coining the term agnosticism: "His outspokenness was the glory of philosophy and science in his day." Harriet Martineau, to whom Holyoake took an immediate liking, was not shy in making her views known. In an 1853 letter to Lloyd Garrison, editor of the anti-slavery *Boston Liberator*, she wrote:

> The adoption of the term Secularism is justified by its including a large number of persons who are not Atheists and uniting them for action which has Secularism for its object, and not Atheism. On this ground, and because, by the adoption of a new term, a vast amount of impediment from prejudice is got rid of, the use of the name Secularism is found advantageous.[12]

The principles of Secularism as set forth by Holyoake meshed comfortably with another strain of new thinking that grew out of scientific inquiry. In the ferment of ideas now referred to as scientific naturalism, Secularism offered a comfortable home for freethinking radicals of all stripes. Shed of the stigma of atheism, it provided the respectability necessary for acceptance of thinking as disparate as Charles Darwin's theories on evolution and Auguste Comte's concept of Positivism. Holyoake was taken with the French philosopher's works when Harriet Martineau translated them into English under the title *The Positive Philosophy*. Martineau's translation was so masterful that Comte had it translated back into French, considering her version better than his own. His ideas appealed not only to Martineau and Holyoake, but to others of their circle, especially Herbert Spencer and George Elliot. The Frenchman's theory of a "Religion of Humanity," clearly bearing influences from the French Revolution, offered a secularist faith that would crown the third stage of human evolution—a positive stage, following earlier metaphysical and theological stages. Comte never got to London to meet his admirers, dying of stomach cancer in Paris in 1857.

In Holyoake's first major book, *The Principles of Secularism Illustrated,* he conceded Comte's influence on his thinking: "Secularism accepts no authority but that of nature, adopts no methods but those of science and philosophy," he wrote. "A Secularist guides himself by maxims of Positivism ... concerning himself with the real, the right, and the constructive." He liked to quote Comte's maxim for scientific progress: "nothing is destroyed until it is replaced."[13]

Holyoake, along with, his "four rights," laid out the responsibilities of secularists, as if he were addressing the "selection of earnest men" that he had called to come forward in his first speech on Secularism at the Hall of Science in December 1851. The secularist "will avoid indiscriminate disparagement of bodies, or antagonisms of persons ... whose sincerity he will not question, whose motives he will not impugn."[14] It was a design for respectful debate, something that would be lost sight of in the heat of fractious political turmoil. "Secularism encourages men to trust reason throughout, and to trust nothing that reason does not establish."

Was Secularism to become a creed, a philosophy, or an organization of men—and women—dedicated to the promotion of rational thinking? Holyoake's emphasis in *The Principles of Secularism* appeared to lie in the direction of an informed cadre of disciplined followers. Membership in this elite would be granted to those whose "actual knowledge of secular principles be satisfactory, and evident earnestness to practise them be apparent."

Holyoake's years in journalism had given him a good understanding of what the public is interested in, and what it cares and does not care about. He recognized that if Secularism was to succeed, it would have to win public opinion to its side:

> So long as people believe Secularism not to be wanted, indeed impossible to be wanted—that it is error, wickedness, and unmitigated evil, it will receive no attention, no respect, and make no way. But show that it occupies a vacant place, supplies

a want ... and it at once appears indispensable. It may be like war, or work, or medicine, or law, disagreeable or unpalatable, but when seen to be necessary, it will have recognition and support. We are sure this case can be made out for Secularism.[15]

By now, Holyoake was framing the first, tentative expression of what Secularism would mean to society in the future. He put education atop his priorities, and stressed the difference between secular education and Secularism itself. "Secular education simply means imparting secular knowledge separately—by itself, without admixture of Theology."[16] And here he identifies the impartiality of his brand of Secularism toward religion: "The advocate of Secular education may be, and generally also is, an advocate of religion." In George Holyoake's vision, Secularism would accept believers and non-believers as long as the public space—the desks of public classrooms and the offices of the public realm—carried with them no religious tests. In articulating this view, Holyoake was setting the stage for the greatest battle of his life, the battle over whether Secularism belonged to atheists alone, or to all who could agree to practice their religion outside the public square.

Holyoake bent his approach to science, society, and religion in ways that would enhance the impact and acceptance of Secularism. He used his connections with the scientific community to gain support of the intellectual class. Important in this were Herbert Spencer, Thomas Huxley, and John Tyndall, the Irish physicist who established in the 1850s the connection between atmospheric CO_2 and what is now known as the greenhouse effect. George Henry Lewes often served as the facilitator of these contacts, having taken a serious interest in science himself. He studied physiology and nutrition, and questioned the high consumption of sugar in the English diet.

In later life, Holyoake's social circle would expand to include such figures as the four-time British prime minister, William Gladstone, and the poet, Alfred Lord Tennyson. Of all the contacts Holyoake would make, no one left him with a more lasting impression than the writer Harriet Martineau. They would become close friends and in her support of Secularism—although she took no active part in its promotion—she offered unstinting encouragement to Holyoake. He would visit Martineau often and his fascination for the candor of her intellect grew each time he saw her.

13

She Heard No Evil, but Saw Much

On a rock-encrusted knoll one-half mile outside Ambleside, in the English Lake District hundreds of miles from the fogbound, gas-lighted streets of London, perched a little gabled house, built of grey stone. You could reach it only by horseback, and it was better not to try in spring or fall when rain turned the trail to a muddy morass. Even winter, with the route usually more tractable by sledge, could be difficult. As you approach the knoll you leave your coach at the steep rock face that rises behind a garden with a cottage, a cow-house, a pigsty, and a root shed. You take a winding path that runs from the road to the pinnacle of the knoll where the house sits astride a terrace overlooking all around it. It was to this peaceful setting that George Holyoake came in 1852, invited by Harriet Martineau, the "most womanly woman" he had ever met, and of whom it was said, when she was but twenty-eight years of age, "a great light had arisen among women."[1]

Martineau had bought the knoll and the land below it in 1845. She planted a garden on a pie-shaped chunk of meadow where a pony had grazed. Her new property amounted to two acres in all. She managed the purchase with money advanced by a generous cousin. Martineau designed the house herself, taking care to ensure every room had a clear view of the hills and vales around them. Holyoake gained entrance through a covered porch opening onto a fairly large, well-lighted drawing room. It served as both dining room and study, and every wall was lined with bookcases. Sunshine flooded in through one of many windows that Martineau had insisted on, optimistic that the tax based on the number of windows in a house would soon be lifted. It was. The only other room on the main floor was the kitchen, "as airy and light and comfortable for her maids as her drawing-room was for herself."[2] Upstairs held her bedroom, a servants' room for her two maids, and a guest chamber.

13. She Heard No Evil, but Saw Much

Harriet Martineau, at first disparaged by Lord Brougham and his Society for the Diffusion of Knowledge as "the little deaf girl from Norwich," would later find him one of her most constant admirers. She was recently returned from America when she wrote to invite Holyoake to Ambleside. "I should like a good long conversation with you on the Abolitionists and American slavery."[3] The note, lacking any touch of personal intimacy, reflected the fact that an invitation from a single woman to a married man to stay with her in her home was a daring act by Victorian standards.

Now fifty, and fifteen years Holyoake's elder, Martineau had become one of the great literary figures of the nineteenth century. Those who knew her work best counted her as the world's first woman sociologist. Holyoake thought she was "the greatest political woman in English history" for her many tracts of economics and politics.[4] After struggling for years on the few shillings she earned in writing for a Unitarian church magazine, she built her reputation on the runaway success of *Illustrations of Political Economy*, a series of fictional accounts explaining the workings of the economy. They were the first books on economics that common people could understand, and they outsold Charles Dickens during much of her life. When she turned to novels, she chose the Haitian black revolutionary Toussaint l'Ouvreture for a hero-worshipping pseudo-biography, *The Hour and the Man*. After touring the United States her critical eye led her to write *Society in America*, expressing praise for the "grandeur and beauty" of Niagara Falls but staunch opposition to the institution of slavery.

Martineau's sixty books and many newspaper articles enabled her

Harriet Martineau, brilliant thinker and friend of George Holyoake, explained economics to common people (Lebrecht Music & Arts/Alamy Stock Photo).

to support her parents after the collapse of the family textile business in Norwich. She thought the collapse the greatest thing that had happened because it liberated her to pursue a life of her own choosing. Of his visit to Ambleside, Holyoake would remember, with an evident sense of achievement and contentment:

> On Sunday, the day after my arrival, she drove me to Wordsworth's house and other places of interest. At my request she extended the drive to Coniston Water, some miles away, and on to Brantwood, the place Mr. Ruskin (art critic, social observer, philanthropist) afterwards bought of Mr. Joseph Cowen, who held a £7,000 mortgage on it.[5]

"I hope you will come as often as you conveniently can," she wrote to Holyoke later. "My good girls, Caroline and Elizabeth, send you respectful thanks for your remembrance of them."[6] There is no record of a second Ambleside visit, but following many casual encounters at meetings and social events, Holyoake was called again to her presence. This time, it was her London home at 55 Devonshire Street, Portland Place. Her note was couched in the proper formalities: "Miss H. Martineau will be happy to see Mr. Holyoake at tea on Wednesday next, if he can favour her with his company at eleven o'clock, February 5, 1855."[7] She had only recently been diagnosed with heart disease and a uterine tumor, either of which might carry her off at any time.

Martineau was generous in her support of fund-raising appeals whenever Holyoake ran out of money, due to losses on his many newspaper ventures, illness, or other reversals of fortune. She took a double subscription to *The Reasoner* and, she told him, "I always read the *Reasoner*—every line of it. You must allow me to thank you, in the name of everything that is wise and good. For the glorious temper you manifest, without break or flattering, towards foe and friend." Of greatest importance to Holyoake, but in no way influencing the genuine affection and even love he felt for Harriet Martineau, was the fact she was a convinced secularist and a steadfast atheist.

"I sent for you," she told him when they had tea in London, "that you may bear witness that I die on your side. An attempt will be made to represent that my opinions have vacillated. I wish you to know my opinions at this time. We have to vindicate the truth as well as to teach it."[8] The invitation had come, according to Holyoake, at a time when "her friends were instructed to expect her death daily." She told him she had never been happier in her life. "Christians will not be able to make a 'death bed' out of me."

Harriet Martineau represented the vanguard of a nineteenth century British intellectual elite who took to Holyoake's Secularism as a philosophy entirely in line with the new thinking about scientific naturalism. The central component of this new line of reasoning taught that everything that exists can be observed and studied; all else is fantasy, built on unsupported imagination. Evolution, as expounded by Charles Darwin, fit squarely into this concept. Secularism, George Holyoake's contribution to the new rationale, became accepted partly because in its efforts to work out new rules for civic life, it fit logically within the framework of scientific naturalism. Writers, scientists, academics and philosophers saw the two schools of thought as twins of an oncoming age of "scientism."

Harriet Martineau respected Holyoake both for his irreligious views and his staunch advocacy of the equality of women. He demonstrated this conviction in his support of female suffrage and equal marriage privileges and property rights for women. There was no subject Holyoake hesitated to raise with Martineau. When he was invited to the home of W.E. Forster, the Whig politician and Lord High Chancellor who had earned the nickname of "Buckshot" Forster for having shots fired at Irish protestors, Mrs. Forster walked "by my side as went down to dinner." Being a stranger, he was uncertain whether he should offer his arm. When he asked Martineau later, she told him that "being a guest. I was for the time being an equal, and might have complied with the opportunities of the hour with propriety."[9]

Harriet Martineau, unlike Annie Besant or Harriet Law, never actively campaigned for Secularism nor did she lecture on its behalf. Her influence as an atheist was as a sympathizer and a supporter of secularist aims, and her prominence gave Secularism credibility at a time when its ideas were beginning to filter into English society.

Martineau overcame obstacles that would have restricted most people to lives of idleness and boredom. The sixth of eight children born to a family of Huguenot extraction, she was sent to a boarding school in Bristol. Finding herself frustrated in her desire to pursue a religious education, she began to write out her thoughts as a distraction from the disappointments of her life. Stricken with a mysterious disease in childhood, she lost her sense of taste and smell and most of her hearing. She studied the Bible for hours, attended Sunday School endlessly, but had began to harbor doubts as early as eight. How could people be blamed or rewarded for their actions if God had previously determined their fate? Her family's allegiance to the liberal Unitarianism of the day saved her from being haunted by visions of hell and the devil—which filled the dreams of many of the young girls who grew up to be freethinkers—but she encountered constant criticism from her younger brother James, a future minister and philosopher of considerable fame, who told her she was too young to question what she was hearing from the pulpit. In her teenage years Martineau "studied the Bible incessantly and immensely ... getting hold of all the commentaries of elucidation I could lay my hands on."[10]

As an adult, Harriet Martineau had to hold a large trumpet to one ear that magnified the sound waves reaching her. To complete her catalogue of medical ills, her tumor caused crippling back pains that kept her abed. She claimed her agonies were overcome in six months of hypnotic treatments, or mesmerism as hypnotism was then known. Her doctors suspected the tumor had somehow moved. Holyoake marveled at how "she acquired her large knowledge, her wonderful judgment of character, [and] her unrivalled mastery of political questions of the day." All this had been achieved despite the fact she could "hear no great singer, actor, or orator ... take no part in public meetings." If it was true that no scurrilous rumors, rancorous gossip, or other manifestations of evil came to her ears, there is no doubt she saw much that was wrong in the country, and spoke out about it.

In contrast to the rigid bounds enclosing most of Victorian society, the freethought movement, of which Secularism had become a major part, welcomed—without always agreeing with—the free expression of women and their ideas on religion, marriage, and sexual morality. George Holyoake had established himself as a feminist in an era before the term was ever known. Women were active at all stages of the freethought movement, from the earliest declarations of atheism by prominent journalists and authors, to the era of Charles Southwell, George Holyoake, and Charles Bradlaugh. Many historians, however, have neglected the role played by women in the freethought movement. This blindness led one, David Nash, to erroneously conclude: "When looking at the role of women ... in Secularism the historian is struck by their sheer absence."

Before Harriet Martineau and George Eliot, there were outspoken women in earlier times, two notable examples being Richard Carlile's wife Jane and his mistress Eliza Sharples. Jane joined Carlile in Dorchester jail when she was convicted for carrying on his publishing and bookselling business. Despite his wife's sacrifice, Carlile fell in love with Eliza Sharples, calling her his "moral wife." A third pioneer feminist, Harriet Law, was converted to Secularism by Holyoake and become a well-known and effective speaker for the cause. Another, Annie Besant, a companion of Charles Bradlaugh, would become notorious in the 1870s and 1880s for her outspoken advocacy of birth control which would see she and Bradlaugh face trial for blasphemy.

Martineau had decided, when she was forty-two, that "the scheme, the nature, or fact of the universe, could not be explained as the product of a divine being." She readily embraced Charles Darwin's evolutionary theory. "In the present state of the religious world, Secularism ought to flourish," Martineau declared. She wrote to Holyoake enthusing over Darwin's *Origin of Species*: "What a book it is!—overthrowing (if true) revealed Religion on the one hand, & Natural (as far as Final Causes & Design are concerned) on the other. The range & mass of knowledge take away one's breath." In her 1851 book, *On the Laws of Man's Nature and Development*, she had been outspoken on theism: "There is no theory of a God, of an author of Nature, of an origin of the Universe, which is not utterly repugnant to my faculties."

Holyoake, in an 1847 issue of *The Reasoner*, had expressed his pro-feminist views in "Hints to the Advocates of the Rights of Women." He urged establishment of a woman's journal in support of freethought. Ten years later, such a magazine with the name of *Woman's Journal* was launched by several feminists. In 1855, Holyoake had written that since the "legal restrictions which marriage imposes upon women are so disrespectful ... marriage itself is not entitled to much respect." When Martineau published *Household Education*, a book she considered one of her most important, Holyoake assigned his wife to review it in *The Reasoner*.

While both Holyoake and Martineau were advocates of women's rights, both held conservative views on sex. Martineau was especially scandalized by the *menageries des trios* (or *quatre*) of the novelist George Eliot (Mary Ann Evans) her common-law husband George Henry Lewes, and Lewes' wife Agnew Jarvis, and Holyoake's friend and supporter Thornton Hunt. Her distaste for their sexual proclivities did not lessen Martineau's enchantment with Eliot's great novel *Middlemarch*, nor Holyoake's appreciation for Hunt's financial assistance. In *Society in America*, Martineau offered women two choices: "either be ill-educated, passive, and subservient, or well-educated, vigorous, and free only upon sufferance."

Their lives were connected by an unusual coincidence. Holyoake had entered the Manchester Oddfellows contest for five essays and won all five. Martineau entered three essays in a Unitarian Association contest on how to communicate Unitarian values to Roman Catholics, Jews, and Muslims. All three won. She shared with Holyoake a concern for European revolutionaries who were challenging monarchies in France, Russia, and Austria-Hungary; her works were banned in the latter two.

Harriet Martineau was no beauty; she was plump, severely dressed, and plainly coiffed. Charles Darwin was pleased to see she was "not ugly." But George Holyoake thought Martineau "grew handsomer as she grew older," acquiring "a queenly dignity." She never married but was pursued by numerous suitors. It appears she never got over her first love, a troubled New Yorker, John Hugh Worthington. After a brief engagement, he committed suicide in 1826, the year her father died. Another ardent would-be lover was Erasmus Darwin, brother of Charles. On arrival home from his *Beagle* expedition, Charles found Erasmus spending day after day "driving out Miss Martineau." He wrote to his sister that Erasmus had been with Martineau from morning to night and that "if her character was not as secure, as a mountain in the polar regions, she would certainly lose it. How fortunate it is that she is so very plain."[11] Eventually, Erasmus's ardor cooled as he suffered continuing rejections.

Like Holyoake, Martineau had a difficult relationship with some of her family. She claimed her mother, a music lover, abandoned her to a wet nurse and was in denial about her deafness. She conceded they had a good relationship in later years. When she published *Man's Nature and Development*, her brother James reviewed it for a magazine under what Holyoake considered "the offensive and ignorant title of 'Mesmeric Atheism.'"

For years, Harriet Martineau put off writing her autobiography. She couldn't forget what she'd gone through in writing *Life in the Sickroom*, a book that turned attitudes toward medical authority upside down. Doctors railed at her for suggesting the patient should take control of their illness. When she finally set down her life's story she did so in a three-volume work she produced in three months. She had its publication delayed until after her death. Holyoake thought "no autobiography produced in its day had a greater impression."[12]

George Holyoake had the ability to develop relationships on levels reflecting the circumstances in which he met people: understanding for those who sought learning from him, patience for those who disagreed with him, and respect for all but those who would oppress him. These qualities, a fact undeniably true of his relationship with Harriet Martineau, enabled him to make a success of a close relationship with a woman without acting on the familiarity that would tempt some men.

Harriet Martineau was born June 12, 1802, at Norwich, and died June 27, 1876, at Ambleside, long outlasting forecasts of an early passing. She did not entirely share the view that she was due for an early death. On March 4, 1850, she had written to Holyoake: "I may hold out a long time yet. Long enough, perhaps, to complete my autobiography, to which I add something every day when I am strong enough."[13]

Harriet Martineau willed her body to medical research. "There is no instance of any distinguished Christian who did this," George Holyoake claimed. In his eulogy in a London newspaper, Holyoake wrote that she did what "eminent authorities on political economy declared to be impossible—namely, to weave its principles into stories, and to make novels illustrating them attractive." Her strength, he added, was that she "saw social facts and their influences with a vividness no other writer of her day did."[14]

Harriet Martineau's name adorns the east face of the Reformers Memorial in Kensal Green cemetery in London. Her chiseled name bears evidence of her enduring presence among those, like Charles Darwin, Thomas Huxley, Herbert Spencer, and George Holyoake himself, whose originality and inventiveness contributed to the intellectual pre-eminence of nineteenth century Britain.

14

A Funeral in Wales and Rallying the Faithless

Late on the evening of Saturday, November 20, 1858, the air filled with fog and the ground hardened by frost, George Holyoake set out from London to attend the funeral of Robert Owen in Newtown, Wales. He traveled with friends via the Great Western Railway and reached Shrewsbury, the end of the line twenty miles shy of the Welsh border, at three o'clock Sunday morning. Switching to a horse-drawn mail coach for the last four hours of the journey, Holyoake found it a relief to be free of the stench of London, where the sewage-laden Thames River was giving off the vilest of smells. He relished the sight of the snorting breath of the horses and the sound of the blowing bugle of the coachman as the team plunged through the fog. When the horses sideswiped a hedge, the guard offered to wrap a baggage strap around Holyoake, who was riding atop the carriage. "I acquiesced, and in a short time nearly had my head pulled off."[1] They stopped at an inn where the men stomped their feet to warm themselves, smoked cigars, and drank hot ginger beer. When the coach passed over the Welsh border, everyone removed their hats, a mark of respect for their lost friend and idol.

News of Robert Owen's death came to Holyoake in the Friday editions of London newspapers, and on Saturday morning the postman delivered a letter from Owen's son, Robert Dale Owen. "It is all over. My dear father passed away this morning [the 17th], at a quarter before seven, as gently and quietly as if he had been falling asleep."[2] Owen was eighty-eight and had been in poor health, but his death came as a shock. Despite their differences in age, the life of Owen, the man Holyoake most admired in the world, had run on a parallel track with his. Owen's famous pronouncement that all religions were false had come the year of Holyoake's birth, 1817. Holyoake had first seen the great man in Birmingham in 1836 and had become one of the early social missionaries of his Society of Religious Rationalists in

1840. Their views later diverged: Owen thought he had found a rational religion; to Holyoake, there was no such thing, but his admiration of Owen remained undiminished.

Owen had returned from America virtually penniless, dependent on a trust fund from his children that gave him £300 per year. "Where the priest has given us barren prayers and the politicians promises," Holyoake wrote, "Mr. Owen dispensed his gold with a princely hand."[3] Owen lived at Sevenoaks, southeast of London, up to the last days of his life. He summoned what strength he still had to travel to Liverpool and deliver a paper at a meeting of the National Association for the Promotion of Social Science. He had to be dressed and carried in a sedan chair from his hotel to the meeting hall, a two-hour operation. With Lord Brougham and Lord Russell on either side of him, Owen managed to deliver all but the last paragraphs of his speech. Lord Brougham terminated the talk by clapping and declaring, "Capital, very good, can't be better Mr. Owen!"[4]

Owen was determined to die in his Newtown birthplace, which he had not visited for seventy years. When the carriage entered Wales he is said to have raised himself from his litter to give a cheer. He took room No. 3 at the Bear's Head Hotel in High Street and ate a dish of flummery, the gruel that had scalded his stomach as a child. Owen went to his old home next door which was now a shop, to buy some notepaper. The shopkeeper suspected the identity of his distinguished visitor. Owen's son, Robert Dale Owen, now the U.S. minister to the Kingdom of Naples, arrived to care for him. Robert Owen's last words were, purportedly, "Relief has come."

Holyoake, accompanied by W.H. Ashurst and William Pare, the one-time Birmingham registrar who had married George and Eleanor, walked alongside the coffin as it was borne to St. David's Church for the service. They moved to the ruins of the thirteenth century St. Mary's Church, no longer in use, where Owen was buried alongside his parents on a slope leading to the Severn River. The Rector, the Rev. Mr. Edwards, forbade anyone from speaking at the graveside. Businesses in the town closed for the day, even though not a single person who had lived there in Owen's time was still alive. "The public of the present day," the *Globe* of London observed, "are hardly aware of the importance that was at one time attached to the theories and movements of the old man who has just died."[5] Another newspaper reported of the funeral: "The streets, windows, housetops, every possible eminence, roadside, and lane, were crowded with spectators."[6] Holyoake regretted that the church allowed Owen the rites of Christian burial. If it had not, "we would have performed the last offices of humanity in our own way."[7]

14. A Funeral in Wales and Rallying the Faithless

Through debates, lectures, and the pages of *The Reasoner*, George Holyoake carried the message of Secularism to the English public. His call for a social order beyond the constraints of either atheism or religion attracted freethinkers, intellectuals, and a growing number of inquiring minds within the scientific community. At a time when churches were losing the faithful, the opportunity to cleanse the English mind of religion by rallying the faithless might not come again. Holyoake knew that what had been a working class concept now must reach into the middle and upper classes if society was to begin "attaching primary importance to the morality of man to man." Having taken part in the building of both the Owenite and the Chartist movements—he was a member of the last boards of both—he knew the value of nationwide organization. Holyoake was a joiner—he sat on the executive of at least twenty-two organizations and when a cause lacked an organization to join, he would start one.

How does one appeal to hard-pressed workers to support a cause that promises no increase in wages or reductions in hours? The churches offered the faithful eternal life; what could Secularism promise the faithless? More than anything, it offered a social outlet for men who had few distractions in their lives and did not wish to go to church. Secularism gave them a sense of belonging, especially when meetings were held at the local public house, the favorite gathering place of beer drinking Englishmen. It was the one place where they felt free to express themselves, notwithstanding the criticisms pubs drew as places where the working men drank away wages that would be better spent on their families. Because of such criticism, coffee houses and Temperance hotels became the preferred locations for meetings. Typical was Thornton's Hotel in Huddersfield, a sizeable market town in West Yorkshire where Holyoake stayed when he lectured at the Philosophical Hall in 1860. Thornton's had every facility for meetings: a small auditorium where the proprietor, Joseph Thornton, sat on a platform to chair discussions; a restaurant; and a games room for drafts and chess.

Among other venues were the Turkish baths, brought to England in 1856 by David Urquhart, the Scottish diplomat and Member of Parliament who years earlier had tried to enlist the youthful Holyoake in a subversive political cell. Urquhart had learned about the Turkish baths while on a peace making mission to that country. He opened the first one in Manchester. At a time when most men washed themselves standing naked in a basin of water, the baths offered both a hygienic and a social alternative to the pubs. They became a fad among secularists, with many opening baths in towns across England. Holyoake promoted them in *The Reasoner* and often took advantage of secularist-owned baths in Edgeware Road and the Golden Square in London.

Holyoake always maintained that not everyone was suited for

membership in a secular society. His preferred candidate was a man of "decent moral character" who would be "tolerably reliable as to his future conduct." He shouldn't be of "an impulsive nature, ardent for a time, and then apathetic or reactionary." He should be a man of esteem among his friends—"a man whose promise is sure, whose word has weight."[8] Given these qualities, what might attract a man to regular attendance at secularist meetings? They usually began with a social hymn; two hundred songs meant to inspire and encourage the religious faithless were collected in a book compiled by the printer Henry Fielding, entitled *Secular Hymns for Sunday Schools and Secular Gatherings*. The chairman of the meeting might read an essay on a philosophical or scientific question, or news items collected from local papers. Selections from *The Reasoner* would be read out. Only rarely would an important speaker like Holyoake or Robert Cooper be available. Members would offer their ideas during an open discussion of issues of interest.

Holyoake's latest pamphlets were eagerly discussed at branch meetings. Many bore anti-religious titles: *The Uselessness of Prayer* and *The Impossibility of Proving the Existence of God*. There was much talk of republicanism. Holyoake challenged the aristocratic structure of society, but he regarded the status of the monarchy as a political issue and avoided attacks on Queen Victoria. He conceded his surprise when his name was published as a contributor to *The Leader*, in that "I was regarded as an atheist and a republican." Increasingly, debate at branch meetings centered on the need for secular education in the schools and on legal problems encountered by secularists in a system where a Biblical oath was required to vouch for honest testimony. If wives were in attendance at these meetings, it would be to serve tea and cakes they had brought from home.

Secularism's unquestioned base remained with the artisans and skilled workers and farmers, the kind of people who flocked to join secular camp meetings throughout England. The camps reached a peak of popularity when two thousand met on the grass at Hollingworth Lake in 1860 and five thousand pitched tents at Castle Hill, a thousand having traveled there by train to hear Holyoake and other secularists. Historian Edward Royle likened the meetings to "a recreational activity similar to a modern football match."[9] At the same time, a wave of evangelical fervor was sweeping the country, with traveling preachers attracting equally large crowds.

Secular camp rallies, pub meetings, and Turkish baths did not, however, bring in money for the ever cash-short secular societies that were springing up across the country. That could only come from paid subscriptions to papers like *The Reasoner*—its circulation never more than five thousand—and *The Investigator*; from the sale of tickets to lectures where tea with cakes was often offered; or from contributions from well

14. A Funeral in Wales and Rallying the Faithless

off supporters. Most of the revenue from lectures—never more than a few pennies a seat—usually went to the speaker. Newspaper subscriptions and occasional advertising were never enough to support the radical press and *The Reasoner*, always in debt, paid a mere subsistence salary to Holyoake. He estimated his income from lectures in 1856 at £42 19s, and he earned another £50 from his books and articles. This left him dependent on supporters like Ashurst, Martineau, and John Stuart Mill, who donated a few pounds at a time, or took part in more formal fund-raising efforts such as drives that were put on in 1853 and 1858. The sum of £642 was presented to Holyoake in August 1858, followed by a further £500 the next year.

Although there were local Secular societies in more than one hundred English communities, no count was ever made of formal membership. Estimates run to about one hundred thousand fairly active sympathizers, with perhaps twenty thousand members of local societies. Robert Cooper, a socialist schoolteacher who had lectured for the Owenite movement, saw Secularism as the natural successor to the Rational Religionists. Where Owenism had been strong, Secularism flourished. Its connections with Socialism are more tenuous, but the ebb and flow of interest in Secularism appeared to match, according to observers, the economic pulse of English life. When times were especially hard, such as in the recession of 1858, interest in "subversive" movements like Secularism picked up.

Cooper's lecture tour of Lancashire had led in 1852 to the first national Secularist meeting, under the auspices of the Manchester Secular Society. Holyoake chaired the meeting, then returned to his cares in London. The London Secular Society came into being the next year and a conference was called for Leeds to form a National Secular Society. It never came off and it was not until May 1855 that Holyoake put together a committee at Fleet Street House that was to organize Secularism nationwide. He saw Fleet Street House as a College of Propaganda for Secularism, training speakers, issuing pamphlets, and coordinating—but not controlling—local societies. To document past accomplishments, Holyoake issued a *History of Fleet Street House* in 1856. It did little to spur his new strategy although places like Leicester, Derby, Birmingham, and Nottingham had set up their own groups, with thirty-five branches in operation by 1857.

Holyoake next published a wide-ranging and biting analysis of religions in *The Trial of Theism*. It was a largely philosophical work in which Holyoake stressed the high moral character of the secularist point of view:

> It [Secularism] regards ethics as a possible science. Secularism seeks to supply the material and social conditions under which, whatever of goodness (relative or absolute) exists in human nature, may manifest itself unchecked. It would place the

intellect under the dominion of true ideas, and show to others that virtue is an advantage as well as a duty.[10]

Holyoake faced constant distractions in his efforts to build public support for Secularism. He was still fighting the Tax on Knowledge war. He took up the cause of the Sunday League, advocating the opening of recreational facilities on Sundays. He satirically suggested two Sundays a week, one devoted to "repose and piety" and the other to recreation. In 1857 Holyoake stood for Parliament in the Tower Hamlets constituency on behalf of the Labour Representation League but withdrew in favor of the Liberal candidate. He'd campaigned for household suffrage, women's rights to property, triennial Parliaments, and measures to improve social conditions. Holyoake later reflected that in making so many "manifold proposals so long before their day, the reader will not wonder at my not being elected."[11]

By 1859, Holyoake's frail health again took him out of action. Exhaustion and a serious case of eczema which badly disfigured him sent Holyoake to bed. Friends took him in for months at a time and paid for him to have a three-week stay in Paris. He feared he was losing control of his life at the very time when the great cause of Secularism needed him most.

George Holyoake had a strong empathy for hard-pressed farmers who had to sell their products for barely more than the cost of raising crops and animals, only to see prices multiply in the hands of middle men. The heartless economic chain of enforced privation went on to the towns, where shop owners were at the mercy of wholesalers who fixed prices at levels that allowed little profit. At the end of the chain were consumers, mostly townsmen who labored in factories at wages barely sufficient to buy the mainstays of their diet: bread, flour, and potatoes. Co-ops vowed to put an end to such practices as adulterating flour by putting sawdust into it. All of these ills, Holyoake had long realized, could be overcome if people banded together in co-operation "in order that gain may be fairly shared by all concerned."[12] These principles were enunciated by Robert Owen, and put into practice by early groups such as the Rochdale Society of Equitable Pioneers, whom Holyoake had encountered during a speaking tour in the 1840s. Mostly ill-paid weavers in the town's textile factories, they established their own store to sell food at lower prices than those charged by privately owned grocers.

Did Holyoake's enthusiasm for the co-operative movement blunt his interest, if only temporarily, in Secularism? A continuing dread of indebtedness, and the unending struggle to balance the books at Fleet Street House wore him down. Emotionally, his primary attachment was to *The*

Reasoner. The paper stood as the main freethought journal in England throughout the 1850s, outstripping in circulation and influence such titles as Owen's *New Moral World*, William Cobbett's *Weekly Register*, as well as the *Poor Man's Guardian*, and the *Republican*. Holyoake's constant flow of books and pamphlets further entrenched his position, dominant in every sense but financial.

Taking stock of the paper's progress, Holyoake had written in 1856 of its varied content: articles by the editor; papers by distinguished contributors; reports of progress by organizations advancing "positive philosophy"; book reviews; and "earnest and relevant discussion" of Secularism. Well-educated readers would have appreciated such articles, but *The Reasoner* might have been more successful if Holyoake had appealed to a broader readership. The paper was deadly serious in its approach to theological issues and Holyoake used humor only in a satiric sense. Occasionally, he wrote short pieces of a distinctly modern tone, some in the style of the Talk of the Town section of today's *New Yorker* magazine. One anecdotal item was headed *Those Rapping Spirits:* "At the request of Dr. A., I went one evening lately to see Mrs. Hayden, and conversed with the assumed 'spirits.' The deceased person I thought of she told me was present, and sundry rappings followed. I could not prevail upon myself to ask any questions, and Mrs. Hayden put them for me. The answers were partly right and partly wrong. [She] seemed to me to act in good faith and is an ingenious looking person."[13] No out-of-this-world bodies, Holyoake concluded, had been contacted. *The Reasoner* existed mainly as a means of sharing news among radicals and keeping up communications among them. But it could have used more such light-hearted items.

Even if Holyoake had lightened the content of *The Reasoner* it would not likely have solved any of the problems now besetting him. Robert Cooper had become one of his severest critics, complaining that Holyoake monopolized the funds flowing into the secularist cause, but disparaged its most ardent advocates. Other, younger voices were also raised in dissent, none louder than that of Charles Bradlaugh. He was an outspoken young man still in his twenties, boisterous, confident, and whose presence in a room could not be missed: he stood over six feet tall and weighed in at fourteen stone. In his speeches, one observer warned, "the Sledge Hammer falls heavy sharpened with wit & tempered by eloquence."

Charles Bradlaugh, like Holyoake, had been raised in a staunch Christian family. It was of either Irish or Danish extraction—they weren't sure which—and Charles's father was a clerk to a firm of London solicitors, his mother a one-time nursemaid. Charles, born in 1833, was enrolled in a National School at the age of seven. When he turned twelve he was put to work as an office boy at his father's firm. Becoming a Sunday School teacher, Charles took great interest in the Thirty Nine Articles of the Anglican Church. When he compared them with the four Gospels he found they did not agree, and wondered why. He wrote a respectful letter to the Rev. John Graham Parker, minister of St. Peter's Church in Hackney Road, asking for his aid and explanation. The response he received was hardly either. The Reverend Parker accused young Charles of making atheistic inquiries and suspended him for three months from his teaching duties.

The quarrel split the family, and Charles found himself thrown out of home. He was taken in by Richard Carlile's mistress, Eliza Sharples and began to make himself known in the city's freethought community. When Bradlaugh was only seventeen, Holyoake introduced him as a speaker at a secularist meeting on October 10, 1850, in the Philpot Street Hall in London.

Bradlaugh's subject was "The Past, Present, and Future of Theology." Holyoake thought he looked more like fourteen than seventeen, but that he spoke with "readiness, confidence, and promise."[14] A newspaper correspondent who happened on the scene described the youth as having "such an uninformed mind, that it is really amusing to see him ... making all history to suit his private convenience." Bradlaugh's voice would strengthen with maturity, making him one of the most compelling of the lecturers to flock to the public platform. After his first speech, he published a pamphlet, *A Few Words on the Christian Creed,* and disappeared from notice. Lacking the means of supporting himself, Bradlaugh enlisted in the Seventh Dragoon Guards of the British Army. On receipt of a legacy from a great aunt, he purchased his freedom and returned to London in 1853. Bradlaugh obtained work with a solicitor where he took advantage of what he'd learned watching and listening to his father.

In the narrow world of English Secularism, Holyoake tracked Bradlaugh's growing notoriety. He would have been struck by the young man's strident atheism that came increasingly into conflict with his own determination to abandon that identity in favor of a more moderate presentation of Secularism. Holyoake refused to publish Bradlaugh's *The Bible: What it Is: Being an Examination thereof from Genesis to Revelation.* He feared its ridicule of Scripture would undercut his own efforts to present Secularism as a less threatening, more acceptable philosophy than atheism. Nevertheless, he had to admit that Bradlaugh was an effective advocate of his beliefs.

Bradlaugh felt vindicated when Edward Truelove, who had taken over *The Investigator*, the London freethought paper, from Robert Cooper, asked him to become its editor. Bradlaugh used the pen name of "Iconoclast" in his searing attacks on religion. Freethinkers enjoyed his work, but

14. A Funeral in Wales and Rallying the Faithless

Bradlaugh's inexperience in business matters contributed to the paper's failure to secure its financial footing. It closed in August 1859 and Bradlaugh returned to odd jobs in solicitors' offices, mixed with speech-making in the city's parks and tours of the provinces as a secularist speaker. Holyoake noted that as a result of one of Bradlaugh's lecture tours of the north, "a good deal of wholesome discontent is manifested in clerical quarters." Bradlaugh was helping to rally the faithless and Holyoake knew that Secularism, a decade after his invention of the word, was in need of articulate voices even if they did not always agree with him.

15

The High Cost of a Clash of Ideas

It was an evening for celebration, and the freethinkers of London who flowed in and out of the tea room of Anderton's Hotel exchanged congratulations on "the extinction of the liabilities" of Fleet Street House.[1] Anderton's was not the fanciest of London's hotels, but it had a reputation as a "trysting place for barristers, solicitors, journalists and others having business in and about Fleet Street," and was known for the quality of its food.[2] The hotel's choice fare included rare turtle, "dressed every day in the highest perfection." There would be no turtle at Anderton's tonight, or any other meat, as those who had paid 1s, 6d for their tickets to this "Congratulatory Meeting" were offered only a choice of tea with sandwiches of watercress or cheese and onions. After a fund-raising campaign overseen by two of Holyoake's most ardent supporters, William J. Turley and John G. Crawford, a purse of £500 had been raised to pay off Holyoake's chronic indebtedness in publishing *The Reasoner*, supporting European revolutionaries, and lobbying parliamentarians to adopt secular proposals—open Sundays, abolition of Biblical oaths, the riddance of Bishops from Parliament, and other ideas calculated to extinguish religious influence in English public life. John Crawford, treasurer of the committee that collected tonight's purse thought it unfair that Holyoake had to bear the cost of propagandizing the cause of Secularism. He had given £100 in an earlier campaign, in 1858. William Turley, an equally ardent secularist and well aware that Holyoake had his critics, rose to his defense at every opportunity. He had made a speech to the Friends of Progress in 1858, speaking on "Mr. Holyoake and his detractors."

The night of May 14, 1861, the heavy curtains that covered the windows on one side of the hall would have been drawn back to allow in the evening sun. The coal-gas lamps around the room would have cast shadows into darkened corners when the chairman of the evening, the barrister John

15. The High Cost of a Clash of Ideas

Clark, stood at the podium and called on George Holyoake to acknowledge the felicitations of the crowd. Holyoake, frail and uneasy of step, not fully recovered from illnesses of the past two years, may have leaned forward on the lectern, as if to rely on it for support.

He spoke for nearly an hour. He began by acknowledging "the kindness of this gift" but shifted quickly to an explanation—and a defense—of how he'd operated Fleet Street House, a place "to which Enquirers from any part of the world could turn." It was a costly venture "which put me at a great disadvantage." Holyoake admitted his critics were many but insisted that the principles "long avowed have not been lost sight of." At no time, he added, had he "derived any pecuniary benefit in connexion with the House."[3] Fleet Street House had been there to put out *The Reasoner* when no other publisher would defy the Stamp Tax; to rail against Napoleon II when he paraded through London in 1856 and to translate into English the pamphlets of French revolutionaries; to rally freethinkers to the great demonstration that brought down Lord Palmerston's government and his hated Conspiracy Bill; and serve as a recruiting chamber for volunteers lining up to join Garibaldi's fight to unify Italy. He published all manner of freethought books excepting those "works of an immoral or coarse character." All this was done, Holyoake said, to "raise the character of the Secular party, and to show to the world that if we criticized the theological views of our countrymen, we at least had convictions of our own."

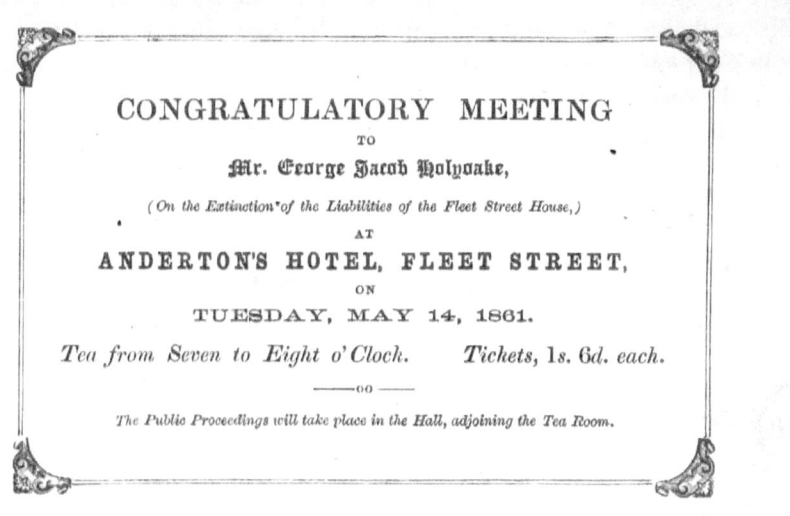

Ticket to a tea party and meeting at Alderton's Hotel, London, celebrating payment of *The Reasoner's* debts, 1861 (courtesy Bishopsgate Institute).

Some may have seen the speech as a heroic recitation of courageous battles, others as a eulogy for a movement that perhaps had peaked and would fade, like the precepts of Owenism from which it sprang, into the silence of history. Holyoake vowed this would never happen; Fleet Street House was safe, he promised, for the duration of its lease to 1868. "We have in view to maintain a free publication of opinions ... where Atheism should have fair play as well as more popular views ... [and] where we would protest against the tyranny of the majority."[4]

Holyoake may have felt faint, certainly he was tired when he finished his speech and accepted the applause of his listeners. He was only forty-four but recurrent illness and the pressures of stressful life were wearing him down. He was tired from helping to organize the English Excursionists who had gone to fight in Italy, and depressed at the fact they had returned home, penniless and had taken out their frustrations by storming Fleet Street House. The mess they'd caused had yet to be cleaned up. Holyoake had been saddened in August 1860 by the death of his old comrade-in-arms, Charles Southwell. Fed up by the constraints of English life, Southwell had emigrated to Australia and then to New Zealand. Richard Carlile, Robert Owen, Henry Heatherington—the list was growing of those who had meant so much to him and now were gone. He was seeing himself a survivor of the freethought movement.

Holyoake was also contending with a new rival for secularist loyalties. Charles Bradlaugh had proven himself not only an energetic and effective orator, but a skilled organizer of secularist branches in the province. Holyoake saw Bradlaugh's involvement in the launch of a new secularist newspaper, *The National Reformer*, as a direct threat to *The Reasoner*, one that could topple the house of cards that held up Fleet Street House. He felt a mixture of anger and humiliation over the fact that Bradlaugh was launching the *Reformer* in Sheffield, a city for which he had sensitive memories; it was there he had received word, as an Owenite missionary, of Charles Southwell's imprisonment, and where he had made his first public declaration of atheism. And now, Bradlaugh had the nerve to advertise the prospectus of his *National Reformer* in *The Reasoner*.

Freethinkers in Sheffield, according to Bradlaugh's daughter Hypatia, adopted her father "as their own ... a bold, able, untiring advocate of the opinions they cherished."[5] Bradlaugh's prospectus set the *Reformer's* capita at £1000 for a weekly paper of "advanced liberal opinions." It promised "antagonism to every known religious system and especially to the various phases of Christianity taught and preached in Britain." Its editor for the first six months would be "Iconoclast"—Bradlaugh, of course—but the *National Reformer* would be managed by a committee chosen by the shareholders. It appeared April 14, 1860, filled with dispatches from

15. The High Cost of a Clash of Ideas

Parliament, news of the co-operative movement, and reports of Secular society meetings.

The National Reformer made a strong impression on the secular movement but Holyoake, despite concern over the new competition, acted as its London agent for a few months. He spent more time in Turkish baths and renewed his interest in the co-operative movement, lecturing on its affairs and writing up its activities in *The Reasoner*. His apparent loss of focus led to the inevitable decision, now that the liabilities of Fleet Street House had been cleared off, to close *The Reasoner* while it was still debt-free. Its last issue appeared June 30, 1861. Holyoake rested at home for a month but by August was back in the fray with a new sheet, a monthly called *The Counsellor*.

The first year of Bradlaugh's *National Reformer* was filled with tumult and controversy. He'd recruited Joseph Barker as joint editor but the two could never agree; Barker's conventionality made a poor fit with Bradlaugh's radicalism. Among other issues, they split over Bradlaugh's support for a radical book on birth control, George Drysdale's *Elements of Social Science*. Barker thought it disgusting in its advocacy of "preventative sexual intercourse" and easy divorce. Their differences led to a showdown at a directors' meeting in Sheffield in August where Bradlaugh was upheld and Barker resigned in a temper tantrum. He went off to start another freethought paper, *Barker's Review*, but within a couple of years was describing himself as again a Christian.

By the end of 1861, Holyoake's struggle to get *The Counsellor* off the ground was floundering. Knowing he faced an uphill struggle and anxious to maintain the unity of Secularism, he accepted—much to the horror of his brother Austin—an offer from Bradlaugh to merge the *Counsellor* with the *National Reformer*. Having agreed to continue the business and pay the annual £74 rent for Fleet Street House, Austin threw up his hands. The lease was canceled and Fleet Street House closed for good.

Bradlaugh left it to Holyoake to prepare an agreement setting out the terms of their collaboration. Holyoake proposed to edit three pages a week for which he would be paid two pounds of Bradlaugh's five pound a week budget. Disregarding all cautions, he began work on the *National Reformer* in January 1862, declaring himself in favor of "One Paper and One Party." His choice appeared to be vindicated when news of his arrival bumped the *Reformer's* circulation up to eight thousand. Optimistic plans were drawn up to launch a National Secular Association and for a time it appeared the new spirit of cooperation would bring local secular societies into a single national federation.

Whether he admitted it to himself, Holyoake's new status was a comedown, putting him in the category of a mere space rate writer, a position usually occupied only by ambitious young men at the beginning of their careers. Faced with surviving on even less income than he'd drawn from *The Reasoner*, he cut expenses by moving from Tavistock Square to Dymoke Lodge in the semi-rural surroundings of Oval Road in Regent's Park. Holyoake wrote to J.S. Mill to report "I have a pleasant home here surrounded by more than half an acre of plantation. A Bengal gentleman called it a bungalow."[6] Holyoake's children played hide-and-seek amongst its shrubs, reminding him of his boyhood on Inge Street in Birmingham.

The modesty of Holyoake's home life, for all the limits it imposed on the food budget and even the smallest luxuries, did not prevent Helen from employing a servant. Most middle class and even lower middle class families had at least part-time help in the home drawn from the ranks of uneducated girls of working class families. Holyoake's friend Edward Greening tells the story of how Helen engaged a Salvation Army lass to clean and help with the cooking. "The girl told Mr. Holyoake, with a natural smack of self-appreciation, that she had 'got religion.'" Holyoake is said to have replied, "Very good, but do you sweep clean under the mats?"[7]

∼∼∼

George Holyoake realized that he and Bradlaugh, both strong willed men, held conflicting views on many of the issues confronting Secularism. Britain was passing through a decade of unprecedented social upheaval as masses of once loyal church-goers abandoned their pews, while demands grew for the removal of religious qualifications from key positions in the professions and government. Holyoake filled his three pages in the *National Reformer* with gentle chidings of Christian fallacies, cheerful news of co-operative movement successes, and critical reviews of books, journal articles, and newspaper stories. Bradlaugh, for his part, charged ahead to slay new dragons. He made birth control advocacy part of *Reformer* policy and helped start a Malthusian League, dedicated to promoting the warnings of imminent over-population emanating from the pen of Thomas Robert Malthus,[8] economist and Anglican cleric who preached that population growth would always outrun the food supply. But it was Bradlaugh's insistence on atheism as the basis of Secularism that gnawed constantly at the Holyoake-Bradlaugh partnership. Where Holyoake was prepared to accept anyone into secular ranks who agreed to the elimination of religious tests from public life, Bradlaugh stepped up his fierce attacks in Christianity. "He was, therefore, the most Christian-hated reformer of the century, and that means of any century," observed G.W. Taylor, in a 1957 chronology of British Secularism.[9]

Atheism, the denial of the existence of God—Bradlaugh said he could not see, taste, or smell him—was the rock on which the intended unity of

15. The High Cost of a Clash of Ideas

Secularism floundered. By itself, it was no new thing in nineteenth century Britain. Richard Carlile and others had espoused atheism in post–Enlightenment England but its roots ran back at least to classical Greece when the philosopher Epicurus wrote there was no need to fear death because after death there was "nothing." In Rome, Lucretius wrote his epic poem, *On the Nature of Things*, expanding Epicurean philosophy, foretelling evolution, and giving the mind a physical source of distinct particles. His humanistic message virtually disappeared until the poem's rediscovery in the fifteenth century. The advent of Christianity as an official religion in fourth century Rome, meanwhile, led to the suppression of independent ideas, hampering material and social progress for almost a millennium.

The creeping disavowal of Christianity generated contempt and hatred of unbelievers in the Middle Ages. David Berman observes in *A History of Atheism in Britain* that the Church of England professed its non-existence, a strategy of denial aimed at inhibiting atheism's presence. By the late seventeenth century such avoidance had fallen out of favor and in 1697 Parliament passed an Act "for the effectual supressing of blasphemy and profaneness." The law made it punishable to "deny the Christian religion to be true, or the Holy Scriptures to be [not] of divine authority."

The counterattack quietly accumulated strength over the next century. Percy Bysshe Shelley published *The Necessity of Atheism* in 1811 and *The Refutation of Deism* in 1814. The floodgates finally opened. An 1822 work, *Analysis of the Influence of Natural Religion*, believed to have been written by George Grote, set freethought gushing into the public arena. Carlile reprinted various atheistic works, Charles Southwell, among others, took up the call as an Owenite social missionary, and George Holyoake converted to atheism on Southwell's imprisonment for blasphemy. It was this penalty that led Holyoake to examine "religious opinion more closely than I had before, and it ended in my entire disbelief."[10]

While Holyoake's views would evolve and he would demonstrate tolerance toward believers, if not their beliefs, Bradlaugh underwent no such re-examination. Their relations became more testy by the day. "The only two men of note in England who maintained that the Secular was Atheistic," Holyoake would remember, "were Dr. Magee, the late Archbishop of York, and Mr. Bradlaugh."[11]

~~~

The partnership of Holyoake and Bradlaugh, entered into with optimism and what must have been a considerable dash of naiveté on Holyoake's part, lasted less than three months. Both would pay a high price in their clash of ideas. The directors of the *National Reformer*, alarmed at the paper's lagging circulation and mounting financial losses, called an urgent meeting for March 23 in Sheffield. They had a plan to curb costs: give up weekly publication and make the *Reformer* a monthly newsletter printed on foolscap paper. Bradlaugh opposed the scheme, Holyoake supported it, and Bradlaugh resigned but quickly changed his mind and put himself up for re-election. Holyoake stood against him but when the proxy votes were counted, Bradlaugh had won, 106 votes to 85 for Holyoake.

Bradlaugh was now free to carry through with a decision he'd announced to Holyoake the day before the meeting. He was changing the terms of their agreement; Holyoake would continue to draw his two pounds a week but he'd have only two columns per week, rather than the three pages over which he'd had editorial control. Holyoake would have none of this. He resigned, and demanded £100 in compensation along with £81 18s, representing his weekly fee for the balance of the year. The directors appointed an arbitration panel to overcome the deadlock. Its three members illustrate the conflicting personalities besetting the movement. J.G. Crawford, one of Holyoake's reliable benefactors, was appointed on his behalf, with William J. Linton, Holyoake's long-time nemesis, named for Bradlaugh. A picture engraver, Linton thought Holyoake "inconsistent and slippery" and remembered they had parted with "harsh words which.... I cannot honestly call back or soften."[12] As must have been expected, Crawford and Linton were unable to agree. A third man, William Shaen, was called in as umpire. He came down on Holyoake's side, leading Holyoake to write in his diary of July 31, 1863, "Arbitration awarded to me."[13] He'd won his case, but he would never collect from Bradlaugh.

Ink in his blood, Holyoake could never remove himself from either the lecture circuit or the press. He immediately launched a new weekly, *The Secular World and Social Economist*. By August, he had to cut it back to monthly. In January 1865 he changed its name, reviving the *Reasoner* title, and continued it as a once-a-month magazine. Traveling about the country, Holyoake had returned to Cheltenham in 1864 to speak on "Changes in Religious Opinion." His welcome was hardly warmer than he'd experienced more than twenty years before. Arriving to speak at the Corn Exchange, he found the gas had been cut off and the lord of the manor had secured a legal notice to evict his hosts. A large room was found in a local hotel where Holyoake gave his talk. (Charles Bradlaugh suffered no less embarrassing consequences when he took to the platform. In one case, six policemen dragged him from Parson's Field in Plymouth when he attempted to speak there in 1860. A charge of breach of the peace was later dismissed.)

One of the great political issue of the 1860s was not the right to engage in public debate or to promote social or religious causes, but the privilege of casting a ballot. Could the common man be trusted with the vote? That was the question that preoccupied politicians, be they Whig, Liberal, or

15. The High Cost of a Clash of Ideas 159

Conservative. George Holyoake thought he had an answer to the fear that illiterate workmen, if given the vote, would rally behind radicals whose policies would wreck the economy and bring on social disorder. The way forward, Holyoake argued in his 1865 pamphlet, *The Liberal Situation: Necessity for a Qualified Franchise,* would be to put would-be voters to an intelligence test. This would be fairer and more practical that the existing rule that to vote, a man's rent must be no less than £10 a year. Holyoake feared Englishmen might do as the French had done, and vote away their liberty. His idea was both impractical and unpopular; he would send "franchise examiners" around the country to test men on their civic knowledge. He called it an "intelligence franchise" and John Stuart Mill told him *The Liberal Situation* was "one of the best of your writings and well calculated to stir up the thinking minds among the working classes to larger views of political questions."[14]

Supporters of universal manhood suffrage, including the new National Reform League, assailed Holyoake as a traitor. That did not stop him from taking part in rallies that aroused London to fears of insurrection. Ten thousand men met in raucous protest at Trafalgar Square, filling the square, hanging signs on Nelson's Column, and spilling across Charing Cross Road to the Church of St Martin-in-the-Fields. Twenty thousand crushed against the gates of Hyde Park; 150,000 protestors filled the Park in 1867. Only then did a new Reform Bill become law, adding 900,000 voters and nearly doubling the size of the electorate. The better-off members of the working class—mechanics and other artisans—at last had a share in the electorate of town after town across England.

George Holyoake's split with Bradlaugh over his role at the National Reformer was both deep and permanent. Their paths would cross often in the future and they would sometimes find themselves in agreement, but Secularism's unity had been shattered. Investors in the money-losing *National Reformer* were glad to accept Bradlaugh's offer to take over ownership. He ran the paper his own way, it struggled toward profitability, and in its issue of September 9, 1866, he announced a program for a new national secular organization. The National Secular Society came into existence two weeks later, based at first on individual membership, then becoming an umbrella organization of local societies. Its aim: "to promote human happiness, to fight religion as an obstruction, to attack the legal barriers to Freethought."[15] Its objects: "Freethought propaganda, secular schools and instruction classes, mutual help and a fund for the distressed."[16]

The one issue Holyoake and Bradlaugh could agree on was abolition of the Christian oath in legal proceedings. In one of the more flagrant examples of hundreds of such instances of atheists being deprived of their rights, bookseller Edward Truelove in 1854 tried to lay a charge of theft against a man who had stolen a book. He was told that only Jews and Quakers were allowed to give a simple affirmation of truth instead of swearing on a Bible; such a privilege did not apply to atheists. The thief went free. Holyoake was twice summoned for jury duty but rejected for his atheism. "I was myself an outlaw until I was fifty-two years of age," he recalled, "without the power of obtaining redress where I was wronged, or of punishing fraud or theft from which I suffered, or of protecting the life and property of others, where my evidence was required."[17] After many attempts, a Parliamentary Oaths Act was passed in 1866 but for several years it deprived atheists of their rights: any affirmation had to be made "in the Presence of Almighty God." Charles Bradlaugh would be twice elected to Parliament as an atheist and would battle until 1888 before being allowed to take his seat by affirmation.

Long before, Holyoake had accepted Bradlaugh's invitation for two nights of debate in London in 1870, on March 10 and 11. They argued, on the first night, that "The Principles of Secularism do not include Atheism," and on the second, that "Secular criticism does not involve skepticism." What they were actually debating was whether one could be a Secularist without being an Atheist, and whether one could be a supporter of Secularism without also being a religious skeptic. Holyoake argued for the affirmative in both cases. Neither were strangers to debates. It had been seventeen years since Holyoake had debated the Rev. Brewin Grant and he'd had innumerable encounters since; this year alone Bradlaugh would debate five men in separate face-offs.

Austin Holyoake was in the chair both nights and kept a careful neutrality. The debates followed the classic format; opening half-hour statements by both men followed by half-hour rebuttals. They listened to each other patiently with only an occasional interjection to clarify a point of contention. The audience had no chance to ask questions but made its presence known by the frequent references in the transcript to Cheers, Loud Cheers, Hear hear, and Laughter. This being well before the Marquess of Queensberry's rules of gentlemanly fisticuffs conduct, the two circled each other cautiously in their opening remarks, as might two combatants in a prize fight, measuring each other before launching frontal assaults in their rebuttal speeches. Holyoake probably felt stressed, knowing his opponent's youthful energy and more powerful speaking style. Bradlaugh, emboldened by his success in forming the country's first national secularist organization, brimmed with self-confidence.

Holyoake led off the opening night by charging that with England's first Education Act[18] then before Parliament, "the greatest impediment in

15. The High Cost of a Clash of Ideas

the way of its being made secular ... is the misconception that Secularism necessarily involves Atheism and skepticism." Atheism is independent of Secularism, he argued. "The Secularist does not include himself among Christians, does not need to profess Christianity, but holds himself quite independent, occupying his own ground."[19]

Bradlaugh's response was to question the difference between Secularism and atheism. "What is the difference between finding belief in God impossible, and being an Atheist?" He wasn't denying God may exist; it was possible things might exist that one hadn't personally experienced. He challenged Parliament not to be turned away from secular education "because the bishops and the clergy are crying out that Secularism is really Atheism. Although at present it may be perfectly true that all men who are Secularists are not yet Atheists, I put it to you as also perfectly true, that in my opinion the logical consequence of the acceptance of Secularism must be that the man gets to Atheism, if he has brains enough to comprehend." (Loud cheers.)[20]

So it went through the two nights, Holyoake accusing Bradlaugh of wandering "through this land proclaiming the principles of Secularism as though they were Atheism, and arguing with the clergy." It was Holyoake's most direct attack on Bradlaugh, and he accused him of weakening the secular movement. "Look at the poverty of their public resources.... Look at the few people of local repute that will consent to share their name and association. Why do they not do it? Because they find no definite principle set down which does not involve them in Atheism and Infidelity."[21]

Holyoake and Bradlaugh departed civilly, if not as friends. In September, Bradlaugh invited Holyoake to become vice-president of the National Secular Society. He refused, saying he told Bradlaugh "I could not take the office ... without confusing the public mind as to the essential difference between Secularism and Atheism which I deem it so important to keep clear."[22] The clash between George Holyoake and Charles Bradlaugh marked a turning point for the secular movement. While most branches across England and Scotland elected to join Bradlaugh's NSS, Holyoake's pioneering work with his "positive program of reform" had by then set the stage for progress toward a more Secular state.

16

The Co-operative Man Makes a Change of Direction

Traveling to the furthest reaches of England and Scotland, George Holyoake was on the move lecturing on Secularism and advocating the benefits of the Co-operative movement, the second great interest in his life. He faced skeptical crowds, errant hecklers, and aggressive police, but never physical injury—except in encounters with London traffic. The streets of the capital bustled with horse-drawn carriages, cabs, and wagons and Holyoake, perhaps because of near sightedness or due to simple carelessness, was knocked down with alarming regularity. Leaving a meeting one evening of the Board of the Co-operative Federation in Leman Street, Whitechapel, he had "incautiously stepped into the roadway to hail a cab, when a lorry came round a corner behind me and knocked me into the mud, which was very prevalent that day." One of the bystanders who picked him up gave him a handkerchief to wipe his face and head, "both being blackened and bleeding."[1]

Holyoake told an inquiring policeman he was on his way to Fleet Street to attend a reading by the French novelist, Émile Zola. "'I think, sir,' said the reflective policeman, 'we had better take you to the London Hospital.'" Holyoake had not forgotten his son had died under the hooves of a cabby's horses. Examination revealed he had no broken bones but his nose and forehead "were bound up with grim-looking plasters." The repairs gave him "the appearance of a prize-fighter, who had had a bad time of it in the ring." His insurance company canceled his policy.

The loss of his accident insurance reminded Holyoake of the benefits of co-operative ventures in production, wholesaling, and retailing—the three pylons supporting Britain's economy. As Charles Bradlaugh gathered adherents to his National Secular Society, Holyoake drew satisfaction from the pioneering role he played in promoting and recording the rise of co-operatives throughout the United Kingdom. Success in retailing came to the co-ops by selling goods at near wholesale prices and sharing profits with customers, based on the purchases they'd made. The dividend, paid when it reached £5, was a revolutionary concept when Holyoake first promoted it, and remains a mainstay of co-operative stores. Such modern adaptations as airline "frequent flyer" miles and points rewards for customer loyalty stem from this simple innovation.

In Holyoake's view, it was necessary to enlist more Englishmen in the movement and that workers as well as customers should benefit. All of these efforts flew in the face of established privilege, and none enjoyed rapid acceptance. Successive acts of Parliament were needed, beginning with the Industrial and Provident Societies Act in 1852. Not until 1869 would British Co-operatives take steps to unite in a federation; fifty-seven would meet in London that year to acclaim William Pare as their first secretary.

~~~

Without surrendering his dedication to Secularism, Holyoake spent much of his energy in the late 1850s and the 1860s on publicizing the history and benefits of the Co-operative movement. He brought out his book, *Self-Help by the People; History of Co-operation in Rochdale*, in 1858. Co-operatives, in his view, represented "the most prosperous system yet devised for the amelioration of the workers of England."[2] The book caught on immediately. Horace Greely of the *New York Tribune* published an edition in New York. Spanish, French, and German editions followed. J.S. Mill quoted passages in his *Principles of Political Economy*, doing, according to Holyoake, "more than anyone else to call attention to the Rochdale Pioneers."

Attention to detail was not always Holyoake's greatest virtue; his Co-operative histories, of which he published half a dozen over the years, were sometimes challenged on their historical accuracy. William Cooper, secretary of the Rochdale Pioneers, returned proofs of the 1858 book with the comment, "It has been said that in some places in your history, movements that took place at different times appear as if they occurred simultaneously."[3]

The memory of Holyoake's first speech on the merits of Co-operation remained fixed in his mind for the rest of his life. He published an account from memory in the first edition of his *History of Co-operation* in 1875. He had given the speech in 1843 to a group of weavers who worked the textile mills in the Lancashire town of Richmond. To be able to recall a speech of more than thirty years before tests credulity; Holyoake was known for a precise memory of principles, if not of details. He remembered the town clerk having loaned his meeting room on Yorkshire Street, overlooking "a low, damp marshy field."[4] Holyoake watched as the audience assembled: "They came in one by one from the mills, looking as damp and disconsolate as their prospects." Ten of the weavers had summoned up £28 between them but were still a year away from opening their first store.

Do it now, Holyoake told them. "What you save will be your own, and your stock will grow, and you will get things as good as your neighbours."[5] He hinted at the value in limiting the size of families. "The only persons whom over-population profits are those who hire labour, because numbers make it cheap. Your condition is so bad that fever is your only friend, which kills without exciting ill-feeling, thins the labour market, and makes wages rise." He challenged his listeners to act on what they'd learned about the co-operative spirit. "If you really think that the principle of the thing is wrong, give it up, announce to your neighbours that you have come to a different opinion." He finished by expressing his conviction that "the right men could do the right thing." Some in the audience thought "a real fanatic had come to Rochdale at last."[6] Holyoake would visit Rochdale often in the years after that speech and each time he was asked to make his first stop at the co-op store.

Holyoake's view of co-operation was as a system for gaining

Holyoake House, headquarters of Co-operative Union, Manchester, opened in 1911 and was dedicated in Holyoake's memory (courtesy Sharon Norman).

workingmen their rightful share of production. Writing in *The History of Co-operation*, he expressed co-op propaganda in a parable:

> A savage can catch only ten fish a day. The capitalist lends him a net and he catches 200, when the capitalist takes 190 of the fish for the use of the net. That is a good thing for the capitalist. But in due time the capitalist buys the river, when he is able to—and when it suits his purpose he does—exclude the savage from catching fish any more. That is a bad thing for the savage. The policy for the savage to pursue is to get capital and buy his own net, and keep all the fish he catches. This is the theory of Co-operation.[7]

The weavers of Richmond saw the merit in co-operation, and by 1865, twenty years after launching an almost penniless venture, they had enrolled 5,326 members and amassed capital of £78,770. Sales for the year were £196,234, with a profit of £25,146.

Consistent with his dedication to Secularism and Co-operation, Holyoake looked for opportunities to support his causes through political action. In 1868, a re-constituted Liberal party under the leadership of a former Conservative, William Gladstone, defeated Benjamin Disraeli's Tories on a confidence motion in the House of Commons. The issue was a resolution by the Liberals favoring disestablishment of the Church of Ireland—a spin-off of the Anglican Church. The country went to the polls with a greatly enlarged electorate and George Holyoake, having joined the Reform League, stood as an independent labor candidate in Birmingham. Opening his campaign at the Town Hall, he billed himself as a hometown boy: "My ancestors lie here; I know most of, and naturally care much for, Birmingham."[8]

Holyoake supported disestablishment of the Irish Church not only because he was an atheist; it would free Catholics from having to pay the hated Anglican tithe. He spoke of the time a clergyman of the Irish Protestant Church had "the sons of poor Widow Ryan shot before her eyes for the non-payment of tithes." If he was elected, Holyoake assured his listeners, "We shall have compulsory education.... Pauperism will be put down as the infamy of industry.... We shall have the ballot [instead of open voting].... Open voting is merely an insolent device for getting at those electors who do their duty." His opening speech marked the high point of his campaign. Leaders among Birmingham's workingmen wanted a candidate "fresh from the workshop," not some "highfalutin' apostle of newfangled ideas."[9] The fact Holyoake's campaign was financed by a £50 donation from a Liberal supporter did not help. Birmingham wanted real Liberals in Parliament, and elected party stalwarts to all three of its seats.

Holyoake was not at all distressed by the Liberal success. He admired William Ewart Gladstone from the start, recognizing in him a man who was willing, like himself, to change his mind when facts demanded he do so. Gladstone, born in Liverpool of Scottish parents, was the fourth son of one of Britain's wealthiest slave-owning families. His father owned 2,508 slaves on nine plantations in the West Indies and received a settlement of £106,000 (£83,000,000 today) when Britain abolished slavery in 1834. One of Gladstone's admirable qualities, in Holyoake's mind, was his willingness to broaden the income tax to cover more of the middle class, and his opposition to Britain's Opium Wars on China, waged from plantations in India. Gladstone's view that religion was better the reserve of "individual conscience" left room for Holyoake's atheism and helped cement their close and warm relationship of later years.

Holyoake's blood, however, ran more heavily of ink than politics. He returned that year to editing when he teamed up with Edward Owen Greening, to launch the first national Co-operative newspaper, the *Social Economist*. Greening gave up his own small journal on condition that Holyoake should be "editor, conductor and manager." The success of the *Social Economist* may have been a factor in the petition Holyoake received from thirty-two men, most of them both Co-operators and Secularists, urging him to relaunch *The Reasoner* after a nine-year hiatus. They were feeling isolated as a result of Charles Bradlaugh's preoccupation with affairs in London, straining his relations with Secularists in northern England. Holyoake was assured of half the profits from a new Reasoner Company, and the first issue of the reincarnated paper, in January 1871, described it as "A Secular and Co-operative Review." It was printed by the Manchester Co-operative Society and half its space was given over to co-operative news. *The Reasoner* came out monthly, but it lasted only until July 1872.

"It is the first duty of a Secular Society to keep itself clear of the charge of Atheism," Holyoake had written in the new *Reasoner*.[10] It was a reminder that the prime issue dividing him and Bradlaugh was his rival's insistence that Secularism be built on a foundation of atheism. He added: "Some societies, simply anti-theological, have taken the secular name, which leads many unobservant persons to consider the term Secularism as synonymous with atheism and general church-fighting; whereas Secularism is a new name implying a new principle and a new policy."[11] This sly dig at Bradlaugh in one of Holyoake's memoirs, published long after their quarrel and after Bradlaugh's death, suggests how lasting was the enmity between the two.

Holyoake's commitment to the unity of the nation's co-ops came as a sharp contrast to what had been his lack of interest in forming a national Secularist organization. He was a member of the committee that organized the first co-operative national congress, held in London in May 1869. It led to the formation of the Co-operative Union Ltd. in Manchester in 1870, with 183 societies enrolled. It was a historic occasion; the organization

16. The Co-operative Man Makes a Change of Direction

established that year is still functioning, housed since 1911 in Holyoake House, the Manchester building named in his honor.

Controversy followed Holyoake throughout his life. As the co-operative movement struggled to find the most practical road to success, its unity was threatened by many disagreements. As early as 1858, Holyoake was asked by James Salisbury, secretary of the Paddington Equitable Co-op Society, to allow his name to stand as one of its arbitrators. "Your well known attachment to the co-operation principles precludes the necessity for any comment from me," he wrote.[12]

No issue was more bitterly argued in Co-operative circles than distribution of the profits of co-op stores. Should profits (the "divi") go only to customers or should they be shared with workers? Holyoake's *Social Economist* partner Edward Greening detected "a perhaps inevitable cleavage" between "idealists" who wanted labor to "share in profits, responsibilities, and control of the workshop" and men of the "practical school" who "stood for giving everything or nearly everything to the consumer." According to Greening, Holyoake "took the side of the 'bottom dog.'" Holyoake used his favorite weapon, a pamphlet, to argue that dividends be split between customers and workers. To his dismay, the "practical school" won. "The right of the workers to share in profits and control was then jeopardized," Greening wrote, "and Holyoake at once became their champion. From that time he never ceased to strive for recognition of Co-partnership, and to the day of his death maintained that attitude."[13]

The issue flared up again at the 1873 Co-operative Congress when Holyoake, this time on the opposite side of the fence, argued that producer co-ops that paid dividends to workers should give the same consideration to customers. He was consistent in supporting the principle that benefits should flow to both workers and consumers. Anything less than sharing of the fruits of co-operation served merely to promote competition, he argued; co-ops might try to outdo each other in their inducements to gain customers. The argument soon petered out, put largely to rest by wage increases made possible by the growth in the British economy.

Another of the myriad of social protest movements that rose up in Britain during the nineteenth century was Republicanism, a cause borne out of unequal distribution of wealth, and one with many aims. Its emotional core lay in opposition to the monarchy but it also found expression in resentment of the privileged life of the aristocracy—the peers of the realm who were the nation's largest landowners, and the wealthy manufacturers and merchants whose influence extended from the manor to High Street. Holyoake shared the sentiments of Republicans but Charles Bradlaugh, as in most issues that linked the two men, was the more aggressive. In 1871 Bradlaugh had helped organize a meeting in Trafalgar Square to protest grants to the Royal Family. When Home Secretary Charles Walpole ordered it banned, Bradlaugh warned it would go ahead, violently if necessary. Walpole rescinded the ban a half hour before the rally was due to begin, making Bradlaugh a hero. He became president of the Republican Club and in his inaugural address declared he was "living the lives of ten men." He stepped aside temporarily as president of the NSS, the position going to an affluent benefactor, Arthur Trevelyan,[14] who unlike either Bradlaugh or Holyoake, was a total abstinence advocate. Other protest meetings followed, finally forcing Walpole's resignation. Bradlaugh called for impeachment of the Royal Family, declaring in his pamphlet, *The Impeachment of the House of Brunswick,* that he loathed "these small German breast-bestarred wanderers, whose only merit is their hatred of one another. In their own land they vegetate and wither unnoticed; here we pay them highly to marry and perpetuate a pauper-prince race." That done, Bradlaugh again took up the NSS presidency.

Holyoake had by now lost two more of his sisters, Elizabeth in 1864 and Matilda in 1867, as well as his mother that year. He would have felt conflicted about his mother's passing, sad for his loss but not entirely forgiving of her and his father's neglect of his wife and baby during his imprisonment in Gloucester.

In Holyoake's accounts of his time as an editor of radical journals, a crusading secularist, and a champion of Co-operatives, there is little mention of his family. His warmest memories are recalled in reminiscences of his childhood. Other family mentions involve his jail time in Gloucester, or the deaths of parents, siblings, or children. He speaks sparingly of his children, a trait probably shared by most Victorian fathers. He makes only a few references to his wife, albeit with affection and respect. He mentions her death only in passing and is equally close mouthed about his remarriage.

We know Holyoake's family offered little or no support to his wife and child while he was in prison. The resulting estrangement may have formed the basis for a question he posed in *Sixty Years of An Agitator's Life*: "How many family feuds and party feuds have arisen from a single saying, perhaps spoken in anger, in most cases never intended to be understood in the sense it was taken? Yet incurable animosity has come of it, and a vendetta which has lasted for years through the lives of a family or the duration of a party."

Years later, Holyoake would sum up his commitment to Co-operation in his *Jubilee History of the Leeds Co-operative Society*:

16. The Co-operative Man Makes a Change of Direction

> I knew Co-operation when it was born. I stood by its cradle. In every journal, newspaper, and review with which I was connected I defended it in its infancy when no one thought it would live. For years I was its sole friend and representative in the press. I have lived to see it grow to robust and self-supporting manhood.[15]

The co-operative movement was a logical but not entirely natural twin to Holyoake's Secularism. His involvement in it sprang from his concern for the welfare of ordinary Englishmen. It also signified Holyoake's remarkable ability to re-invent himself. Having grown up a committed Christian, he moved to atheism after witnessing abuses that he saw as rooted in Christianity. Maturing, he jettisoned atheism and invented Secularism as a more acceptable branding. His adoption of the Co-operation cause solidified his ranking as an exponent of economic reform. In all of these incarnations, he impressed colleagues with his rational and logical approach. Edward Greening wrote that "his untiring courtesy and consideration, his fearless honesty of purpose, his life of long self-denial for principle brought him appreciation from high and low."[16] Extending his interests from Secularism to Co-operation matched his proclivity to join every protest organization that sprang up in the United Kingdom in the nineteenth century. No one has ever attempted to make a count of the number of groups he joined—it probably exceeded one hundred. He demonstrated an honesty of conviction and a willingness to deny himself both leisure and comfort, qualities not always present in leaders of his or any other time.

Part V

Goals Gained

17

Charles Bradlaugh, Birth Control and Mrs. Besant

Annie Besant hoped the lecture by Charles Bradlaugh advertised for Sunday evening, August 2, 1874, at the Hall of Science at 142 Old Street in London, would help her settle on a replacement for the religion she had abandoned.[1] She entered watchfully; she was twenty-seven, separated from her Anglican clergyman husband Frank Besant, and had decided if there was an organization dedicated to freethought, she ought to join it. She learned about the National Secular Society by reading the *National Reformer* and had written to the paper to ask if one must be an atheist to become a member. Assured one need not, she sent in her name and learned she could pick up her membership certificate any Sunday evening. Annie Besant found the Hall "crowded to suffocation" with a thousand people cheering Charles Bradlaugh's arrival. As the "tall figure passed swiftly up the Hall to the platform" her eyes followed him, "impressed and surprised" at his strong face, his massive head, and keen eyes. After the lecture Bradlaugh went among the audience to give out certificates. He handed one to Besant, with the query, "Mrs. Besant?" They talked about her letter regarding atheism and much later, when she asked Bradlaugh how he knew her, he laughed and replied he did not but "he felt sure I was Annie Besant."

One could hardly fail to notice Annie Besant, an attractive woman of stately bearing, a head of curly dark hair, and a penetrating gaze. Born Annie Wood in London to parents with Irish roots, she was taken in at the age of five by a well-to-do family following her father's death. They saw to her education and sent her as a teen-ager on trips to Europe. She married Frank Besant at twenty and moved with him to the Lincolnshire village of Sisbey. She soon had doubts about how God "could be good and yet look on the evil and misery of the world unmoved and untouched." When

172

she refused to take Communion, her husband obtained a legal separation, kept their son Arthur, and sent Annie and daughter Mabel to live with her mother. He settled a small monthly allowance on her and she made her way to London, still Mrs. Besant. "I stood no longer a Christian, face to face with a dim future."[2]

After meeting Bradlaugh, Besant began visiting him in his "two tiny rooms" in Turner Street. He had sent his wife and two daughters to live with his father-in-law, and together they discussed the errors of Christianity, Ireland's desperation for home rule, and the need to improve the living conditions of Englishmen. When Besant, already an accomplished writer, showed Bradlaugh her manuscript *On the Nature and Existence of God*, he told her, "You have thought yourself into atheism without knowing it."[3] Bradlaugh attended a speech Besant made on "The Political Status of Women" at the Co-operative Society Hall. He thought it "probably the best speech by a woman he had ever listened to."[4] He hired her for the *National Reformer* and Besant's first article appeared in the August 30 issue, less than a month after their encounter at the Hall of Science. Annie Besant's meeting with Charles Bradlaugh would change both their lives, jolt the secularist movement, embarrass the British judicial establishment, and by their promotion of birth control, help change the sexual habits of millions of couples, contributing to a reduction in family size and a slowing of population growth.

Glamorous Annie Besant crusaded for secularism, birth control, and theosophy. With Charles Bradlaugh, she was acquitted of obscenity for reprinting an American birth control manual (Chronicle/Alamy Stock Photo).

In the more than twenty years since George Holyoake first promulgated the principles of Secularism, the demands for social change in Western society had acquired a relentless pace. Earlier struggles for manhood suffrage, workers' rights, and the elimination of child labor had been partially successful, although Parliament was still dominated by MPs committed to the status quo. Holyoake had sat on the boards of the main reform movements—the Owenite Religious Rationalists, the Chartist movement, various Reform groups, in addition to his pioneering of secularist principles of equality. The freethinking movement, building on the defiance of Richard Carlile and other early nineteenth century crusaders, was now ready for a new challenge. It found it in birth control, a not entirely recent subject of contention but one which would now envelop Charles Bradlaugh, Annie Besant, and George Holyoake in fresh and sometimes bitter controversy.

The prudery of Victorian society made it difficult to conduct any discussion of reproduction and family size in a rational manner. Church leadership, both Anglican and Catholic, held that a sexual relationship could occur only in marriage and that its sole purpose was the procreation of children. Richard Carlile had taken issue with this in his 1826 work, *Every Woman's Book or What is Love?* Robert Owen's son, Robert Dale Owen, published *Moral Physiology* in 1830. Another important development came in the United States in 1832 in Dr. Charles Knowlton's ground-breaking pamphlet, *The Fruits of Philosophy: An Essay on the Population Question*. Its seemingly erudite title obscured the fact it accurately described sexual functions and explicitly set out means of birth control. He also argued that celibacy among priests and nuns was unnatural and represented a "war against nature." The book was widely circulated by freethought publishers in Britain, notably James Watson who had partnered with George Holyoake in 1846 in launching *The Reasoner*. Holyoake later acquired Watson's inventory when he bought him out and continued to sell the book at 147 Fleet Street. Austin Holyoake wrote his own pamphlet on birth control, *Large or Small Families*.

Sales of *Fruits of Philosophy* might have escaped police attention had not an opportunistic Bristol printer and bookseller, a Mr. Cook, published in 1876 a corrupted version into which he inserted what were considered lewd anatomical sketches. He was convicted of obscenity. The printing plates had belonged to Charles Watts who had acquired them from Watson's widow. Watts went to Bristol intending to defend the book, was himself charged, and when he realized how it had been disfigured, he pleaded guilty. Released on his own recognizance of £500, he promptly sailed for Canada where he took up a freethought "pastorate" in Toronto, not returning until 1891.

Bradlaugh was furious that Watts had pleaded guilty to distributing an obscene publication. He fired him from his sub-editorship of the *Reformer*.

"The Knowlton pamphlet is either decent or indecent," Bradlaugh wrote. "If decent, it ought to be defended. If indecent, it should never have been published. To judge it indecent, is to condemn, with the most severe condemnation, James Watson, whom I respected, and Austin Holyoake, with whom I worked. I hold the work to be defensible, and I deny the right of anyone to interfere with the full and free discussion of social questions affecting the happiness of the nation."[5]

Both Bradlaugh and Annie Besant were now sufficiently worked up over what they saw as freedom of the press and the public's right to information, that they formed their own Freethought Publishing Company for the express purpose of republishing *Fruits of Philosophy*. They both knew the risk they were taking but were determined to "test the right of publication." Bradlaugh was appalled by the widespread infanticide and abortion then common in England, which he put down to ignorance about birth control.

George Holyoake was disturbed when he received an unexpected letter from Charles Bradlaugh and Annie Besant advising Besant was a partner in the new firm and that they would be shortly publishing a revised version of Knowlton's pamphlet. Holyoake knew Besant would be held equally responsible with Bradlaugh, and thought it ungentlemanly of him to expose her to such risk. Holyoake was also concerned that his name, and that of Austin, now dead, would be dragged into the affair over the fact they had printed and sold *Fruits of Philosophy* at 147 Fleet Street. Holyoake was a conservative on many social issues and was troubled by the coarseness of Cook's edition that had resulted in Watts's conviction. He thought the better course would be to drop any plan to re-issue it. He wrote to Mrs. Besant to tell her:

> If you intend to publish the work, it means ruin to you as a lady. At that I am concerned. If the Partnership does not intend to reprint it, what Mr. Bradlaugh says has no meaning. My brother Austin being dead, I wish Mr. Bradlaugh not to introduce his name. Neither his name nor mine was ever on Knowlton's book as publisher in chief. ... I bore "the flag" into prison in worse days than these; and would carry it onto the treadmill, if necessary, now. But I cannot think of vesting the defence of the liberty of publication upon a quack like Knowlton—imposed upon us by an artifice in days of struggle.[6]

Mrs. Besant's response was to thank Holyoake for his "most kindly meant" letter but said they must agree to disagree. She promised to "revise carefully" the book's "unduly coarse" passages. She later sent Holyoake a copy and he was dismayed to discover they had made only "grammatical amendments." When Bradlaugh's friend Touzeau Parris invited Holyoake to join a defense committee set up to support Bradlaugh and Besant, he declined. "In this question that concerns neither Free Thought nor a Free

Press, I have elected to stand aside," he replied.[7] Holyoake prepared himself for a storm of controversy.

Charles Bradlaugh's concern for freedom of the press appears to have been matched by a desire for notoriety for himself and the National Secular Society. Rather than waiting for police to respond to a complaint, Bradlaugh and Besant made the rounds of the city's legal offices on Friday, March 23, 1877. They delivered copies of the pamphlet to Mr. Martin, the chief clerk of Magistrates at the Guildhall; Detective Sergeant Green at the Old Jewry police station; and the City Solicitor. They left letters saying they would be selling the Knowlton pamphlet the next day at their shop in Stonecutter Street, between four and five o'clock.

The sale had also been announced in the *National Reformer* and on Saturday a crowd gathered to buy the book. Bradlaugh suspected detectives were among the customers that day and he was not surprised when a squad of police headed by Detective-Sergeant Outram showed up with arrest warrants on April 6. Bradlaugh and Besant were marched to the police station at Bridewell Place, charged with publishing an obscene book, and brought before Alderman Figgins, a Magistrate. After a brief hearing they were released on their own recognizance and instructed to return for trial on April 17. Detective William Simmonds testified he had bought a copy from Mrs. Besant on March 24, paying her sixpence. Bradlaugh had stood beside her at the counter and heard their conversation. A second detective testified to having bought *Fruits of Philosophy* from Mrs. Besant that day.

The trial provided a new sensation for the Victorian press and they made the most of it. Accounts filled the columns of London newspapers and were widely printed in the provincial press. After the first court appearance of Bradlaugh and Besant, the *Globe* noted: "On leaving the court they were accompanied by number of friends, and were loudly cheered leaving Guildhall-yard."[8] Later accounts reported similar demonstrations of support. "Long before the appointed hour," the *Morning Post* reported on April 18, "the court was crowded to its utmost limits, and many hundreds remained in the corridors of the Court of Common Pleas."

While the trial went forward, questions arose as to who was responsible for the prosecution. On May 4, the City Solicitor, Mr. Nelson, declared in writing that "the Corporation of the City of London has nothing and never has had anything to do with the prosecution."[9] He added that "in general terms" the prosecution was instituted by the police. Colonel James Fraser, commissioner of police, when asked about this, referred only to the sworn information which simply bore the name of Detective Simmons who had made the incriminating purchase. When Bradlaugh asked another jurist, Mr. Justice Lush, for the name of the responsible prosecutor, he replied that he (Lush) should know who it was, but regretted he had no power to help him. Beyond that enigmatic response, no answer was ever forthcoming.

Bradlaugh always insisted that his aim, according to one newspaper report, was "simply to raise such a discussion as would set at rest the legality of the publication. He deemed that everyone ought to show respect for the law of the country in which he lived, and be had no desire or intention of breaking it."[10] As Bradlaugh hoped to avoid a trial in the Central Criminal Court, the haunt of cheap criminals and shilling solicitors, he applied for a writ of certiorari to have the case heard at the Court of Queen's Bench. His application went before Lord Chief Justice Sir Alexander Cockburn, who sat with Justice Mellor at his side, on May 7. After hearing Bradlaugh's argument, the Chief Justice observed that if "the object is the legitimate one of promoting knowledge in a matter of human interest, then lest there should be any miscarriage resulting from any undue prejudice, we might think it a case for a trial by a judge and a special jury."[11] But first the judges would have to read the book. A few days later the Chief Justice reported back. "We think it [the pamphlet] really raises a fair question as to whether it is a scientific production for legitimate purposes, or whether it is what the indictment alleged it to be, an obscene publication." The justices agreed it was a question that needed to be considered by a special jury, and the writ was granted.

When Charles Bradlaugh and Annie Besant appeared for trial before the Lord Chief Justice in the Court of Queen's Bench on June 18, they announced they would act in their own defense. Bradlaugh had learned a good deal of law in his years as a solicitor's clerk and was convinced he knew all he needed to know. He was also confident no obscenity had been committed. He wasn't entirely surprised when he found himself up against a senior member of Prime Minister Disraeli's cabinet, Solicitor-General Sir Harding Gifford, who had been brought in to prosecute the case. Bradlaugh's first move was to offer each member of the jury a copy of *Fruits of Philosophy*. It was something the Crown had apparently given no thought to. As recorded in *The Queen vs Charles Bradlaugh and Annie Besant*, the Solicitor-General thought Bradlaugh's offer "very convenient." The Lord Chief Justice agreed: "It is absolutely essential that the jury shall be thoroughly possessed not only of the substance but of the actual language of the book."[12]

In his opening charge, the Solicitor-General launched a long and tortuous attack on the Knowlton pamphlet and Bradlaugh's Freethought Company. His arguments ranged over the history of British obscenity law, the indecency of books that assailed alleged sexual practices of the Catholic church, and the danger of allowing the public to receive unvarnished information on birth control "not written in any learned language, but in plain English, in a facile form, and sold in the public streets at sixpence"—a price almost anyone could afford. His sense of decorum would not allow him to read any part of the book, but he warned darkly, "on page 34 you will find a chapter on promoting and checking conception." He went on:

> I say this is a dirty, filthy book, and the test of it is that no human being would allow that book to lie on his table; no decently educated English husband would allow even his wife to have it.... The object of it is to allow persons to have sexual intercourse, and not to have that which in the order of Providence is the natural result of the sexual intercourse. That is the only purpose of the book, and all the instruction in the other parts of the book leads up to that proposition.[13]

Bradlaugh and Besant were on their feet for hours during the four days of the trial. Mrs. Besant spoke first. She pleaded a lack of legal knowledge or force of tongue, but said she relied on a "far mightier power ... the goodness of my cause." Free discussion and the spirit of inquiry had "abolished tyranny, swept away the monstrous abuses it rears, and established the liberties under which we live." The prosecution, she argued, "is using the name of Knowlton to smother the right of free discussion and free press in this country."[14]

That argument made, Besant turned her attention to the thing George Holyoake most wished to avoid—his part in past distribution of the Knowlton pamphlet. It had been openly published, she said, by George Holyoake's Holyoake & Co., and then by Austin Holyoake's company. "There is here throughout no concealment of publisher or printer."[15] Anticipating that Bradlaugh and Besant would use his past involvement as a defense, George Holyoake had sent letters to the *Times* and the *Daily News* to say he had never published *Fruits of Philosophy* "in the ordinary sense of the word" and that he had always disliked it.

When Bradlaugh addressed the court on the second afternoon of the trial, he became entangled in points of law and legal precedents, but built his defense on the idea that people had a right to know how to manage their marital relations. If the Solicitor-General was right in saying people should restrain themselves, he maintained, then everything in the Knowlton pamphlet "is instruction necessary to be communicated to the mass of the people." It was the "height of absurdity" for the Solicitor-General to suggest that "this instruction must be confined to the medical schools and not communicated generally to the public."[16] Bradaugh had said he would call forty witnesses, but only one actually turned up. Charles Darwin pleaded ill health, Holyoake refused to testify, and others cited a variety of reasons for their inability to come to court.

The jury, a fractious lot whose arguments could be heard in the hallways, took one hour and thirty-five minutes to deliver its verdict. It was

17. Charles Bradlaugh, Birth Control and Mrs. Besant 179

a clumsy and contradictory outcome to a complex case: "We are unanimously of opinion that the book in question is calculated to deprave public morals, but at the same time we entirely exonerate the defendants from any corrupt motives in publishing it."[17] Lord Chief Justice Cockburn saw it as an unsatisfactory conclusion. "I am afraid, gentlemen, I must direct you, on that finding, to return a verdict of guilty." Hearing these words, the foreman bowed, indicating his assent. The Lord Chief Justice addressed the defendants: "I will not pronounce sentence against you at present but I shall order you to come up this day week, when you will be heard."[18] Bradlaugh and Bessant, free again on their own recognizance, left the Guildhall. "A large crowd which had gathered outside to learn the result cheered the defendants as they passed to their carriage."[19]

Back in court on June 28, Bradlaugh appealed for a new trial; the Lord Chief Justice denied him. "I think we must pass judgement, have you anything to say in mitigation?"[20] Bradlaugh hesitated, then answered in a grave voice, "I respectfully submit myself to the sentence of the court." It was at the end of the long day and Bradlaugh and Besant stood, tired and concerned. Their "defiance by continuing to circulate this book," the Lord Chief Justice declared, had changed an "offence of a comparatively slight character" into "a most grave and aggravated offence." It warranted severe punishment: six months imprisonment in Holloway jail, a fine of £200 pounds each, and two years of recognizance at £500 each. "Would your Lordship entertain a stay of execution pending an appeal?" Bradlaugh asked. "Certainly not," he was told.[21] His face ashen, Bradlaugh turned to his daughter and handed her his wallet. Officers moved forward to take him and Besant into custody, but as they reached the door that would lead to their cells, the Lord Chief Justice spoke again, this time in "milder tones."

"On consideration, if you will pledge yourselves unreservedly that there shall be no repetition of the publication of the book ... we may stay execution."[22] Sir Alexander had just offered to reverse his ruling. Bradlaugh, now sounding contrite, said he had meant to give such an assurance. "Not only will I stop the circulation of this book myself [pending appeal], but I will do all in my power to prevent other people circulating it."[23] He and Besant left the courtroom free on £100 recognizance. On February 12, 1878, a three-man Court of Appeal under Lord Justice Bramwell found the prosecution had failed to set forth the "indecent, lewd, filthy, or obscene" words in the Knowlton pamphlet alleged to be obscene. The decision was unanimous and the indictment was quashed, thus ending the saga of Bradlaugh, birth control, and Mrs. Besant. Bradlaugh revived his Malthusian League and Besant published her own tract on birth control, *The Law of Population: Its Consequence and Bearing Upon Human Conduct and Morals*. She felt the Knowlton pamphlet was outdated and not entirely accurate and she knew she could do a better job.

~~~

The end of the trial was soon forgotten in a flare-up of anti–Russian feelings brought on by British and Russian rivalry over Afghanistan. It was the start of what Rudyard Kipling called the "Great Game," a contest for influence in Central Asia that would go on for a century. On a Sunday afternoon a month after the Bradlaugh-Besant appeal court decision, a small riot broke out in Hyde Park between Conservative government supporters whose shouts filled the air with "war-urging pretentiousness," and a gathering of peacemongers that happened to include Charles Bradlaugh. The Tory demonstrators later marched over to Harley Street and broke the windows of the residence of William Gladstone, leader of the Liberal opposition. A music hall performer had received a Royal patent for a ditty that George Holyoake thought "calculated to excite the contempt of foreigners."

> We don't want to fight
> But by Jingo if we do
> We have the ships, we have the men,
> And have the money too.

Feeling that "a belligerent meeting was better held on a Saturday than a Sunday [as that] would give the combatants time to recover before their workshop duties on Monday commenced," Holyoake wrote a letter to the *Daily News*.[24] It was headed, "The Jingoes in the Park." He said the leaders of the Jingoes, whom he described as music-hall politicians, were better left to their own devices on church day. The term Jingoes and Jingoism used in his letter caught on as representative of "the habitués of the turf, the tap-room, and the low music halls, whose inspiration is beer, whose politics are swagger, and whose policy is insult to foreign nations." Jingoism was the second invention by Holyoake of a new word, coming twenty-seven years after his coining of the term Secularism.

~~~

In 1877, when Charles Bradlaugh had obtained a permanent separation from his wife, his two daughters joined him in his tiny apartment in Turner Street. The younger girl, Hypatia—named after Hypatia, the ancient Greek pagan philosopher—wrote in her biography of her father, *Charles Bradlaugh*, of being seated on the floor to sort pamphlets because "chairs were a scarce commodity at Turner Street."[25] She disliked the rooms because one dared not open the windows due to the stench that came in from the street. In February 1878 the family moved to 10 Portland Place, Circus Road, and Mrs. Besant came to live with them, bringing along her daughter Mabel. It was a "queerly arranged house" in which the Bradlaughs and Annie Besant occupied the first floor (second floor to North Americans) and the basement, where they took their meals. The ground or main floor held a firm of music sellers.

For two people separated from their spouses to live together was a challenge to the morality of the times. There is little doubt that Charles Bradlaugh and Annie Besant had bonded during their legal tribulations, developing a mutual affection that may have been platonic or passionate. No evidence exists to establish the exact nature of their relationship although Bradlaugh always insisted they were merely friends. Annie Besant wrote admiringly of Bradlaugh's politeness: "One very charming characteristic of his was his extreme courtesy in private life, especially to women."[26] Bradlaugh had, she added, an "outward polish foreign rather than English." The trial strengthened the bond between them, but it also led to tragedy for Besant. Her husband gained custody of daughter Mabel in a suit that argued her morals were endangered by living in the same house as Bradlaugh.

Annie Besant never allowed a personal setback to dissuade her from her struggle to strengthen Secularism and win social reform for the masses, She earned the enmity of factory owners when she supported the Matchgirls' strike in 1888. These were girls who worked in deplorable conditions at the Bryant & May factory, making matches with tips of sulphur and white phosphorus. Many suffered painful mouth and jaw conditions as a result of inhaling fumes. A delegation of one hundred of the 1,400 strikers went to Besant's home to plead for her support. She addressed meetings and got Charles Bradlaugh, by now an MP, to speak on their behalf in Parliament. She attended negotiation sessions with management and argued for abolition of fines and penalties often imposed on the women, and for safer working conditions. A settlement was reached and the company agreed to stop using white phosphorus.

Besant toured the United Kingdom on behalf of Secularism and wrote dozens of books and pamphlets before meeting, in 1890, Helena Blavatsky, the founder of theosophy. Besant broke off with Bradlaugh over her socialist ideas—he was a rugged individualist—and she soon became a full-time advocate for Blavatsky's occultist religious movement. She published her autobiography, *Through Storm to Peace*, in 1893. Holyoake thought she should have entitled it *From Storm to Storm*. Besant settled in India and emerged as a leading figure in the Indian National Congress that would lead that country to independence. Annie Besant's grounding in the Secularism of George Holyoake and Charles Bradlaugh influenced Mohandas K. Gandhi and Jawaharlal Nehru in their formation of policies for the future of the sub-continent. She established several schools and colleges in India before dying in Madras, at the age of 85, in 1933. A life devoted to the service of others had carried her through skepticism of her Christian faith, to atheism and Secularism, and finally to her devotion to an eastern religious philosophy and her support for the liberation of Britain's largest and most profitable colony. No other woman of her time had a greater influence or a more profound impact on the world around her.

18

Going Blind, but Keeping the Vision of a Secular State

In the autumn of 1874 George Holyoake fell disastrously Ill. He was stricken during one of the most exhausting times of his life, giving lectures on Secularism, meeting deadlines for newspaper articles, and writing a history of the Co-operative movement. He was also mourning the passing of his brother, Austin, who had died in April. It was rare for Holyoake to be free of infections of various types; influenza, recurrent colds, discomfort and pain, or exhaustion brought on by overwork, stress, and malnutrition. Now came his closest brush with permanent disability as the cataracts clouding Holyoake's eyes thickened and he went entirely blind.

Word of Austin's illness had reached Holyoake during a speaking tour of the provinces—Manchester where he spoke on "The Christian Imagination" and Leicester on March 2—and he rushed back to his brother's bedside in London. Holyoake had worked more closely with Austin than with any other person and his death plunged him into despair and dismay but did nothing to lessen his frenetic pace.[1]

Holyoake put out a quick pamphlet, *In Memoriam*, to record his brother's life. It followed three he had published in 1873; one on the life of John Stuart Mill, another on Co-operation, and the third, on *Secular Responsibility*. He wrote it in rebuttal to the charge of a Christian minister that Secularism taught irresponsibility.

> The Christian can excuse himself with the plea that moral evil is the will of Providence. If he prays against evil he counts himself exonerated, and that he is better and holier than other men. The Secularist transfers no responsibility to Providence. He teaches that society is responsible for its own condition. Were secular principles connected with irresponsibility, or conduct, our adherents would be more numerous.[2]

Holyoake struggled through 1874 to finish his two-volume history of the Co-operative movement. He would cover the pioneering period between 1812 and 1844, and then move on to the current era in which he had witnessed first-hand how Co-operation was improving of the lives of people all over the United Kingdom by offering quality goods at fair prices and giving members a share in any profits.

It was likely the stress of this work, combined with his continuing efforts to promote Secularism, that brought Holyoake down. He may have been at his desk when he became aware of what was happening to him. The room would have darkened, making it difficult to read what his pen had recorded. If he complained to Helen, as he likely did, she would have put him to bed. Two physicians were called in, Drs. George Bird and Hugh Campbell. Weeks passed before an eye specialist, Mr. Brudenell Carter, examined him. Carter concluded that the pupils of both of Holyoake's eyes were "tied down by multiple adhesions," preventing light from reaching the retina. Operating under primitive conditions, he managed to scale away scar tissue without further damaging Holyoake's eyes. Holyoake's grateful thanks went to Carter for "the restoration of my sight."[3]

Friends feared Holyoake's career was finished. Walter Morrison, a Co-operative advocate who had befriended Holyoake, raised a fund of £2,254 to assist him. After giving Holyoake £500, an annuity yielding £100 a year was purchased. To the surprise of all, Holyoake recovered, as indomitable as in every earlier illness. He regained his sight, finished writing his *History of Cooperation*, and published both volumes in 1875.

In the thirty year period between 1850 and 1880, a troika of new influences—Secularism, science, and liberalism—ascended to prominence in British life. Each would have flourished of its own vigor in the exploration of new frontiers. Thrown together in the same time and place, their common roots in free inquiry bound them to each other in a lasting and natural affinity. George Holyoake's vision of Secularism focused on the material and natural world of which he viewed science as the predominant interpreter. Secularists, as freethinkers, acknowledged this in naming their meeting places Halls of Science. "Science has shown that we are under the dominion of general laws, that there is no special Providence, that prayer is useless," Holyoake wrote.[4]

Secularism's slow seep into English society was by now changing the thinking and behavior of many of Holyoake's countrymen. This was especially the case in education, where relaxation in the 1870 Elementary Education Act of control by the Church of England had allowed for non-denominational religious teaching. That was not, of course, good

18. Going Blind, but Keeping the Vision of a Secular State

enough for the advocates of secular education. They formed organizations like the Birmingham Education League to press for the total elimination of religious classes. Their growing strength could be seen in the opposition they aroused. Conceding that the League was "prosecuting its agitation with considerable industry," the *London Evening Standard* refused to believe "that public feeling is beginning to favour the policy of the opponents of religious education. There has never been any doubt as to the motive of the Radical Secularists in striving to depress the denominational system. They are opposed, as a matter of abstract principle, to the teaching of religion."[5]

This was a time when science moved to the fore, a period in which Britain established both the supremacy of its empire and its leadership in intellectual thought.

The term scientist had been coined as recently as 1833. The first course in natural science was established at Oxford University in 1850; scientists were examining the White Spot on Saturn and thousands of papers were being written on every conceivable scientific subject. The causes of tuberculosis, cholera and anthrax were being investigated, and anesthetics were being used in operations.

At the head of British scientific achievement stood Charles Robert Darwin, naturalist, geologist, and biologist whose 1859 *Origin of the Species* opened a new epoch in scientific inquiry. Reluctant to confront his Christian faith over evolution, Darwin limited himself to declaring, "Light will be thrown on the origin of man and his history."[6] He left it to his and Holyoake's friend, Thomas Huxley, to publicly enunciate the principles of the new science. Huxley did so, willingly, as "Darwin's bulldog."

In 1869, Huxley's devising of the term agnosticism filled a yawning vacancy in non-religious terminology. Perhaps it was just a play on words. Was there really any difference between agnostics and atheists? Agnostics were uncertain of God, but because atheists had no experience of God did not mean he might not exist. Huxley's substitution of agnosticism for atheism, like Holyoake's alternative of Secularism, provided polite society with a more acceptable term. As George W. Foote, an unflinching atheist, put it, "An agnostic is an atheist with a top hat."

The forward march of Secularism and science came in confluence with the rise of a new political liberalism, a concept that involved a role for public responsibility in the well-being of the individual. It was a radical idea and it contrasted sharply with the *laissez-faire* principles of classical liberalism, the predominant political philosophy for the past two hundred years. Walter Bagehot, influential editor of *The Economist*, helped open the door to the new liberalism with his attack on *laissez-faire* in 1848: "…a sentiment very susceptible of hurtful exaggeration."[7] Advocates of classical liberalism, he wrote, were opposed to efforts at a national education; they fought compulsory sanitary reform and resisted aid to the starving peasantry of Ireland.

The Liberal Party, formed out of remnants of Whigs and Radicals in the 1850s, became the political arm of the new liberalism. Its chief exponents included John Stuart Mill, formerly a classical liberal, who carried the new philosophy into the House of Commons as an MP in 1865, advocating labor unions, women's suffrage, and farm co-operatives. Under Opposition pressure, the Conservative government of Lord Derby brought in the Second Reform Act in 1867, virtually doubling the size of the electorate. For the first time, some working class males were enfranchised. The first Liberal Prime Minister, William Ewart Gladstone, took office in 1868 for the first of four terms he would serve, ending in 1894. He headed what would today be considered a reformist government. In an important step toward secular statehood, Gladstone achieved disestablishment of the Church of Ireland (Protestant) and struggled for, but never secured, home rule for that island. Queen Victoria disapproved of him, his policies angered the upper class but the public called him "The People's William." Holyoake was both a friend and admirer, and breakfasted often with him. "He was as open in his friendship as in his politics," Holyoake remembered.[8]

As important as the fresh winds of science and liberalism were in creating an appetite for secular statehood, George Holyoake's personality and approach in his advocacy of Secularism also came to play a significant role. His gentle personality, reserved style of speech, and courtesy toward critics, especially in the church, helped to make Secularism a less threatening prospect for Britain. He made a practice of attending church when he was on lecture tours or "near the home of some distinguished preacher." Evidence of the respect churchmen came to show him is found in the fact that after a speech in Birmingham in 1869, the Rev. Septimus Hansard publicly thanked Holyoake for his "religious speech."[9]

Holyoake's cautious approach eased his efforts to attain respectability and attract support in the upper levels of British politics and society. His admirers ranged from Alfred, Lord Tennyson, the Poet Laureate of Great Britain, to the Marquess of Queensbury, who designed the rules governing the sport of boxing. Their friendship endured despite the Marquess's fealty to Charles Bradlaugh's National Secular Society and the peer's uneasy connection to the cause: "I cannot say I feel satisfied with the associations I find Secularism has drawn me into."[10]

18. Going Blind, but Keeping the Vision of a Secular State 187

Secularism would require changes to laws affecting how schools dealt with religion, the ways in which the courts interpreted common law, and the privileges that the Church of England, as the country's established church, enjoyed in levying tithes, appointing public officials, and escaping taxes. Progress, slow but inevitable, had begun well before Holyoake's 1851 declaration of Secularism. A historical summary put it this way:

> Those who were unwilling to subscribe to the Church of England's articles of faith faced significant obstacles to education, civic participation, and professional advancement. They could not graduate from or hold teaching positions at Oxford or Cambridge, sit in Parliament, or hold public office. These obstacles had been removed with the repeal of the Test and Corporation Acts (1828), Catholic Emancipation (1829), the decision to make English state schools nondenominational, and related measures. Without going so far as to disestablish the Church of England and remove its bishops from the House of Lords, successive governments had so limited its power over public life that full disestablishment was a step that few still thought was worth taking.[11]

The public sphere—the courts, schools, and public services—were becoming increasingly secular as Britain moved toward a Secular state. Society eased itself out of the straight jacket of stultifying uniformity, while the high clergy, enriching themselves at the expense of the common people, found their privileges severely curtailed. The exercise of freedom of religion—and from religion—became a matter of personal choice. The Bishop of Manchester bemoaned the new alignment in an 1879 sermon at St. George's Church in London. He revealed that in a "thickly populated and degraded district of Manchester" a religious census had shown that in 276 of 518 houses, a clear majority, "there was not a church or chapel-going member, or any one professing any form of religion whatever."[12] George Holyoake took note of the changes overcoming British society.

> Everyone observant of public controversy in England, is aware of improved tone of late years. This improved tone is part of a wider progress. Increase of wealth has led to improvement of taste, and the diffusion of knowledge to refinement of sentiment. The mass are better dressed, better mannered, better spoken than formerly. A coffee room discussion, conducted by mechanics, is now a more decorous exhibition than a debate in Parliament.[13]

Holyoake and Charles Bradlaugh shared the common goal of transforming England into a Secular state, but neither could agree on exactly how this could be achieved. Rivalry mixed with occasional co-operation would always mark their relationship. When a young secular disciple, George W. Foote, disagreed with Bradlaugh's handling of the *Fruits of Philosophy* controversy, he found a ready listener in Holyoake. Together, they launched a new paper in 1876, the *Secularist*. Holyoake left most of the editing to Foote and disliked much of what his young partner was writing. He became convinced Foote was using him to embarrass Bradlaugh, and said so in a piece he wrote for the *National Reformer*. That did it for the partnership. Holyoake moved on to start yet another journal, the *Secular Review*.

Amid bickering, Holyoake stood fast in his views on such issues as atheism and birth control that were dividing the Secularist movement. He attended the 1876 convention of the National Secular Society in Leeds where a bid by Foote to replace Bradlaugh was defeated. Holyoake found himself invited to the speaker's platform where Bradlaugh, doing what he could to keep Holyoake in the fold, invited him to become a vice-president. It was a final attempt to heal the divisions within Secularism. Holyoake accepted, but never took an active part in the Society's activities.

Holyoake's departure from Foote and the *Secularist* was a factor, ironically, in the formation in 1877 of a new organization, the British Secular Union. Now that Foote had control of the *Secularist*, he joined with Charles Watts, who also had fallen out with Bradlaugh over Knowlton's birth control advocacy, and together they promoted the new anti–Bradlaugh organization. The BSU appeared to be as strongly committed to Atheism as was the NSS under Bradlaugh but Holyoake gave it his support. It was short-lived, petering out by 1881. The fights over atheism and birth control had begun to resemble the internecine warfares of Protestantism, and Holyoake was fed up. He retreated into his deepening association with the co-operative movement, convinced that in doing so he was also advancing the cause of Secularism. Foote started his own paper, the *Freethinker*.[14] His furious, often satirical attacks on Christianity led to a year's imprisonment for blasphemy in 1883. His disgust with Bradlaugh's exclusion from the House of Commons despite his election as an MP in 1880 led to their reconciliation. Foote would succeed Bradlaugh as president of the National Secular Society in 1890, serving until 1915.

It is to Bradlaugh's stubborn credit that one of the major steps toward a Secular state came as a result of his insistence that he be allowed to take his seat in Parliament by declaring a simple act of affirmation, rather than taking the traditional Biblical oath. Acts passed by earlier Parliaments, including the Jewish Relief Act of 1858, had eased the customary requirement that new MPs swear "on the true faith of a Christian." Quakers had been allowed since 1833 to swear to an oath that excluded any mention of God. Catholics were permitted to enter Parliament since 1829 provided they swore to "solemnly abjure any intention to subvert the present Church establishment."

None of these liberalizing steps were enough for atheists, or for Bradlaugh. In a remarkable demonstration of public support of secularity, he won election as an avowed atheist in the Parliamentary seat of Northampton in 1880. His request to affirm instead of taking the religious oath was denied, and he was briefly detained in the Clock Tower under Big Ben. After winning two general elections and two by-elections he was still

18. Going Blind, but Keeping the Vision of a Secular State

denied his seat and it was not until 1886 that Bradlaugh was finally allowed to take his seat on swearing the Christian oath. Two years later, he gained passage of a bill giving MPs the right to take their seats on affirmation of truth and loyalty rather than by swearing a Christian oath to God and the Queen.

∼∼∼

The upheaval of freethinking in Britain between 1850 to 1880 unleashed a social and political transformation unmatched at any other time in the nineteenth century. One must turn the calendar forward to the 1960s, marked by the civil rights movement and anti–Vietnam War agitation in the United States, and anti-nuclear and youth-oriented demonstrations of protest in the United Kingdom, to find a similarly transformative era.[15]

George Holyoake's agitation to change the character of British life had begun in a prison

Charles Bradlaugh at the Bar of the House of Commons, by Walter Sickert. Only after winning four successive by elections was Bradlaugh allowed to take his seat in the House of Commons (Manchester Art Gallery, UK/Bridgeman Images).

cell in Gloucester County. He went "on the warpath" on his release, carried his crusade to London, and later propagandized Secularism throughout England, Wales and Scotland. Edward Royle, a pre-eminent historian of freethought in Victorian England, saw Holyoake's creation of Secularism as "basically an agitation for a scheme of rights: the right to think for oneself; the right to differ; the right to assert difference of opinion; the right to debate all vital opinion.... Looking back on the events of 1842 and Holyoake's subsequent agitations, men could see this as a turning point."[16]

No more than one percent of the population—if that—actively supported the Secularism of George Holyoake and Charles Bradlaugh. That Secularism achieved the foothold it did was due to the logic and force of their arguments, coupled with a begrudging recognition by church leaders that the public thirst for a more tolerant society could not be much longer denied. Secular laws began to move power from Westminster and the councils of the Church of England to local citizenry: the Married Women's Property Act of 1883 gave women the right to hold property separate from their husbands; the Local Government Act of 1889 gave responsibility for poor law relief, roads and asylums to local councils. The modern age was coming into shape.

This evolution came at a fortuitous time in the life of George Holyoake. Had he attempted to introduce Secularism twenty years earlier than his pronouncement of 1851, he would have been ignored; society was not ready to hear of a new worldview with an independent stance toward religion. Had Holyoake waited another twenty years he would have been irrelevant; the irresistible appeal of secularity would have been proffered by others. He bridged the gap at a crucial moment in history.

Holyoake had explained his vision of the Secular state in an 1877 article he wrote for the free thinking *Boston Index*, and which he reprinted in his *Secular Review*. In its origins, he wrote, Secularism "saw that the faculties of men were bound by this life—that the knowledge of another life is denied to us; we have only the hope of it. Therefore we conclude that the secular is the sacred sphere of duty. The theologian measures morality by the will of the unknown, the secularist measures morality by material consequences."[17]

Holyoake took up the issue of Secularism and the working class when he sent a copy of *The Secular Review* to his Liberal friend, William E. Gladstone. Telling him it was the last journal he would edit—it wasn't—Holyoake suggested "it may be just worth glancing at" for its coverage of "Free Thought and Secular thought among the working people who try to think according to the dim and limited light of their lot." He told Gladstone, newly appointed Chancellor of the Exchequer (finance minister) that he had not forgotten a question he (Gladstone) had put to him during a breakfast at the minister's Harley Street home.

> How may the people be interested in public measures devised for their benefit? Were Paradise opened and the people had not sense to know it they would not go up the steps. The hungry birds on the Thames side would not eat at my window table until it complied with the conditions of bird logic. The conditions of association among the people are only in a humbler degree the same as among gentlemen. In a club

18. Going Blind, but Keeping the Vision of a Secular State 191

> gentlemen have refreshments according to their taste; read what books they please; discuss what topics they choose. The working people want to do the same. Being concerned in their daily lives they have no sense of distinctness and deference for each other as gentlemen have. To allow them into association [society] only needs to concede them the liberties of gentlemen.[18]

In those few lines, Holyoake summed up the fundamentals of the future secular state: democratic, respectful of human rights regardless of class, gender, or race; with a system of governance free of religious control but impartial to the private practice of all religions (or none) and invested with the moral responsibility for the well-being of its citizenry. He was defining the aspirations of the modern liberal democracy under the banner of Secularism—a state marked not merely by the absence of an official religion, but a state that has a decent regard for the individual's yearning for material good, self-expression, and freedom and fulfillment, and which provides the institutions that encourage the realization of these ideals.

19

An Innocent in America Finds the Ties That Bind

A winter storm was burying New York City in snow when George Holyoake and his daughter Emilie boarded the Cunard liner *Catalonia* in the "hurricane month" of December 1882. It looked less like a ship than "one vast boulder of snow."[1] The liner had been moored a week at a Lower Manhattan dock without steam and her cabins were cold. The *Catalonia* carried 1,500 passengers into four days of the "best-conducted" sea before a north-west gale blew her near on her side, wallowing in the Atlantic until the waters quietened off Ireland. Emilie stayed in their cabin while Holyoake, bruised and tossed about, retreated to the saloon so as to escape being washed overboard. He found one benefit: "There is no dust at sea," unlike London, where his books and papers were daily "covered with the nimble particles."[2]

The return of George and Emilie Holyoke to England brought to an end the second of two forays he made in 1879 and 1882 into the political and social complexities of the New World. His trips were ostensibly to promote the idea of a settler's guide book that would prepare emigrants for life in their new homelands. It is unclear whether he went on his own accord or on behalf of the British co-operative movement. In either case, he traveled as a voluble exponent of emigration, a stark turnaround from his youthful championing of "Home Colonisation"—co-operative communities set up and run by workers—as an alternative to starting new lives overseas. He would now advise the poor to "save a little capital at co-operative stores, and join the great fortunes of those nations where freedom and equality dwell and where wealth awaits all who have fortitude, common sense, courage, and industry."[3]

In contrast to the "eagerness and gladness" that the prospect of a journey or the sight of the sea had once given Holyoake, he felt no such emotions on his first voyage to America in 1879. He crossed alone, still suffering

19. An Innocent in America Finds the Ties That Bind 193

the malaise that followed his fight with blindness. His life had become uninteresting. "While traveling in America, I felt no exaltation. On my return I was not conscious of being better or worse. Yet all the while I was entirely changed."[4] What he saw in America—its cities spewing out new industries and its countryside bedecked in scenic grandeur—had driven any sense of weariness from his mind.

Holyoake disembarked in New York from the SS *Bothnia* carrying on his arm a rug presented to him at the Gloucester Co-operative Congress. It was small enough, apparently, for use as a throw or a wrap to cover his shoulders. He took a room at the Washington Hotel, No. 1 Broadway, where from the fifth floor he looked out on the Bowery and the Castle Gardens. The hotel was filled with old ship captains who talked of cargoes, storms, and shipwrecks in every language but English. It left him feeling "utterly solitary and lost."

As Holyoake traveled from Boston to Santa Fe and Quebec City to Chicago, he sent off articles to the *Co-operative News* back in Manchester and wrote dispatches for other publications, ranging from the *Nineteenth Century* magazine in London to the free thinking *Boston Index*. The articles became the stuff of two books, *Among the Americans and a Stranger in America,* and *Travels in Search of a Settler's Guide-Book of America and Canada.* It would be an "absurd pretension," he conceded, to regard either as a "book upon America." They were each but "a mere fireside story of what interested me."[5] In this, Holyoake was too modest by far. The books contain illuminating insights into what he found in America at a key point in its development. More important, they reveal much of Holyoake's own sentiments, prejudices, and innate qualities of personality, honed by six decades of study, strife, and persuasion—in all of which he retained a gentle innocence as he pushed ahead with ideas that were once reviled and unpopular, but were now becoming conventional wisdom in the late Victorian Age.

Holyoake naively trusted the Canadian and American governments to do his bidding in the preparation of guide books that would educate prospective immigrants on matters as diverse as land to be had by purchase or by homestead, the climate, conditions of health, markets for labor—all things enabling "an emigrant to go out with his eyes open." In neither Washington nor Ottawa were officials easily convinced to take on such a project. Holyoake found himself a sixty-two-year-old Innocent in America, a mirror image of Mark Twain's *Innocents Abroad*, both recounting experiences in unfamiliar lands at approximately the same time. Both traveled as America was entering the Gilded Age of Twain's fevered imagination, a period when the post–Civil War United States turned its attention from freeing (but not liberating) its slaves, to pushing Indians out of its most valuable western lands, while building a new industrial colossus. France would call the time La Belle Époque and Britain would know it simply as the Victorian Age—a turning point when Holyoake's Secularist propagandizing and co-operative advocacy would help change the thinking of millions.

The United States had entered a period of rapid economic growth that followed the Panic of 1873 when fortunes were lost on land speculation, and the Reconstruction Era had come to an end in 1877. The Supreme Court, casting aside all efforts to improve the lives of ex-slaves, would rule that discrimination by race in employment, transportation and public services was perfectly proper. In Washington, President Rutherford B. Hayes would listen patiently to Holyoake's entreaties for a settler's guide book, give him 475 maps of seventeen American states, and do nothing, In Canada, where Holyoake would lunch with the Premier, Sir John A. Macdonald, he found a country dealing with a different kind of challenge: two nations (English and French) that had been "warring within the bosom of a single state."

In both the U.S. and Canada, Holyoake found, times were getting better for workers, despite the suppression of labor unions and the exploitation of illiterate immigrants. Real wages, according to U.S. government statistics, rose from $380 in 1880 to $564 in 1890. Railroads were the big preoccupation of governments and railroad barons. A transcontinental railway crossed the U.S. in 1869 when a Golden Spike was driven into a railway tie in Utah; Canada would have to wait until 1885 for its Last Spike marking completion of the Canadian Pacific line in the mountains of British Columbia. At the time of Holyoake's second visit in 1882, New York was celebrating the building of the Brooklyn Bridge, the world's first rodeo was being held in Pecos, Texas—bringing closure to the gunfighting days of the Old West—and a traveler like him could set his watch by standard time in the five new continental time zones. Holyoake was never far from the rails. Hearing strange noises on his first morning in New York, he looked out his hotel room window and "found the elevated railway almost running through my bedroom." It was New York's answer to urban transit and Holyoake agreed "the elevated railway is a wonderful contrivance of iron architecture; nevertheless beautiful streets are disfigured by it."[6]

Like other accomplished travelers, Holyoake combined careful planning with good luck. He found himself meeting leading citizens in every city he visited; they often brought invitations to stay in their homes rather than at a hotel. It was by such fortuitous circumstance when Holyoake looked up his old classmate from the Birmingham Mechanics' Institute, Dr. Frederick Hollick, in New York. Hollick handed him a letter from the secretary of the C-operative Colony Aid Association. E.E. Barnum was writing to ask Holyoake to visit him at the association's newspaper, *The Worker*. "He became my friend and was my friend always." A former church minister, Barnum accompanied Holyoake about New York and took him to

19. An Innocent in America Finds the Ties That Bind 195

Saratoga by train to see the New York State Republican convention. He also led Holyoake about at night "lest my being unable to see in the dark" might cause him to lose his way.

The pattern persisted throughout Holyoake's two trips. He went to Boston to meet Wendell Phillips, anti-slavery fighter and crusader for native rights. Phillips had once dispatched a letter to *The Reasoner* critical of something Holyoake had written, so he presented himself at Phillips's door "as his ancient and alien adversary." Phillips took him about Boston and arranged for him to meet Ralph Waldo Emerson, the essayist and poet. Holyoake found Emerson "Though tall, still erect [with] bright eye and calm grace of manner."[7] Holyoake gave his first American speech in Boston at the invitation of Josiah Quincy of the eminent American Quincy Adams family that had given the United States two presidents—John Adams and John Quincy Adams. Holyoake spoke at Stacy Hall, where the freed slave, Lloyd Garrison, had been dragged from the podium and nearly lynched.

Holyoake made friends quickly, one of his new acquaintances being Seth Hunt, the treasurer of the Connecticut City Railroad, who took him to his namesake town of Holyoake, Massachusetts. He gave a lecture on co-operation in this town on the Connecticut River, in sight of Mount Holyoake "which overlooks the splendid and fertile valleys through which the silver snake-like river winds four hundred miles."[8] The town's founder, Revolutionary War hero Elizur Holyoake, reared a son, Edward, who was an early president of Harvard University. Edward's son became a doctor and performed a surgical operation at the age of ninety-two. Holyoake was told the family's ancient coat of arms showed holly and oak, thus giving the letter *a* to the name.

Holyoake never allowed his secular convictions to prevent him from visiting churches and mixing with ministers. He had no choice on his first ship to America when he took a third-class cabin and was double-bunked with the Rev. James J. Good of Philadelphia who was returning from the Holy Land. There were twelve clergymen on board which was fine with Holyoake because he was sure if anything went wrong with him "they would use friendly intercession in the quarter where they had influence—and get it all put right." He gave his first speech to a church congregation at the Free Church of Florence, Mass., to a group of Sunday School teachers. He remembered he had been one himself. He spoke many times in churches and found the piety of the worshippers simple and fearless. "They did not, as we do in England, pay any attention to what people thought of them. They did me the honour to believe that it was impossible that I could abuse their trust."[9]

In Brooklyn, Holyoake heard a sermon by the Rev. Mr. Beecher, who he had met while visiting Niagara Falls. Beecher's sermon observed that

Christ had written nothing himself and those who claimed to record what he said were mostly illiterate. "It was impossible," Holyoake thought, "not to be impressed in favour of Christianity preached with this manly candour." On a side trip to Providence, Rhode Island, Holyoake spoke to the Free Religious Society on "Unregarded aspects of human nature." It was an unremarkable speech, except for a concluding comment reported by the local newspaper: "He believed that the secular element of things was as important as the religious element; that science was a revelation obtained by the intellect, and that morality could exist apart from religion."[10] At Cornell University, the acting president, the Rev. Dr. Trussell, invited Holyoake to speak to 450 students. He introduced him "as the apostle of the most important doctrine that this century will publish to humanity."

Of all the places of worship Holyoake visited, he found two Negro churches in Washington "cleaner brighter, more cheerful structures than any Wesleyan or Congregationalist chapel in England."[11] He sat near a "magnificent Negress; she wore a small, spotted, close-fitting dress; she reclined listening, like a handsome tigress, voluptuous as Cleopatra." The music, he thought, was "most strange." Each person sang in a "trill always rising in energy. The final appeal to God in which prayers ended was in a wild musical tone that seemed able to pierce the skies and reach the throne of heaven."

Holyoake was introduced to the North American press soon after his arrival in New York City. *The Associated Press* story on his arrival went to 120 papers and he was interviewed by the city's journals—*The Mail, The Tribune, The Times, The Daily News, The Herald*. He spoke to a gathering of journalists at the Press Club. Holyoake was both amused and confounded at the stories written about his interviews. "The interviewer is an inquirer, and he visits you partly from courtesy, partly for the sake of news. Sometimes I read reports of interviews I did not know, until I reread the heading and found they related to me."[12] In Denver, the headline on his interview identified Holyoake as "a great man." He was often referred to as General Holyoake. A reporter in Las Vegas asked him what he thought of a great comet that was then visible in the sky. Would it fall into the sun and what would the sun do if it did? Holyoake answered innocently that it seemed to be well-behaved and as it had been loafing about the skies for two thousand years, it must know its way about. He was astonished when papers described him as an authority on comets.[13]

Before leaving New York State, Holyoake was invited to speak at what had become the newest cultural phenomenon in America—gatherings of upwardly mobile church-goers seeking culture and education by taking in speeches and concerts while camped out on the shore of Chautauqua Lake. It was in the westernmost part of the State. A future president,

19. An Innocent in America Finds the Ties That Bind 197

Theodore Roosevelt, is said to have called the Chautauqua movement—which morphed into hundreds of similar summer camps in towns all over the country—"the most American thing in America." Chautauqua brought culture and adult education to communities that otherwise had no access to intellectual thought. Holyoake arrived at the "pow wow" expecting to find a definite plan of procedure. There being none, he drew up a set of tongue-in-check resolutions, one asking that each speaker "be allowed reasonable time for denouncing everybody and everything."

Holyoake's innocence of American life showed in his comments about what he saw. "Children in America are regarded as apt to act upon their own will rather than upon the will of their parents." He did not find this so in families he had the opportunity of observing; they were manifestly affectionate and obedient. But he was right is judging them to have more free freedom than children in England "where we have a somewhat unwise domestic paternalism, which encourages a costly dependence." They hang around home longer than they should. "The American habit of training their children to independence has much to be said in its favour."[14]

But what kind of independence? Holyoake quotes with favor the words of *Chicago Times* publisher Joseph Medill, spoken to a Senate committee: "The educational system of America ... does not train our youth in habits of useful industry. Its purpose is not to increase the effectiveness of labour [but] to imparting dead languages, elegant literature, and higher mathematics ... all well enough for the boys of the wealthy leisure class, but is not best suited to equip the future bread-winners for their work."[15] The answer, Holyoake was sure, was "industrial education."

Of all the American cities Holyoake visited—New York, Boston, Chicago, Philadelphia, St. Louis, Las Vegas—he was most impressed with Washington, "the most superb in its brilliant flashes of space." He added; "Washington is the only city I have ever seen which no wanton architect or builder can despoil."[16] It was a planned city in every aspect and even in the twenty-first century retains a human scale, dictated by a rule that no building can exceed the height of the Washington Monument. Holyoake makes no comment on what may be Washington's least favorable feature; its climate of stultifying heat and humidity in summer and fog and chill in winter.

Holyoake got a first-hand view of American politics in Washington, where he was led about by Colonel Robert Ingersoll, celebrated freethinker known as "The Great Agnostic." They had admired each other from a distance; they were each other's English and American counterparts, they shared common views on the great issues of the day—religion, slavery, women's rights, birth control—and were both persuasive writers who sprinkled their works, as well as their talks, with humor, anecdote, and calls to action. That both would become lost figures in history would have been seen as inconceivable. Each was the leading freethought lecturer of his country, delivering dozens of talks to audiences that numbered in the thousands.

Robert Ingersoll was born, the son of a Congregational minister, in a village in the Finger Lakes district of New York. A hard taskmaster, his father loved his children but beat them, instilling in the boy what would be a lifelong disapproval of corporal punishment. Ingersoll taught school, studied for the bar, and during the Civil War raised a regiment for the Union and gained the rank of Colonel. He was captured but released by a Confederate general on a promise to fight no more. A promising political career with the Republican party evaporated when he "came out" as an agnostic but he was held in such repute that he was allowed to nominate—unsuccessfully—James G. Blaine for President in 1876. Ingersoll's view of religion could be summed up in his declamation on the centenary of American independence: "One hundred years ago our fathers retired the Gods from politics." Of women, Ingersoll left no doubt of their fate under Christianity: "As long as woman regards the Bible as the charter of her rights, she will be the slave of man." Holyoake could not have expressed those views more succinctly.

Colonel Robert Ingersoll knew everybody who was anybody in Washington. He invited Holyoake home for dinner to meet Frederick Douglas, the "noble slave" who had escaped the South and become an Abolitionist speaker. In one of the most noted acts of post–Civil War Reconstruction, President Hayes appointed Douglas the U.S. Provost-Marshall for the District of Columbia, the highest post occupied by an African American. Holyoake "drank [on that night only] champagne of finer quality than I had before tasted in America." After meeting Douglas, Holyoake concluded that "coloured people, having regard to their self-possession and deliberateness of manner, seemed to me a royal race as compared with the excited white people who stampede after a fortune, contract disease in getting it, and drop with a spasm into the grave, without having looked at the world into which they have been projected."[17] Never a money-grubber nor one who sought comfort or status, Holyoake would have been reflecting some of his own values onto the people he was observing.

Of American politics, Holyoake bemoaned the system of patronage surrounding Presidential appointments in which 100,000 jobs turn over after every change of President. "Each of these aspirants has on the average as many personal friends who devote themselves to getting him installed. So there are two millions of the most active politicians in the country always battling for places. There is wonder that the progress made in America occurs at all."[18]

He was equally damning of Americans who thought the United States would be the better for a king. "I conversed with many who longed for an aristocracy. There are people who decry and give dismal accounts of popular government. Others I found, as we find them in England, making quite a reputation by denouncing the supposed tyranny of others, with a view to outing a real one of their own in its place."[19] Holyoake had lost none of his passion for democratic equality, which he noted was not as evident in America as its boasters would have one believe.

Holyoake's daughter, Emilie Ashurst Holyoake, kept close to his side on his second visit to North America in 1882. She was motivated either out of caution for her father's health, or her own desire to see the New World. Prime Minister Gladstone, appreciative of Holyoake's support, assigned him a £100 grant. They passed by Niagara Falls—"the maddest of all waterfalls and cataracts ever known"—on their entry into Canada. Holyoake was much impressed with the college of agriculture they visited in Guelph, Ontario, but was taken aback when an eminent editor told him there was no need for a settler's guide-book because everything a settler needed to know had already been written up. Undeterred, Holyoake and Emilie traveled on to Toronto, Ottawa, and Montreal to another waterfall, Montmorency Falls, in Quebec. At Montmorency Falls they encountered a French-Canadian beggar who "excelled all beggars in his vocation, cap in hand. He did not ask, but demanded, a gift."

In Toronto, Holyoake and Emilie met Prof. Goldwin Smith, an English-born academic who was regarded as Canada's leading public intellectual of the day. He was a leader of the Canada First movement which, belying its name, advocated union with the United States. Holyoake found Smith at The Grange, a fine stone home and "the most English manorial house I had seen in that country or America. Quaint, strong, and capacious, with endless dark-panelled rooms, bright with paintings and with other signs of historic opulence."[20]

The highlight of their visit to Ottawa was a luncheon with Premier Sir John A. Macdonald, the hard-drinking, high-living head of the Canadian government. Brought to Canada as a child from Scotland, he built a law practice in Kingston, Ontario, and played a leading role in the Confederation of British colonies into the new Dominion of Canada. One day, Holyoake records, Sir John "made some remarks which threw more light on European conceptions of Canada than any other I heard. He said artists were the defamers of Canada. They all paint the snows, the sledges, and ice, and the people in furs. The ripened fruit, magical vines, the golden harvests, the forests, the flowers, the splendid rivers and glories of tropical seasons the great land has, we never see painted."[21] Macdonald turned Holyoake over to J.H Pope, the Minister of Agriculture. Pope took up the idea of the Settler's Guide-Book and assigned John Lowe, his chief secretary, to the writing of it. It was published a few months later and Holyoake personally received four hundred requests for copies.

The final stages of Holyoake's second North American visit took he and Emilie to the American Southwest and the land of the rapidly vanishing Old West. On the way, they visited Kansas City where Holyoake's good luck ran with him. He was invited on a torrid day to visit a co-operative sugar bakery. Interrupted by an invitation to go for a drive, he found on his return that the bakery had collapsed, burying five people in its ruins.

Holyoake came away with a somewhat superficial impression of the lives of the Mexican peon class of the region—descendants of Spanish-Indian natives who had filled the region before it was annexed by the United States. He envied the Mexican woodcutter who "takes three days to cut his wood in the most romantic dells in the universe. He loads his asses in the morning sun. Spends a day in roadless gorges, takes another day in the quaint sunny city of Sante Fe selling his bundles. ... With money in hand he buys a pint of whisky, of quality very doubtful, the backbones of a couple of sheep, some coffee, or pepper, or some other spice. He does no more work while those provisions last. ... Other Mexicans rear goats and drive them at leisure a hundred miles to market."[22] Holyoake thought, God preserve them from civilization.

Such days in the sun were not to last long for George and Emilie Holyoake. The *Catalonia* reached Liverpool shortly before Christmas 1882. They thought they were safe when they reached the bar of the Mersey River but they were held near its estuary for thirty hours due to tide and fog. They feared running aground or jamming into another ship. "Our prudent captain avoided both." When they did make dock, they had to wait for the cargo of two earlier arrivals to be unloaded. "We had to wander about in the frost and snow more than two hours."[23]

Once settled back in London, Holyoake resumed the friendly correspondence he had enjoyed with Colonel Ingersoll. Their letters betray mutual admiration. Ingersoll wrote on January 1, 1883, to say, "We have missed you every day, and every day we talk about you and yours. There is no living man for whom I have greater respect and admiration."[24] Holyoake replied: "My days have all been brighter since I received your letter."

In his trips to America Holyoake preached the benefits of co-operation but spoke rarely on Secularism. "English Secularism, is as little known in America as American and Canadian secularism, is understood in Great Britain," he would write in *English Secularism: A Confession*

19. An Innocent in America Finds the Ties That Bind

of Belief. Holyoake had gone to America an Innocent, and returned, if not a worldly sophisticate, at least with a deeper understanding of the divisions that differentiated English-speaking peoples on either side of the Atlantic, and the common heritage of language and history that bound them together.

20

"The Queen Is Dead, Long Live the King!"

George Holyoake's trips to America expanded his conception of the global society that was emerging in the wake of oceanic steamer traffic, railways linking Europe together and crisscrossing the American continent, and the stringing of telegraph wires along their routes. His trips also whetted the yen for travel for a man who in his youth had mistrusted "all people not English." Now well into his sixties, Holyoake set out as a traveling ambassador for Britain's Co-operative movement. He had visited France and Holland in earlier years, and during the 1880s became a popular figure at international Co-op Congresses in Milan; Bologna; Tours, France, and other centers.

Thousands of other Britons had also caught the travel bug as the British Empire extended its reach around the world, carried by merchant traders from Manchester to Bristol, the money lenders of the City of London, the power and prestige of the Royal Navy, and the protective skirts of Queen Victoria. Her reign ran on and on, with most Britons knowing no other monarch during their lifetime; many assumed she would be with them always. Britain's domain extended over twenty percent of the world's land surface and numbered some four hundred million people. If there was any one name associated with Britain's "imperial century" it was Thomas Cook, a cabinet-maker who launched his eponymous travel agency in 1841 by taking holidayers on short day trips by rail. He carried 150,000 visitors to the Great Exhibition that George Holyoake attended in London in 1851 and was soon taking rich Englishmen on sea voyages to Egypt and India. Americans also got into the act; fifty thousand Europe-bound tourists departed by ocean liner in 1880; that figure would double in the next decade as wealth flowed upwards and property-poor British earls began to look to American heiresses to save their estates from foreclosure.

Holyoake was a devoted if often absent father and was especially attached to his youngest daughter, Emilie. When she was a little girl and Holyoake visited Holland in 1869, he sent her amusing letters to which he had glued newspaper cuttings illustrating Dutch boys akin to the one who stuck his finger in the dyke to prevent a flood. "Here in Dutchland where all the streets are made of water I met a little boy very much like Frank [a brother] carrying a placard. Read it. 'De zuster' is Dutch for the sister. I suppose 'Broeder' Frank (for the Dutch say broeder for Brother) has lost his 'Zuster.' Soon after on the Amstel Bridge I met another boy. There he is putting up what Broeder wanted to know. You see [a boy with a poster]. Here is the notice: 'De Zuster is all right. There she is.'"[1]

Sometime in the early 1880s—Holyoake is vague on details—he and Helen moved, after eighteen years, from Harrow-on-the-Hill in northwest London to Brighton, the fashionable Regency resort on the English Channel. They settled into a first floor apartment of the Eastern Lodge at 36 Camelford Street and Holyoake dabbled in municipal politics, aspiring to but never achieving a seat on the local council. "After some weeks of enjoyment," Holyoake wrote of their life following his return from America, "bronchitis came" to Helen. Physicians were called, but she died on January 11, 1883. "Ceaseless watching and aid day and night averted the customary stress of that malady, so death came by failure of the heart's action, and the serenity and sweet sense of rest at the end was so absolute that I called in the nearest physician to assure me that it was really death."[2] The obituary he wrote drew attention to the "great pleasure" she brought to their household with her "elementary sense of taste—though not acquired in the schools. Her preference was for one or two things of real worth and beauty; she was impatient of a crowd of commonplace objects ... [and] had the same taste in dress, which was always simple and seemly, which was no mean satisfaction to me, to whom proportion in things is a form of pleasure which never palls."

Holyoake gave Helen a secular burial that he conducted himself. C.D. Collet sang the same Harriet Martineau hymn, *Beneath the Starry Arch*, that he had sung at the funeral of Maximillian, their boy killed in a traffic accident many years before. She was buried beside him in Highgate Cemetery, London. Emily Tennyson, wife of Alfred, Lord Tennyson the poet, sent two letters of condolence, the first on news of Helen's illness and the second after her death.[3]

Holyoake now had to think about how best to mix Secularism and Co-operation in ways that would advance both causes and provide him with sufficient income to cover his frugal way of life. He chose the same old mix: writing on religion, politics, and his favorite causes, for any papers that would give him space; and speaking to any audiences that would fill a lecturers' collection plate. He would also need his own paper in which he could expound his radical views without editorial interference. After six months back home he launched *The Present Day* in June 1883. He viewed it as a vehicle to restore Secularism to its original broad base. He had thought it up, he told friends, while cruising the St. Lawrence River on his last American visit.

Holyoake intended that *The Present Day* would eschew atheism and focus on the wider moral meaning of Secularism and the duty it imposed on every man and woman to work for the material well-being of their neighbors. He severely criticized the "new Freethinkers" who, he felt, were guilty of the same outrages of denying the right to freedom of belief that they had once deplored in their opponents. The new orthodox thinking that he opposed would find a future parallel in what might be known in the modern age as "political correctness." For all his distress with what he saw as inflexible voices in Secularism, he took care to balance *The Present Day* with news of the Co-operative movement and accounts of other political and social issues.

Forever a crusader against taxes on the poor, Holyoake used the paper to good effect in his role as chairman of the Travelling Tax Abolition Committee. It was a pressure group set up to urge repeal of the tax on the fares of third-class railway passengers, a class of carriage Holyoake was intimately familiar with. The campaign went on for twenty-four years. The tax was reduced to a penny a mile before it was finally abolished in 1884. Holyoake published *The Present Day* for more than three years until, exhausted, he closed it down and turned to a less demanding daily routine.

The most important political development of 1884 was the passage, with William Gladstone now Prime Minister, of the Representation of the People Act, also known as the Third Reform Act. It expanded the electorate to 5.5 million by giving the vote to men in the country on the same basis as townsmen: payment of rent of £10 a year or holding land valued at £10. A companion bill redistributed constituencies to give more seats to the cities, but forty percent of adult males and all women were still without the vote.

When the member of Parliament for Leicester resigned, Holyoake set his sights on his third run for public office in the knowledge that if he were elected, he would never agree to swearing on the Christian oath, an obstacle that was keeping Charles Bradlaugh out of the House of Commons. He must have realized that the Leicester Liberal Council would be unlikely to choose a candidate burdened by such a handicap, notwithstanding the fact Leicester was one of the most radical of English towns, with a long secular tradition. His letter seeking the nomination was straight forward: "If you think it worthwhile to assist in opening a door in Parliament through which a gentleman and an honest man can enter without shame or humiliation, I offer you my services." The Council, casting its net widely, invited

Herbert Spencer to stand but he declined. Holyoake's fifty votes were insufficient to win him the nod and he retired to Brighton to contemplate his connections with the Co-operative movement.

~~~

Holyoake's busiest years in the Co-operative movement were about to begin. With co-operative enterprises taking hold throughout western Europe, Holyoake found himself called upon to explain the movement's principles and methods to audiences in Holland, France, Italy, and Germany. In 1885 Holyoake attended the first Congress of the French Co-operative Movement in Paris, accompanied by his daughter Emilie. Holyoake spoke little French and when he was seated with the president of the Congress, he excused his lack of fluency with the fact he'd had only a half hour's notice to make the trip, which gave him little time to study French. He took more enjoyment from a side trip to the northern French town of Guise to see *La Familistère,* a co-operative community set up by Jean-Baptiste Godin, a local industrialist. Workers owned and managed the complex, which would remain under communal ownership until 1968.

The next year, Holyoake traveled to Milan, Italy for the Congress of Italian Co-operators. The trip turned into an adventure when Holyoake and his traveling companion reached Monza, where they were to visit an Italian professor. They became separated and Holyoake, knowing no Italian, refused to pay a charge to leave the train and chose to stay onboard. When it stopped at a large city a soldier was found who could speak English. He explained to an excited crowd that Holyoake was the "delagato Inglese" to an important convention. It was then that Holyoake discovered he was in Milan. He addressed the Congress with the aid of an interpreter and spoke of his support for the struggles of Mazzini and Garibaldi to obtain Italian unity. These lines probably gained him more applause than anything he said about Co-operation. His homeward trek was via Genoa, Nice and Nimes, where he was entertained by the foremost French co-operator of the day, M. de Boyve. He returned to France in 1887 for a Congress in Tours and to Italy to attend a Congress at Bologna.

Holyoake's mind would have been on more than Co-operation during these trips. He had met a lady, Mary Jane Parsons, and had married her on May 25, 1886, when he was sixty-nine. Almost nothing is known of her except that she brought her daughter Gertie to live with them in Brighton. Holyoke commuted monthly to Manchester to attend meetings of the Co-operative Union and worked on a Co-operative history, *Self-Help a Hundred Years Ago.* Disappointment came his way when Gladstone's Liberals split over the Prime Minister's support of Home Rule for Ireland, and lost the 1886 election to the Conservative party.

The next year's Co-operative Congress in Manchester saw further honors heaped on Holyoake. He gave an inaugural address as president for the year. The *Manchester Evening News* reported his speech cast a glance at the England he had known as a young man, and he told his own parable of the fishes: "A savage, says Mr. Holyoake quaintly but forcibly, can catch only ten fish a day. The capitalist lends him a net, and he catches 200, when the capitalist takes 190 of the fish for the use the net. That is a good thing for the capitalist. But in time the capitalist buys the river and forbids the savage catching any more fish. A bad thing for the savage. His salvation is to get capital, buy his own net, buy a river or a share in it, and keep all the fish he can catch. This is the theory and practice of co-operation."[4]

Throughout his life Holyoake encountered rivals and skeptics, but few enemies. There is no known source, therefore, for the rumors that came out of Ireland in 1890 that he had become a Catholic. A newspaper in Dewsbury, Yorkshire—a town with a tradition of firing a gun every night at ten o'clock—announced: "From a statement made and published by Mr. Holyoake, it appears that he has embraced the Roman Catholic faith."[5] An item Holyoake had published in *The Present Day* about being offered a share in ten thousand Catholic masses if he would convert, had been embroidered to make it seem he had indeed returned to Christianity. The purveyor of the mischief was never identified.

The long and testy relationship between Holyoake and Charles Bradlaugh—which had become more placid in recent years—eased when Bradlaugh resigned the presidency of the National Secular Society in 1889. He was ill. When the executive met at the Old Street Hall of Science, Holyoake moved a motion to acknowledge the "friendliness exhibited in some religious assemblies in offering up prayers for Mr. Bradlaugh's recovery."[6] It was adopted unanimously, an indication that the barriers between Secularism and English churches were slowly being overcome. Any remaining antagonism between the two rivals came to an end with Bradlaugh's death January 30, 1891. That such an apparently healthy and robust man should pass away at the age of only fifty-eight came as a shock to all who knew him. Bradlaugh suffered from Bright's disease—known today as nephritis—and died of cardiac hypertrophy after several seizures. Holyoake stood with the large crowd, a young Mahatma Gandhi among them, that gathered for Bradlaugh's burial in the Brookwood Necropolis in Sussex.[7] At Bradlaugh's request, it was a silent service. An hour after most departed, "a lingering band of devoted men had got the shovels from the workmen and were one by one obtaining the last sad privilege of casting their handful of earth into the grave."[8] The following Sunday Holyoake delivered a eulogy at the Hall of Science in London:

20. "The Queen Is Dead, Long Live the King!"

He was the most illustrious fighting propagandist they had ever seen. Freedom could not be obtained by any party if they shrank from the price to be paid for it. Bradlaugh knew this, and he paid the price. He was a great man because he had genius—the genius of liberty, the genius of discovering how to advance the cause of the people in ways that nobody else saw. He understood the difference between wishing and willing. His creed was to take the world as he found it, and try to make it better.[9]

Bradlaugh's daughter, Hypatia Bonner-Bradlaugh, published in her biography of her father some critical notes that Holyoake had written during the birth control trial of Bradlaugh and Annie Besant. These aroused Holyoake's old enmity and he wrote a pamphlet, *The Warpath of Opinion*, in which he challenged the facts as set out in the biography. He also, however, recognized Bradlaugh's effectiveness. "He was the greatest agitator, within the limits of the law, who appeared in my time among the working people."[10]

The mark of an eminent Victorian was to have his portrait painted, and George Holyoake achieved this distinction in 1892 when he sat for three paintings by the well-known artist Walter Sickert. Each shows Holyoake somewhat ravaged by age, tired, cheeks sagging, and beard unkempt. Sickert donated a painting to the National Portrait Gallery, where it remains today. The Munich-born Sickert also painted such figures as Aubrey Beardsley and Winston Churchill. He did a notable pencil sketch of Charles Bradlaugh and a large oil portrait titled "Bradlaugh at the Bar of the House of Commons." The NPG states that Holyoake sat for twenty-one portraits by different artists.

Age was now catching up with the great man, but he resisted the loss of strength, both physical and mental, with his usual determination. He continued to be accident prone: On a Sunday morning in Brighton he was knocked down by a man on a bicycle. The rider apparently

George Holyoake by Walter Sickert, oil on canvas, 30 in. × 25 in., exhibited in 1892 (© National Portrait Gallery, London).

chose to miss two women and hit Holyoake instead. "As I had always been in favour of the rights of women, I said he did rightly, though the result was not to my mind."[11] Holyoake noted in his diary that on his 75th birthday in 1892, "Tho I was at work until two o'clock this morning, I am as well as I ever was on a birthday." A new honor came his way when he was elected an honorary member of the National Liberal Club in 1893 and given a dinner by the Press Circle of the Club.

Illnesses weakened Holyoake in 1894 and 1895 but he took pleasure in publication of his autobiography, *Sixty Years of an Agitator's Life*. Compiled largely from newspaper articles he had written over the years, it provides a chronological account of the main elements of Holyoake's life. His last Secularist book, *The Origin and Nature of Secularism*, came out in 1896. An American edition was titled *English Secularism; A Confession of Belief*.

This book can be read as a sequel to *Principles of Secularism*, published in 1859. The two, written nearly forty years apart, cast light both on Holyoake's evolving maturity toward the main intellectual challenge of his life, and the changing environment in which his ideas were being accepted. With publication of his latest book, Holyoake also demonstrated that his commitment to Secularism had not flagged despite his loss of control of organized Secularism, and the tremendous effort he had put into the Co-operative movement. By either title, *The Origin and Nature of Secularism* is probably, by present day standards, the most readable of Holyoake's works. It is thorough in encompassing the basic principles of freethought and precise in setting out Secularism's emphasis on the material well-being of the people.

> From the first, Secularism has based its claims to be regarded on the fact that only the rich could afford to be Christians, and the poor must look to other principles for deliverance. Material means are those which are calculable, which are under the control and command of man, and can be tested by human experience. No definition of Secularism shows its distinctiveness which omits to specify *material* means as its method of procedure.[12]

A pamphleteer at heart, Holyoake encouraged other radical and freethought writers to put their works into print. Few publishers, however, would risk the derision of the publishing world or the criticism of influential periodicals or churchmen by issuing radical books. To counter this, an informal committee of radical supporters had been subsidizing two or three such works per year. Beginning with the Propagandist Press Committee in 1890 that grew into a much larger Rationalist Press Association in 1899, Holyoake served as president of each group. The RPA logo appeared on dozens of pamphlets and books that sold more than a million copies in its first five years. It was still in business as of 2020.

The outbreak of the Second Boer War in 1899 troubled Holyoake for its undisguised belligerence and he joined the chorus of criticism leveled at the Prime Minister, the Marquess of Salisbury, and his Conservative government in the conflict between the British Empire and the two South African Boer (Dutch) states, Transvaal and the Orange Free State. Holyoake's political idol, William Gladstone, had been Prime Minister during the First Boer War which ended in an embarrassing stand-off. Now, Gladstone was dead and there was no effective opposition to the patriotic hue and cry that blew up in wake of early British defeats. What had been expected to be an easy victory for the Empire turned into two and one-half years of blood-letting before a superior British force occupied all of South Africa. The war overshadowed the end of the 1800s and the advent of the twentieth century, which was marked with solemnity in Britain on January 1, 1901. The New Year's Honours list was published in *The Times* and it was noted that Queen Victoria's physician, Thomas Barlow, was made a baronet. In Washington, more than five thousand people walked into the White House to shake the hand of President William McKinley.[13]

Three weeks later, Victoria, by the Grace of God, of the United Kingdom of Great Britain and Ireland Queen, Defender of the Faith, and Empress of India, was dead. She died, at the age of eighty-one and after sixty-three years on the throne, at six thirty o'clock on Tuesday, the 22nd of January, in her bed in Osborne House Palace on the Isle of Wight. She was the only monarch George Holyoake had known throughout his adult life. There is no written account of how Holyoake took her death, which plunged Britain into deep mourning. Newspapers devoted endless pages to her long life, from her wedding to her cousin Prince Albert of the old Germanic state of Saxe-Coburg and Gotha in 1840, to her many years of withdrawal from public life following his death in 1861. Then the spotlight shifted to Victoria's son Albert, Prince of Wales, who became King Edward VII. His presence on the throne gave Britain the Edwardian era, a short-lived period of relief, renewal and hope that would be discarded with the arrival of the Great War, with all its demons.

Holyoake disapproved of monarchy, as he disapproved of any rank or privilege not earned by merit. He was a Republican, forthright in his views, but he never attacked the monarchy directly or any member of the Royal Family personally. He expressed his distaste for a system of inherited governance, and especially its status as the protector of state religion. He questioned why every summons and every command of a cabinet minister, a judge, or a mayor had to be issued in the name of the Queen. "It seems a disadvantage of the monarchial system," he wrote, "that the name of the head of the reigning House should be attached to all proceedings, great or petty, noble or mean, honourable or infamous."[14]

The passing of Queen Victoria and the advent of the twentieth century spelled *finis* to a remarkable period in history. The old order had not overcome poverty but it had brought peace to much of Europe, industrialization to Britain and the Continent, a vast expansion of settlement in North America, and the spread of the British Empire around the world. Nine months after the death of Victoria, President William McKinley died from an assassin's bullet. His successor, Theodore Roosevelt—Teddy the Rough Rider—would become the symbol of a vigorous new Progressive age. George Holyoake had lived through an epic period of social reform—rights gained by trade unions, extension of the vote and agitation for women's rights, lifting of taxes from the press, reduction of the influence of religion in much of education and lawmaking, the launch of the Co-operative movement and the inception of Secularism. It was an almost triumphalist list of achievement and Holyoake could look with satisfaction on his contribution toward the making a new and modern world.

21

A Life, a Legend, a Legacy

George Holyoake would never forget him. Robert Owen's ideas about socialism, co-operation, and the belief that men could be bettered by giving them a better environment, remained a compelling force in Holyoake's life long after the death of his Welsh-born mentor. Holyoake had felt empowered when he'd first heard, as a part-time student at the Birmingham Mechanics' Institute, Owen's messianic message about the urgency of breaking free from organized religion. He'd relished his days as a social missionary for Owen's Society of Religious Rationalists, and he had stood in silent tribute when Owen was buried in the old churchyard of Newtown, beside the River Severn, in 1858. Holyoake returned to this Welsh birthplace of Robert Owen on a warm summer afternoon in 1902, this time as the honored guest of the Co-operative movement—and the last survivor of the men who had put Owen's body in the ground forty-four years before. He was there to unveil a memorial in recognition of a man who had dedicated himself to the betterment of the lives of workingmen everywhere.

Now a somewhat querulous octogenarian, Holyoake traveled from Brighton, transferring to a Great Western Railway train in London for the journey to Shrewsbury, near the Welsh border, over the route he had taken all those years ago. As a guest of the Co-operative Union, he would have enjoyed the comfort of a first class carriage and when he reached Shrewsbury, instead of transferring to a horse-drawn coach, he switched to a Cambrian Railways train for the final run to Newtown. He likely checked into the Bear Inn and had perhaps taken a room on the same floor of the three-story structure in which Owen had spent the last night of his life. It was then called the Bear Head Inn; its Victorian Tudor style façade still suggested an air of substance and civility to all who entered.

The memorial that George Holyoake unveiled on Saturday, July 12, enclosed Owen's tomb in an iron fence bearing two stone tablets, one a portrait of Owen and the other a bronze bas-relief depicting Owen holding his hand out to a procession of workers. Cardiff's *Western Mail* reported that the crowd attending the ceremony gathered on the bank of the Severn, "here a small stream that one may wade through."[1] There were "representatives of the co-operative movement from all parts of the country." The townspeople, "accustomed to hear Owen spoken of as an infidel, and one, therefore, to be treated with suspicion rather than reverence, looked on, some in sympathy and admiration but more in wonder at this national act of homage to a noble and chivalrous character."

Holyoake's "long and interesting address," the *Western Mail* reported, defended Owen against the criticism that he was an impractical dreamer.

> Owen was a man of more ideas than any public man England knew in his day. He shared and befriended every new conception of moment and promise, in science, in education, and government. Because some of his projects were so far reaching that they required a century to mature them, onlookers who expected them to be perfected at once, say he failed in whatever he proposed. While the truth is he succeeded in more things than any public man ever undertook. He saw, as no man before him did, that environment is the maker of men.... Owen said there were material means, largely unused, conducive to human improvement. This was Owen's aim, as far as human means might do it.[2]

The thread between Robert Own's "angerless philosophy" and the Secularism that George Holyoake pronounced as early as 1851 is clearly heard in these lines delivered in 1902. They harken back to Holyoake's declaration as set out in his *Principles of Secularism*. Its leading precepts, not dissimilar to those enunciated by Owen, were three-fold: Humanism, "the physical perfection of this life"; Moralism, "founded on the laws of Nature"; Materialism, "as the means of Nature for the Secular improvement of this life." To these, Holyoake added: "Secularism is the study of promoting human welfare by material means. It seeks human improvement through purity and suitableness of material conditions as being a method at once moral, practical, universal, and sure."[3]

There were more speeches that night, a second one by Holyoake and others by his fellow editor of the *Social Economist*, Edward Greening, as well as various co-op leaders. They all praised Owen and gave lofty assessments of Holyoake's life. By the time Holyoake left Newtown to return to Brighton, he would have become tired and perhaps embarrassed at compliments being rained on him that might have better been directed to Robert Owen. As with any person growing old, Holyoake's years were moving more swiftly. He could not have comprehended, as a young man, the long stretch of time represented by the forty-four years between his two trips to Newtown. Holyoake was eighty-five now and his life had unfolded in a manner unlike what he might have imagined when he began his studies at the Mechanics' Institute. But Holyoake was getting used to this sort of thing. On his eighty-fourth birthday in 1901, the *St. James Gazette* had paid him tribute as "one of the men who fought for and won the freedom which Englishmen possess today. He was one of the men who were appointed to explain all over the country the social system of Robert Owen, and since then has spoken thousands of times in the greatest halls in England."[4]

Holyoake was still filled with energy and ideas. He spent a week as editor of the *London Sun*, writing daily leaders (editorials) on topics ranging from the Boer War to daily life in the city. His nephew, Mr. Bottomly, was editor of the *Sun* and he saw to it that Holyoake was paid the largest journalistic fee he ever received. When Holyoake's tour of duty had been completed, Bottomly wrote:

> As soon as it became known that Mr. George Jacob Holyoake, the veteran apostle of free speech, a free press, and reform, was to occupy the editorial chair of the *Sun*, it was found necessary to guard the editorial sanctum, even against his old friends, who were anxious once more to look into his sunny face and grasp his hand.... The leading articles which have appeared from his pen have been decided upon and written within the hour, and the brief sessions during the day which have been assigned to him for rest have been occupied by him in the preparation of articles (30 in all) for other departments of the *Sun*.[5]

Holyoake enjoyed his birthdays, usually marked by gatherings of family and friends. His eighty-sixth in 1903 was celebrated at a reception at the South Place Chapel in the Finsbury district of London. Two daughters, Emile, now Mrs. Alfred Marsh, and Eveline, now Mrs. Taylor, attended with him. Press reports told how Holyoake's "remarks aroused his listeners to repeated demonstrations of enthusiasm."[6] A month later, the *Brighton Gazette* published a tribute by local postal workers who called Holyoake a "Father Confessor" to Brighton postmen, "some who burn a candle at his shrine."[7]

Such tributes would have reminded Holyoake of his lifelong struggle to lift people out of poverty. That there were still millions of Englishmen living in want was made clear in 1903 when Charles Booth, a wealthy shipowner and agnostic, published the last of his seventeen volumes of *Life and Labour of the People in London*. He'd sent squads of notetakers into the streets of the metropolis over the past twenty years, recording every detail of the lives of the poor. His books featured elaborate maps where streets with the heaviest concentration of the poor were marked in red and blue. The last seven volumes were devoted to religion's role and claimed, among other things, that the fifty-four churches serving the small population of the City—London's financial district—were unneeded, and would better serve the public by offering music, lectures, and conferences that would bring "an awakening and refining influence." It is certain Holyoake knew of the books and if he read them, he would have taken satisfaction of a sort from the confirmation they gave to his view that education would play a bigger role than religion in uplifting the lives of the common people.

By now, Holyoake was losing old friends, something he had become used to as former comrades in arms died off and he lost family members much younger than himself. No death was more painful that that of his youngest son, Francis (Frank) George, who had died in Manchester in 1902 at the age of forty-seven. A few days after Holyoake's eighty-seventh birthday, he suffered an attack of vertigo and fell to the ground. Doctors took it as an indication of a cardiac problem, his first serious sign of aging. Holyoake retreated into correspondence with friends. He enjoyed exchanging letters with Albert Grey, the fourth Earl Grey, a radical Liberal aristocrat who had dubbed Holyoake "the father of Co-operation." When Lord Grey was appointed Governor General of Canada in 1904, he wrote to Holyoake: "There are no letters I enjoy more than yours. They are always full of buoyancy and faith and hope and courage. I hope I shall see you before I go to Canada to say good-bye and to thank you for all the encouragement and inspiration which your example has been to me for many years."[8]

George Holyoake's last important work, a second memoir, was published in two volumes in January 1905. *Bygones Worth Remembering*, like its predecessor, *Sixty Years of an Agitator's Life*, was drawn largely from newspaper articles. It is more loosely structured and generally lighter in tone, a haphazard gathering of tales and insights from a long and exuberant life. In February his diary entry read, "Felt often of late like one approaching the edge of the world—but see no more than others what lies beyond." He marked his eighty-eighth birthday by having his bed moved into his library where his papers and books would be close at hand. Both sight and hearing were failing him. He had to pass up his favorite annual get-togethers—the Co-operative Congress, the Rationalist Press Association, and the celebration of the Leicester Secular Society. He managed to "run up" to London in August for a last visit to the National Liberal Club. In September he worked on an article on Woman Suffrage for *Nineteenth Century* magazine, and recorded in his diary, "Numbness, coldness, pain in feet more than of late."[9]

He had chronicled all the changes in his life, from "the first half of my life [when] I ate whatever came to hand and as not enough came I easily observed moderation," to his later years when he "sought to limit each meal to the least quantity necessary for health, [and] not thinking much of meat, I limited that to a small amount." One thing that did not change was his preference for "a soap bath for the body every morning."[10]

Holyoake's daughter Emilie returned to help look after him and she, her husband Alfred Marsh and Holyoake's wife Mary Jane gave him a

Christmas dinner in the library. He focused all his interest on the coming general election which he hoped would bring the Liberal party back to power. His last known literary effort was a letter he dictated to the *London Star* that filled nearly a column and appealed to workers to vote Liberal. The voting that began on January 12 led to a Liberal landslide. Nonconformist Protestants voted Liberal to express their anger at the 1902 Education Act that gave control of local schools to authorities controlled largely by Anglicans.[11] Holyoake, frequently in a comatose condition, revived sufficiently to read telegrams that brought news of the Liberal victory. Putting them aside, he lay back serene and died, peacefully, of heart failure on Monday, January 22, 1906, five years to the day since the death of Queen Victoria.

The body of George Holyoake was taken to the Golders Green Crematorium in London where he lay in a white coffin wrapped in a faded Garibaldian flag that paid witness to his support of the struggle for Italian unity. On the following Saturday, January 27, his body was "borne through a dense crowd" of mourners who seemed to *The Times* "to represent all classes of the community." The Co-operative Union sent eighty delegates from Manchester, two arrived from Italy, and letters and telegrams were received from all of the world. Holyoake's old friend Edward Greening gave the eulogy to the son of a Midlands iron worker who, while a radical and a reformer, had become one of the great intellectual voices of the century. Admirers, hushed in respect, watched as Holyoake's remains were carried through the bronze gates of the Crematorium. There was no religious

George Holyoake's grave in Highgate Cemetery, London (Stefan Dickers/Wikimedia Commons).

service. Two memorial services were held on Sunday, in the afternoon at the South Place Chapel and in the evening at the New Road Church in Brighton. On Monday, Holyoake's family and a few personal friends were present in Highgate Cemetery, London, where his ashes were committed to a grave he had purchased several years before. He had chosen a site close to the graves of two faithful friends, George Eliot and George H. Lewes.

~~~

The British press saw Holyoake's death as the passing of a legend. He was hailed as a great social reformer and a founder of the Co-operative movement but less was said about his Secularism and almost nothing of his atheism. The *London Standard* described him as "a remarkable personality who exercised a powerful influence both on the intellectual thought and on the social and political development of the times in which he lived."

The Telegraph saw him as "one of the foremost of his time ... a kindly, well-intentioned man." *The Pall Mall Gazette* declared "It was impossible not to respect him and the general sum of his achievements." *The Daily News* wrote, "He helped to build a better society, and was a Secularist who followed the golden rule better than most Christians." The ultimate tribute came from the *Chronicle*: "One of England's Grand Old Men."

The provincial press was no less attentive. The *Leeds Mercury* summed it up succinctly: "He will be remembered as a pioneer of the Co-operative movement, and, above all, as one of the forerunners of the Labour movement, whose triumph he has

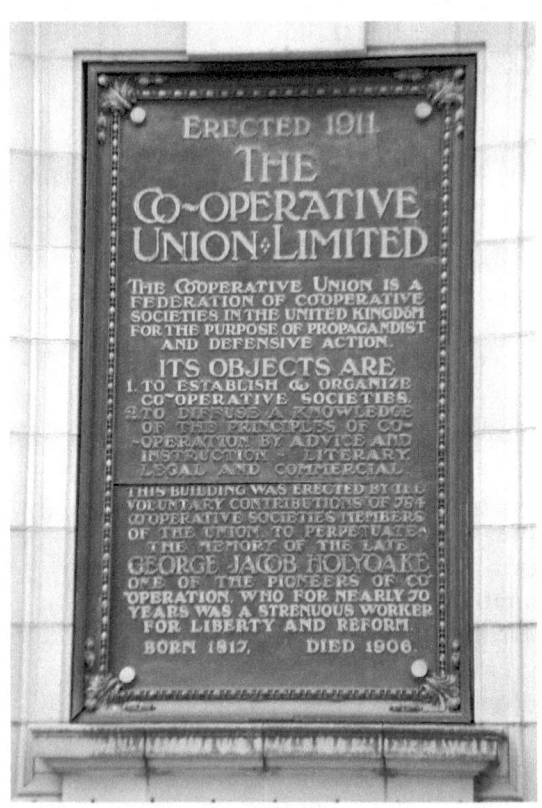

Manchester Co-op plaque honoring George Holyoake, "strenuous worker for liberty and reform" (courtesy Sharon Norman).

witnessed in the last hours of his long and strenuous life, one of the men who fought for and won for Englishmen that freedom of speech which we take as matter of course to-day."[12]

Holyoake's will was probated in London. He had left an estate valued at just under three thousand pounds. While modest, it represented an accumulation of assets through a lifetime in which Holyoake had never sought monetary reward. He had turned down Gladstone's offer of a civil pension, recommending instead that it go to a more needy friend. After providing for bequests to family members, the will instructed that Holyoake's papers and memorabilia go to his daughter, Emilie Holyoake Marsh. She subsequently turned them over to the Bishopsgate Institute for permanent archiving. Holyoake willed a painting of himself by his brother William "to be hung in the public art gallery of Birmingham or in any other room open to the public on Sundays." A painting of Richard Carlile, said to be the only one in existence, was bequeathed to the National Gallery. His leasehold flat at 36 Camelford Street, Brighton, went to his wife, Mary Jane. She survived him by only a few months, dying on May 20, 1906.

Bust of George Holyoake at Holyoake House, Manchester (courtesy Sharon Norman).

The Co-operators of Great Britain retained sculptor Albert Toft to create a bust of Holyoake which was mounted at his gravesite. The National Co-operative Union raised £25,000 to build Holyoake House in Manchester, opening it as its new headquarters in 1911. The centenary of Holyoake's birth was marked in 1917 with ceremonies in Birmingham. A telegram was read from Earl Grey, recently returned from Canada where he had served as Governor General. He described Holyoake as "the architect of a great voluntary cooperative commonwealth" who had rendered "greater service to our country than all the legislators at Westminster."[13]

~~~

George Jacob Holyoake swept through the greatest century of British history the world would ever know. Born in the Regency Period, Holyoake outlived the Victorian Age and by the early Edwardian, he had helped move Western society across a vast gulf of doubt and uncertainty. Holyoake's act of defining Secularism as a system of civil society respectful but free of religion, produced one of the most significant moments of social change in the human journey. Secularization had been practiced to varying degrees for centuries, notably Henry VIII's dissolution of English monasteries in the sixteenth century and the proclamations of rights and freedoms by the eighteenth century American and French revolutions. The process of reducing religiosity in public life continued into the twentieth century and extended to such unlikely countries as Turkey, where sharia law was abolished in 1924. George Holyoake's legacy was assured when he branded secularization with a name, Secularism, and codified a design for civil life restricted not by religious doctrine, but instead illuminated by reason and rationality.

Holyoake's effect on the modern world extended into aspects of public life that would grow out of his secularist initiatives, but were not necessarily contingent on them. These included his fostering of the modern feminist movement through encouragement of the women of his time to organize and demand their right to the vote, to property ownership, and to freely determining the course of their own lives. He lobbied for a progressive tax system and abolition of taxes on essential goods and services. As an advocate for a free Sunday, he preceded by a century the lifting of barriers to free choice in the use of what had been known as the Sabbath. Holyoake's role in gaining freedom of the press and equal representation in Parliament serves as eloquent evidence of his influence on the crucial issues of his time—and ours.

When Holyoake's first biographer, Joseph McCabe, formerly the Father Anthony who wrote *Twelve Years in a Monastery*, began work on *Life and Letters of George Jacob Holyoake*, "Six large trunks of letters and other documents were placed before me. They would have made an intimate and vivid biography of the nineteenth century."[14] Holyoake's strategy to de-emphasize atheism and move the debate to a broader base of morality and public service assured that secularist concepts would be more readily acceptable to mainstream society.

Arguments about Secularism have ranged across a spectrum of debate; some experts maintain that the spread of Islam and the rise of

Pentecostalism in Africa, Latin America, and Asia rendered secularity a "myth" of the twentieth century. Others interpret twentieth century Secularism differently; a study of 109 countries adduced evidence that in every single one, a rise in secularization has been a pre-condition of economic growth.[15] While the connection may be tenuous, the opening decades of political Secularism saw an upsurge in technological development. Following on the telephone and telegraph, the period between 1890 and 1910 witnessed the advent of the oil industry, automobiles, motion pictures, the phonograph, typesetting machines, and the first days of flight. These innovations were rapidly shaping a new modern world and changing life at a speed hitherto unknown in human history.

Secularism as enunciated by George Holyoake has followed divergent paths across the West. In the United Kingdom, where Holyoake's branding of Secularism became foundational to secularization, religion remains entwined with public life. With a head of state who is also defender of an established church, appointed Bishops sitting in Parliament, and a majority of its schools under church control, Britain would hardly appear a model of Secularism. Yet for practical purposes of everyday life, most Britons enjoy a secular environment. The decline of religious affiliation is accelerating and there are few, if any, religious barriers to social and economic mobility. Any reflection of the diversity and democratization of twenty-first century life leads to the inescapable conclusion that this could not have been accomplished without Secularism.

That this is so, is due in good measure to the work of Britain's two secularist organizations, the National Secular Society and Humanists UK (an outgrowth of the Union of Ethical Societies founded in 1896). Both have carried forward campaigns in support of issues that George Holyoake raised in the nineteenth century. Rights that now seem common and everyday—such as the right to sell literature in London's parks that was won in 1920—were hard-fought and took years to secure. The first birth control clinic was opened in 1921, the religious taboo against suicide was overcome with enactment of the Suicide Act in 1961, homosexuality was decriminalized in 1967, and blasphemy was removed from English law books in 2008. An Equality Act in 2010 brought together existing anti-discrimination laws and protected religious and sexual orientation. In 2018, a century after George Holyoake's death, a Blue Plaque to commemorate his life was funded by the National Secular Society and put up at 4 Woburn Walk in Bloomsbury, London. Today, Humanists UK sponsors the annual Holyoake Lecture.

While Holyoake's principled views on the organization of society came to be generally accepted within his lifetime, his support for republicanism and the replacement of the monarchy—which he was reticent to promote vocally—never gained traction. Whether the present high regard the British have for the two queens that have led the country in the past two hundred years—Victoria and Elizabeth—will endure long after the death of the present monarch, is a moot question. The monarchy in Britain has survived scandals and setbacks, including sometimes impetuous attacks in the press. An errant 1994 editorial in the influential *Economist* described the monarchy as "an idea whose time has passed," arguing for its replacement by a republic. The magazine's aristocratic ownership grumbled, and nothing more was heard of the notion.

More enduring is the concept of humanism, a classical philosophy that found a new purpose and meaning within George Holyoake's Secularism. Holyoake did not take part in the formation of the British Ethical Union in 1896 when four local ethical societies, comprised mainly of academics and intellectuals, banded together. Borrowing ideas from the American Culture movement, the new group built on the classical concept of humanism as a culture of generosity. It embraced the now widely accepted nontheistic view that humans are responsible for their fates without regard to some supposed supernatural being. The philosophy of today's humanist movement is aligned with Holyoake's Secularism, members being mostly atheists, agnostics, and other freethinkers.

Global support for secular humanism is found in the 170 societies that are members of Humanists International. These include its largest affiliate, the American Humanist Association, founded in 1941 as a successor to the Humanist Fellowship. Adoption by the United Nations in 1948 of a Universal Declaration of Human Rights reflected in principle, if not in detail, the four "Rights" that Holyoake spelled out in *Principles of Secularism:* the right to think for one's self, to differ, to assert difference of opinion, and to debate opinion.[16]

Today, for all his achievements and his contributions, Holyoake is not well known to the public at large. His legacy, vastly greater than his public recognition, ranks him as one of the most significant of British politicians, philosophers, and writers (all of which Holyoake was) of the past two hundred years. A tolerant society, respect for all individuals, equality of all people, the removal of barriers of class and caste, freedom from but also of religion—these are the qualities of the secular modern world that are most closely associated with the legacy of George Jacob Holyoake.

Epilogue
In Our Time: Secularism Under Siege

> They passed through the city at noon of the day following. He kept the pistol to hand on the folded tarp on the top of the cart. He kept the boy close to his side. The city was mostly burned. No sign of life. Cars in the street caked with ash, everything covered with ash and dust. Fossil tracks in the dried sludge. A corpse in the doorway dried to leather. Grimacing at the day. He pulled the boy closer. Just remember the things you put into your head are there forever, he said. You might want to think about that.
> —Cormac McCarthy, *The Road*, 2007

In 2021, one hundred and fifteen years after the death of George Holyoake, the issues facing society following the Covid-19 pandemic—the inequalities of globalization, human interference in the natural world, climate change, and the degradation of the environment—preoccupied people around the world. These concerns came as echoes to the challenges of thinkers from the Renaissance to the twentieth century. Niccolò Machiavelli and the political maneuvering of *The Prince*, like John Donne's epic English poetry—*Let us possess one world, each hath one, and is one*—reflect the timeless questioning of the inquiring mind, no less than German philosopher Martin Heidegger's search for being or Jean-Paul Sartre's World War II era doctrine of humanist existentialism. Parallel to these thinkers, George Holyoake wrote of Secularism as a method to improve the "material and social conditions" of society. He hoped, as we might today, that "whatever of goodness exists in human nature, may manifest itself unchecked … and show that virtue is an advantage as well as a duty."[1]

While poverty has been much reduced from Holyoake's era, problems of inequality and social justice figure as prominently today as in his time. The "material conditions" that Holyoake sought—improved diets, universal education, better housing—have become dependent, in our time, on our ability—as yet uncertain—to overcome the damages of deforestation, overfarming, and plundering of the seas. We cannot be sure that Holyoake's vision of the virtuous society will necessarily prevail in the future.

Amid the rise of religious extremism and populist authoritarianism, Secularism and its principles of moral excellence independent of religious bias have come under siege. The assault on Secularism is widespread and emanates from many points of the compass. In the West, the attack has been led by U.S. Christian evangelists, Roman Catholic prelates up to and including Pope Francis, and members of the U.S. federal cabinet; in the East, by Islamic fundamentalists in Arab states, Hindu nationalists in India, and Communist party functionaries in China. Authoritarian regimes in countries such as Hungary, Poland, and Turkey, while not overtly anti-secular, have clamped down on freedom of expression and other civil rights traditional in democratic secular countries. In all of these examples, the driving force has been the pursuit of power for the privileges it brings, with the intention of marginalizing secularity and reasserting the dictates of religiosity in temporal affairs.

The melding of spiritual certainty with populist political strategies has invariably resulted in a less liberal and more controlled society: one that is amenable to internal discipline and supportive of the domination of other states and disparate societies. The British Empire, in large part, found moral justification for its nineteenth century expansionist adventures in a Church of England dedicated to the Christianization of heathens. The Empire was succeeded as the global power of the twentieth century by a United States dedicated, with equal fervor, to overthrowing Godless Communism. That both the British Empire and the American Republic sought world economic domination was secondary to the moral aims of a Christian power bent on seeding less favored nations with law and order, human rights, and spiritual values compatible with Christianity. For Britain, it was the Crimean War, the bombardments of Canton in the Opium Wars, conquests in India and Afghanistan, and the Boer Wars; for the United States, after the vanquishing of Germany and Japan in a Second World War made inevitable by the peace terms of the First, the litany of military adventurism included Iran, Vietnam, and Laos, plus Indonesia, Chile, Nicaragua, Grenada, Afghanistan, and Iraq, among others. The Cold War was waged within the familiar framework of defending freedom and right. Only in South Korea were these aims achieved, albeit following a long period of dictatorship after the Korean War. With a new contest for global hegemony now unfolding between the United States and China, the desire to "make

America great again" quickly won the support of religious interests that saw an opportunity to override the secular traditions of a country founded on a constitutional separation of church and state.

The strain of religiosity that has pervaded American public life shows little sign of ebbing, despite the rise in numbers of the religious "nones." A 2020 survey by the respected Pew Institute had half of Americans (49 percent) saying the Bible should have at least "some influence" on U.S. laws, with more than a quarter (28 percent) holding the view that the Bible should take priority over the will of the people.[2] It is not surprising that those with such views should seek passage of laws grounded in religious convictions. Examples include denial of LGBTQ rights, restrictions to abortion, withdrawal of funding to organizations like Planned Parenthood, and cancellation of foreign aid to countries permitting abortion.

The U.S. capital is filled with lobbyists for special interests, which is one reason a little known but highly influential Christian fundamentalist group has largely escaped public attention. To those who know of it, it is referred to as The Fellowship or The Family. For the past seventy years it has exerted a high level of influence over U.S. presidents, their cabinets, and members of Congress. Some of its tactics have been revealed in a controversial book by Jeff Sharlet, *The Family: The Secret Fundamentalism at the Heart of American Power*. Sharlet describes this group as "fundamentalism's avant-garde, waging spiritual war in the halls of American power and around the globe." He sees it as a direct challenge to Secularism, undermining the traditional American separation of church and state. Since its founding in the 1930s by several businessmen who believed that Christianity should favor men of success and not the downtrodden poor, the Fellowship has become deeply embedded in Washington politics. It counts many in Congress, mainly Republicans, as members.

A chief success of The Fellowship is its annual National Prayer Breakfast originated by founder Abraham Vereide and attended by every U.S. president since Dwight D. Eisenhower. The breakfasts circumvent normal diplomatic protocol by providing a venue for foreign leaders to meet the President. Operating from a Washington headquarters known as The Cedars, the Fellowship has reportedly facilitated aid and links to U.S. industry for dictators such as "Papa Doc" of Haiti, Siad Barre of Somalia, and Mega Soeharrto of Indonesia. Fellowship leaders have repeatedly summoned Congressmen and other leaders, including Hillary Clinton, to support evangelical Christian political positions. At its behest, hundreds of millions of dollars of public funding for social welfare have been transferred, largely surreptitiously, from government departments to private faith groups, beginning under the George W. Bush administration.

In such an environment, most politicians are reluctant to express a commitment to humanist values. There are exceptions. Nancy Pelosi, Speaker of the House of Representatives, declined to attend the 2020 National Prayer Breakfast. More than a dozen Democrats are members of the Congressional Freethought Caucus. Its most recent recruit is Rep. Rashida Tlaib of Michigan, a Muslim. Its most notable member is Rep. Jared Huffman of California who has declared himself a "non-religious humanist." The prospect of electing more atheists is not, however, hopeful; forty percent of Americans told a 2019 survey they would not vote for such a person.

It was in this atmosphere that President Donald Trump and members of his cabinet between 2017 and 2021 came down in favor of evangelical political positions. According to Mat Staver, president of Liberty Counsel, a legal advisory organization, about ninety percent of fundamentalist goals were achieved under the Trump administration. "He's been the most pro-religious freedom and pro-life president in modern history," Staver said.[3]

Measured against 2020 guidelines from the U.S. Department of Education on school prayer, the observation holds up. The guidelines outline scenarios in which school officials must permit prayers. Other regulations removed barriers to religious organizations obtaining federal funding. "We will not let anyone push God from the public square," President Trump said as he introduced the new rules.[4] His comments came as American states began to require schools to post the slogan In God We Trust on classroom walls. In 2020 more than $7 billion of Covid relief funds were retransferred to 88,000 churches, according to the American Humanist Association—in the view of many a clear violation of the First Amendment of the U.S. Constitution. These challenges to Secularism were echoed in U.S. Attorney General William Barr's claim, made in a speech to the University of Notre Dame law school, that "militant secularists" were behind a "campaign to destroy the traditional moral order."[5]

President Trump's appointment of conservative judges to the Supreme Court has securely embedded pro-religious views on America's highest court for many years to come. Trump appointees Neil Gorsuch and Brett Kavanaugh tilted the Court further to the right; its interpretations of the First Amendment prohibiting "establishment of a state religion" have weakened rules for separation of church and state. The steps toward repudiation of Secularism have been incremental: a Supreme Court ruling to give government funding for paving of a playground at a Catholic school (opening up churches to receiving taxpayer funds); and affirmation of the right of a Colorado baker to refuse, on religious grounds, to make a wedding cake for a same-sex couple (thereby placing religious scruples above the law of the land).

One of the last liberals on the Court, the late Justice Ruth Bader

Ginsberg, was the most outspoken in resisting such moves. She dissented in a 2019 Court decision that approved the right of a Maryland municipality to maintain a large Christian cross on public land. "Decades ago," she wrote, "this court recognized that the Constitution demands governmental neutrality among religious faiths, and between religion and nonreligion. Today the Court erodes that neutrality commitment, diminishing precedent designed to preserve individual liberty and civic harmony."[6] Ginsberg's successor, Trump-appointed Amy Coney Barrett, voted in her first case to rule unconstitutional a restriction on the size of public gatherings—including church services—during the COVID-19 crisis. With its now-solid conservative majority, the Court is likely to render anti-secular decisions in the decades to come, despite the country's growing religious diversity and increased secularity, especially among younger Americans.

In a clear violation of the separation of church and state as set out in the U.S. Constitution, a law enacted by Congress in 1952 established the first Thursday in May as the National Day of Prayer. According to a government mission statement, it "exists to mobilize unified public prayer for America." A secularist organization, Americans United for Separation of Church and State, sees this contrivance for what it is: "...a vehicle for spreading religious misinformation and fundamentalist Christian doctrine under the aegis of the government—precisely what the framers [of the Constitution] were seeking to prohibit."

The U.S. also faces anti-secular assault from Christian nationalists such as the Proud Boys, the Oath Keepers, QAnon and others who fear what has become a pluralistic society. They include Trump loyalists who fomented a putative insurrection at the Capitol Building on January 6, 2021, and the neo–Nazis who gathered in Charlottesville, Virginia, in 2017 to defend a Confederate monument and chant "Blood and Soil," a Nazi rallying cry.

Although denied a second term, Donald Trump's affinity for bigoted racial and religious views is likely to affect American politics for a long time to come. His successor, Joseph R. Biden, recognizes he has been elected to govern a secular nation. A pragmatist, he is unlikely to permit his Catholic faith—of which he makes no secret—to interfere with his official responsibilities; he accepts the right to abortion and opposes the death penalty. While most humanists welcome Biden's liberal social policies, they see his public invoking of God and prayer and his description of America as a nation "sustained by faith" as a contradiction to the separation of church and state, something that was supposed to have been settled in 1776. Such expressions also disrespect the nearly one-third of the American population—atheists, agnostics and other non-religious—who hold dissenting views. Biden's remarks are, at best, harmless; but at worst, they provide a cloak of respectability for elements who seek to embed their religious convictions in law and legislation. The road ahead for Secularism will be no less rocky than in the past.

Virulent attacks on Secularism have emerged in the American Catholic press. The *National Catholic Register*, which describes itself as the most faithful Catholic news source in the United States, has blamed Secularism for the crimes of Nazi Germany and Soviet Russia, declaring "Secularism in any of its guises is deadly." The article containing this allegation was headed "Beware the Stormtroopers of Secularism" and was illustrated with a picture of Nazi troops in Poland taking a Catholic priest to his execution. Such hyperbole overlooks the fact that both regimes violated a main principle of Secularism: that the state shall have no role in religious matters. The Nazis persecuted an entire population based on its Jewish religious identity, while the Soviet campaign of atheism invaded the secularist right of Soviet citizens to freedom of religion.

The supreme Roman Catholic authority figure is of course the Pope, and Pope Francis has issued stern warnings about Secularism. In his 2019 World Mission Day statement, he warned that "Rampant secularism, when it becomes an aggressive cultural rejection of God's active fatherhood in our history, is an obstacle to authentic human fraternity." During a visit to Egypt in 2017, he said he was there to defend "a vision of healthy Secularism"—one which does not reduce the role of religion in public life. The trade-off for acceptance of Secularism, the Pope appears to be saying, is that religion must continue to dictate public policies on issues that the Church regards itself and the Bible as the sole arbiters.

In order to forestall religiously inspired attacks on Secularism, says American Humanist Association executive director Roy Speckhardt, it will be necessary to "reach out and convince every person of the humanity within all of us, no matter what we believe, no matter the gender with which we identify or the color of our skin." He asserts that rather than relying on ancient books or divine revelation, science offers the best method for finding answers. "We must invest more in reversing the trend toward anti-intellectualism that we see all around us. We must come out as humanists, atheists, and liberals, never passing up the opportunity to put a human face on what's being demonized. And most of all, we must realize that this isn't going to be fixed soon, so we need to steel ourselves for a long and uncertain journey that will give us our best chance of arriving at a better future."[7]

~~~

Across Europe, alarms have sounded that secularization is under threat from right-wing parties that blame it for a loss of faith and spirituality. Hungary's near-dictator Viktor Orban has blamed liberals for "the abandonment of Europe's Christian culture" and has promised to defend against an "attack from outside which is embedded in migration." Together, he claims, they "threaten destruction of the Europe we knew." The German state of Bavaria mandated that government buildings display a crucifix to show the region's "social and cultural identity." The Polish parliament approved legislation to criminalize sex education in schools, while imposing a near-total ban on abortion and equating homosexuality with pedophilia. In Turkey, the most secular of all Muslim countries for the past century, Secularism is in full retreat. Established as a secular republic by Mustafa Kemel Ataturk after World War I, Turkey's secular constitution is being chipped away at by president Recep Tayyip Erdogan. His regime has persecuted dissidents, ordered mosques to broadcast the Quran's "prayer of conquest" from their minarets, sanctioned violence against those who "offend Islam," and has blessed the Turkish deployment of troops in Syria as "jihad." "Religion has returned to Russia and Turkey with a vengeance," according to Aristotle Papanikolaou, of Fordham University, writing in *Orthodox Observer*. In highly symbolic acts, Turkey has restored both the historic Hagia Sophia and the Church of the Holy Saviour, secular museums for more than seventy years, to the status of mosques.

French right-wing leader Marine Le Pen is an avowed secularist but takes an even harder line than the French government on her country's version, laïcité, which bans the wearing of hijabs, or headscarves, by school pupils and imposes other restrictions on the wearing of Muslim religious symbols. Yet, this extremist approach to Secularism has fostered its own problems: a loss of individual rights and further economic isolation of France's six million Muslims. In the French-speaking Canadian province of Quebec a similar law designed to protect Secularism has been likened to a solution in search of a problem; Quebec's tiny minority of Muslims has never represented a threat to culture or civil order. These examples show the need for balance when Secularism is under threat or when politicians find it advantageous to represent that it is when it is not.

The United Kingdom, in contrast, treats its challenges to Secularism with calm British demeanor, partly because it has become accustomed to a long-lived monarchy known since 1917 as the House of Windsor, and an established church, the Church of England. Neither blatantly interferes in British daily life, but there is need for a "serious rethink" of religion's public role, according to Stephen Evans, chief executive of the UK National Secular Society. He points to the British Social Attitudes Survey showing only twelve percent claim affiliation to the Church of England, while fifty-two percent identify with no religion, and twenty-six percent subscribe to atheism. "As Christianity declines and Britain becomes more irreligious and more religiously diverse, the UK needs an equitable and sustainable settlement fit for the twenty-first century," he states.

Religious classes in schools and the presence of unelected Anglican bishops in Parliament are seen by secularists as unacceptable in Britain. While not always enforced, a school regulation requires that schools conduct a daily act of Christian worship. Secularists insist this be replaced by inclusive assemblies of a non-sectarian nature. Private bills have been introduced in Parliament in an attempt to end the appointment of twenty-six Anglican Bishops to the House of Lords. Critics point out that only one other country, Iran, gives unelected clerics automatic positions in its legislature.

The most alarming, if not the most significant, attacks on Secularism have come from elements of Islamic extremism, ranging from the ISIS uprising in Iraq and Syria to repeated terrorist attacks throughout the world—London, Paris, Mumbai, New York, and Nairobi being only a few examples. Inspired by doubtful interpretations of the Muslim faith and the Quran, they represent on one level a renewal of the age-old use of violence to impose religious rule. On another, they show the misuse of religion to motivate attacks against economic and political adversaries. Ironically, far more Muslims than non–Muslims have been killed in such attacks, with Sunni and Shia rivalry the main factor in these bloody outbursts. Christians also have been victims of religious persecution, with a 2018 Pew Research report finding that Christians were targeted in 144 countries, with "extreme" persecution in eleven countries.

France's version of Secularism—Lacité, a more rigid rejection of religious symbolism than in other countries – has put the Republic's staunchest secular partisans, including President Emmanuel Macron, in confrontation with Islamic extremism. Jihadist terror inflicted on France includes the attack on the satirical weekly *Charlie Hebdo*; the assault on the Bataclan concert hall; and killings such as the beheading of school teacher Samuel Paty after he showed his class cartoons of the Prophet Mohammed. In rallies throughout the country following Paty's murder by an 18-year-old Muslim student, demonstrators carried signs reading "zero tolerance to all enemies of the Republic." Macron has promised "a fight to the death" against what he sees as Islamic separatism. Part of the problem may lie in France's rejection of multi-culturalism and its insistence on assimilation of ethnic minorities, a goal that remains distant. In his defense, Macron can point to repeated attacks in other countries; Spain, Italy, Austria, the Netherlands, and England. Most of Europe's terrorist attacks, whether by Islamists or by right-wing Christian fanatics, have been perpetrated by unsophisticated young men of apparently aimless vision, corrupted by online or one-on-one proselytizing.

The use of blasphemy laws is a favorite method of attacking Christians and non-believers in some Muslim countries. The 2020 arrest of Mubarak Bala, president of Nigerian Humanists, on charges of blasphemy over his humanist views was a clear violation of a constitution that defines Nigeria as a secular state. In testimony to a U.S. House of Representatives Foreign Affairs subcommittee, Bangladesh human rights advocate Rafida Bonya Ahmed identified eighty-three countries with blasphemy laws. Penalties on conviction include fines, torture, long-term imprisonment, and death. Ahmed and her husband were attacked in Dhaka by a machete-wielding gang enraged by his anti-religious online comments. Police watched as he was murdered and she was seriously injured. In but one example of similar cases in Pakistan, an illiterate Christian woman, Asia Bibi, spent eight years on death row after being falsely accused of blasphemy by co-workers. When she was freed on appeal, the UK refused to give her asylum in fear it might cause "unrest." Canada accepted her and she later claimed asylum in France.

Blasphemy laws remain in effect in several western democracies including Scotland, Germany, Poland, Italy, and Switzerland. Although rarely enforced, their existence provides Muslin countries such as Pakistan with convenient justification for their own, more draconian laws.

As hated as blasphemy is in these countries, the crime of apostasy—rejecting one's religion—is considered an even more vile act. At least ten countries, according to Humanists International, impose the death penalty for abandonment of Islam. Such laws raise the question of whether Muslim countries will ever accept either Secularism or the presence of other religions. The east African country of Sudan, in a remarkable turn-about by its new transitional government, has pledged that the country's new constitution "should be based on the principle of separation of religion and state." It is uncertain, however, whether military opposition will permit this change.

India, nominally secularist since the days of the British Raj, has been plunged into civic disorder as a result of actions by the Hindu nationalist government of Narendra Modi and his ruling Bharatiya Janata Party (BJP). Its policies are having the effect of turning religions that did not originate on Indian soil—notably Islam and Christianity—into alien essences. The most controversial is a Citizenship Act that provides for refugees who came to India from Pakistan, Bangladesh, and Nepal to be given expedited access to citizenship—providing they are not Muslims. A U.S. government commission on international religious freedom has called for punitive measures against India, citing a "drastic turn downward" in religious freedom. The commission listed nine countries lacking secular freedoms: the Muslim states of Eritrea, Iran, Pakistan, Saudi Arabia, Tajikistan and Turkmenistan, plus Myanmar, North Korea, and China.

China is believed to have detained several hundred thousand Muslims in its far western province of Xinjiang. Alleged "terrorists," they have been sent to indoctrination camps described as a "boarding school management system." It hoped to cleanse them of any lingering Muslim faith. This despite an avowedly Secularist provision in the Chinese constitution that "No state organ, public organization, or individual may compel citizens to believe in, or not to believe in, any religion." Chinese policy, according to the former Canadian ambassador to Beijing, David Mulroney, is to ensure that "Muslim holy places, scripture, music, cultural practices and even traditions of family life are methodically eradicated."

Andrew Copson, President of Humanists International, the global umbrella body for atheist, humanist, skeptic and secularist organizations, is of the view that "Secularism, globally, is under threat." He lays much of the blame on ignorance of what Secularism stands for, and its absence from the curricula of most schools and universities:

> Attacked from all sides: from the left, from the right, by liberal multiculturalists and illiberal totalitarians, abused by racists and xenophobes as a stick with which to beat minorities in the West, subverted elsewhere by religious fundamentalists planning its destruction. But perhaps the biggest enemy of Secularism today is ignorance. Although Secularism has been of fundamental importance in shaping the modern world, it is not as well-known a concept as capitalism or social welfare or democracy. You won't find it commonly studied in schools or even at universities. These days, when all the implicit assumptions of modernity and the open society are under strain, this is a dangerous situation. Reasonable debates about Secularism on the basis of a shared understanding of it, what it means, and where it came from, are in short supply.[8]

Copson's warning sounds a sobering note in what otherwise has been a spectacularly successful re-ordering of the social priorities of the modern world. Today, we stand at a tipping point where we can build more inclusive and accepting public societies, or revert to the prejudices and confining borders of the past. We must also apply secularist principles to head off the "descent into chaos" that the Secretary-General of the United Nations, Antonio Guterres, warns we face. "Humanity is waging war on nature," he has said. "This is suicidal. Nature always strikes back—and is doing so with growing force and fury."

We began this book with an epigraph drawn from *The Pickwick Papers* by Charles Dickens. We end with a quotation from *The Road* by Cormac McCarthy, written one hundred and seventy years later. Both represent a perspective of their times; one a realistic portrayal of an English city bustling with energy at the height of the Industrial Revolution; the other a frightening picture of an American city in some dystopian future where no hope of normal life remains. I have chosen them because I think the first represents the era in which Secularism was born, and the second an era in which, if we are not careful, it could be brought to an end. In contrast to the pitiable outcome of the human experience as contemplated by Cormac McCarthy, we might better aspire to the kind of world envisioned by George Holyoake. He looked beyond his own time, confident that "Secularist principles involve for mankind a future." It would be a future of moral as well as material good, offering an infinite diversity of intellect with equality among humanity, and "all things—noble society, the treasures of art, and the riches of the world—to be had in common." His was a vision of a Secularism that rises above sectarian differences or economic rivalries, and places universal opportunity, and individual freedom, in the hands of all who inhabit our rich and beautiful—but endangered—planet Earth.

Chapter Notes

Introduction

1. "Death of Mr. G.J. Holyoake—An Interesting Life Story." *Leeds Mercury*, January 23, 1906.
2. George Holyoake, *English Secularism; A Confession of Belief*, viii.
3. Joseph McCabe, *The Life and Letters of George Jacob Holyoake*, Vol. I, 76.
4. British Social Attitudes Survey, 2019. The survey reports its key finding of religious decline "is not simply a private matter for individuals and families, but rather a trend with profound implications for our social norms as well as our public institutions. Today, following decades of secularisation and social change linked to industrialisation and the rise of liberal democracy, we can see clearly not only a shift away from religious worldviews, but also the strengthening of confidence in science and technology, which not only permeate our day-to-day lives in practical ways, but also provide an alternative way of interpreting and understanding the world." See https://lgiu.org/briefing/natcen-british-social-attitudes-survey-2019/.

Chapter 1

1. Birmingham Library Archives, files MS3145/5/5/2/20/34; MS3145/5/5/2/7/2; MS21/1/20/61.
2. George Holyoake, *Sixty Years of an Agitator's Life*, Vol. I, 7.
3. *Ibid.*, 8.
4. *Ibid.*, 11.
5. *Ibid.*, 12.
6. The year 1816 became known as "the year without summer" after the eruption in 1815 of the Mount Tambora volcano in the Dutch East Indies (now Indonesia). Ash filled the atmosphere, reducing sunlight and prolonging cold weather. Famine was widespread throughout the Northern Hemisphere.
7. The two occasions immediately previous to the 1817 suspension of the Habeas Corpus Act occurred under Premier William Pitt the Younger, first in 1794 when "a tortuous and detestable conspiracy" was thought to be plotting a revolution of the type France was then experiencing, and in 1798 when the government felt threatened by Jacobin Societies and a plot to kill King George II was alleged. In modern times, the Prevention of Terrorism Act of 2005 and its successors, which empower authorities to detain citizens as well as foreigners without trial, have been assailed as steps toward "the dismantling of the rule of law."
8. Holyoake, *Sixty Years of an Agitator's Life*, Vol. 1, 4–14. The famous Selly Oak has been dated to around 1710. It was demolished for safety reasons in 1909 and its trunk was displayed for many years in the local park.
9. Holyoake, *Sixty Years of an Agitator's Life*, Vol. I, 3. Inge Street is sandwiched between Hurst and Essex Streets in central Birmingham and is today the site of 1840s era Back to Back houses that opened onto courtyards with green spaces. Holyoake's original home no longer exists.
10. *Ibid.*, 3.
11. *Ibid.*, 12.
12. *Ibid.*, 16.
13. The window tax was first imposed in 1696 at a rate of two shillings per house plus additional charges for more than ten

windows. It was abolished in 1851 after complaints that it was a "tax on health, and on light and air." The window tax was one of many imposed in the United Kingdom as an alternative to income tax, bitterly opposed by the propertied class who gained most of their income from rents. William Pitt the Younger imposed an income tax in 1798 to pay the cost of preparing for the Napoleonic Wars. It lasted, under various names, until 1816, when it had maxed out at ten percent. Income tax returned under Sir Robert Peel in 1842 and has since remained in force, through many permutations and varying rates. Peel taxed those with incomes above £150 per year, at a rate of 7d per pound—about three percent. The Crimean War upset Benjamin Disraeli's plan to abolish income tax. In his 1858 budget speech Disraeli described income tax as "unjust, unequal, and inquisitorial" but he was out of office within a year. Re-elected in 1874, the tax remained, yielding some £6,000,000 of the government's annual £77,000,000 revenue. Both World Wars brought stiff increases in income tax rates. Englishmen were beset by taxes at every turn in the nineteenth century. Toll booths operated by Toll Trusts collected fees from travelers on the country's thirty thousand miles of roads. Canal boats faced similar tariffs. Tariffs on imports were the main source of government revenue prior to the advent of free trade.

14. Holyoake, *Sixty Years of an Agitator's Life*, Vol. I, 14.

15. J.A. James, *Female Piety, or the Young Woman's Friend and Guide Through Life, to Immortality*, 66.

16. *Sixty Years of an Agitator's Life*, Vol. I, 33. John Angell James, b. 1785 Blandford Forum, educated Gosport, Hampshire; began preaching Carr's Lane 1805, attracting large crowds. His *Anxious Inquirer* sold over 500,000 copies.

17. Frank Podmore, *The Life of Robert Owen*, Vol. I, 5.

18. *Ibid.*, 22.

19. Robert Owen, *The Life of Robert Owen*, Vol. I, 86.

20. *Ibid.*, 331.

21. *Ibid.*, 246.

22. It is difficult to ascertain the numerical values of 19th century currency in 21st century figures. Worse, it is almost impossible, due to changes in production and in consumption patterns, to measure their relative worth. I have used the percentage change in average UK incomes to arrive at a present-day valuation of Owen's £50,000 worth in 1824. Even that is a guess, drawn from biographer Frank Podmore's assertion that he left New Harmony, Indiana, with £40,000, or four-fifths of his available capital exhausted (*Robert Owen: A Biography*, 327). Jane Austen readers have struggled with trying to guess what Mr. Darcy's annual income of £10,000 would be worth today. An illustration of the difficulty is given by Katherine Toran who writes, in one example: "…if the consumer price index is controversial in modern times, it becomes impossible to use in the nineteenth century. People lived very different lives two hundred years ago. Instead of purchasing food at a local store, they often raised chickens or maintained gardens. Instead of buying their clothes, they made them by hand." See http://jasna.org/publications/persuasions-online/vol36no1/toran/.

23. Arthur Estabrook, "The Family History of Robert Owen," *Indiana Magazine of History*. Estabrook cites Owen as having stated on his arrival in the United States: "I am come to this country to introduce an entirely new state of society; to change it from an ignorant, selfish system to an enlightened social system which shall gradually unite all interests in one, and remove all causes for contrast between individuals." https://scholarworks.iu.edu/journals/index.php/imh/article/view/6280/6277.

Chapter 2

1. The Eagle Foundry was established in 1785 by Richard Dearman. Among the most advanced in England, it boasted of installing, in 1792, a cylinder boring mill. This machine was used to make cylinders, pumps and guns. It was capable of boring a cannon barrel from solid steel. In an 1847 advertisement, the Eagle Foundry lists its products as including cranes, bridges, fences, heating apparatus, garden and field rollers, and stoves. The foundry showed its wares at the 1862 London Exhibition. Of George Holyoake's employment, biographer Joseph McCabe refers to a letter from the owners of the Eagle Foundry, Smith and Hawkes, stating in 1849 that he had worked there thirteen years. McCabe, *The*

Life and Letters of George Jacob Holyoake, Vol. I, 8.

2. Holyoake, *Sixty Years of an Agitator's Life*, Vol. I, 20.

3. *Ibid.*, 20.

4. McCabe, *The Life and Letters of George Jacob Holyoake*, Vol. I, 23.

5. Holyoake, *Sixty Years of an Agitator's Life*, Vol. I, 26. Thomas Attwood, b. 1783 Shropshire, educated Wolverhampton Grammar School, became a banker, economist, and advocate of the "Birmingham school of under consumptionist" economics. MP 1832-1839.

6. *Ibid.*, 32. Attwood was a century ahead of his time in advocating what amounted to the twin tools of credit liquidity and low interest rates that would be resorted to in the Great Depression of the twentieth century. After the Great Recession of 2007–08 this was called "quantitative easing," facilitated through massive purchase of bank bonds by governments. Much greater government stimulus was invoked to cushion the economy in the 2020 Covid-19 crisis.

7. *Ibid.*, 26.

8. Podmore, *The Life of Robert Owen*, 323.

9. Holyoake, *Sixty Years of an Agitator's Life*, Vol. I, 4.

10. George Combe, b. 1818 Birmingham, educated Mechanics' Institute; emigrated to United States becoming physician, gained notoriety in Philadelphia for using mannequins to explain female anatomy, charged with obscenity, escaped to New York, published *The Marriage Guide*.

11. Holyoake, *Sixty Years of an Agitator's Life*, Vol. I, 87.

12. Holyoake, *Bygones Worth Remembering*, Vol. II, 226.

13. *Ibid.*, 229.

14. Bishopsgate Institute, London, Holyoake 1:1, Letter, William Ick, November 27, 1838.

15. Holyoake, *Sixty Years of an Agitator's Life*, Vol. I, 51.

16. *Ibid.*, 52.

17. *Ibid.*, 54.

18. *Ibid.*, 55.

Chapter 3

1. Holyoake, *Sixty Years of an Agitator's Life*, Vol. I, 34. Historically, the Midlands comprise what was once known as the Kingdom of Mercia. The area is generally divided into East and West Midlands, both being the site of early developments in the Industrial Revolution. Major cities include Birmingham, Nottingham, Leicester, Derby, Coventry, Chesterfield, and Worcester.

2. *Ibid.*, 43.

3. Bishopsgate Institute, Holyoake 3:1, *Birmingham Journal*, July 28, 1832.

4. Steven King, *Writing the Lives of the English Poor, 1750s-1820s*. King contends that England reached a level of mass literacy by the 1820s, if not earlier. The majority of the letters to parish relief authorities that King examined were the work of those who signed them, not scribes.

5. Podmore, *The Life of Robert Owen*, Vol. I, 540.

6. *Ibid.*, 462.

7. Holyoake, *Sixty Years of an Agitator's Life*, Vol. I, 115.

8. *Brighton Patriot*, December 19, 1837.

9. Holyoake, *Sixty Years of an Agitator's Life*, Vol. I, 69.

10. *Ibid.*, 70.

11. McCabe, *George Jacob Holyoake*, 8. Holyoake makes no mention of this meeting in his memoirs, but McCabe, who had access to Holyoake's files after his death, insists in his 1922 rewrite of his *Life and Letters of George Jacob Holyoake*, that "he met Owen himself [in Manchester] and had a talk with him."

12. "Manchester Meeting." London *Morning Chronicle*, August 19, 1819.

13. National Co-operative Archive, Holyoake House, Manchester, Letter #7, G.J. Holyoake, September 1838. Helen is referred to as Ellen in some accounts, mistakenly repeating the dropped H in the spoken dialect of the lesser-educated English.

14. William Pare, b. 1805, Birmingham, apprenticed to cabinet-maker father, became a tobacco retailer and reporter; member of the first town council, and vice-president of Owen's All Nations; on Owen's death he was appointed literary executor.

15. Holyoake, *Sixty Years of an Agitator's Life*, Vol. I, 41. William Pare was forced to resign when his appointment was attacked in the House of Lords by Dr. Henry Philpotts, Bishop of Exeter and nemesis of all Owenites. The office of Registrar General, created in 1836, was given responsibility

for the decennial census beginning in 1841. The General Registrar office is now part of HM Passport Office.
16. Bishopsgate Institute, London, Letter, John Watts, June 5, 1839.

Chapter 4

1. Edward Royle, *Victorian Infidels*, 66.
2. *Worcester Journal*, August 25, 1839.
3. Holyoake, *Sixty Years of an Agitator's Life*, Vol. I, 84.
4. *Ibid.*, 45.
5. McCabe, *The Life and Letters of George Jacob Holyoake*, Vol. II, 34.
6. Bishopsgate Institute, Holyoake 1.2, Letter, Frederick Hollick, January 19, 1840.
7. McCabe, *The Life and Letters of George Jacob Holyoake*, Vol. I, 45.
8. National Co-operative Archive, Holyoake House, Manchester, Letter #15, W. Newell (copy) July 22, 1840.
9. Bishopsgate Institute, London, Holyoake 1:2, Letter, James Plant, September 15, 1840.
10. Royle, *Victorian Infidels*, 77.
11. Holyoake, *Sixty Years of an Agitator's Life*, Vol. I, 134.
12. Holyoake, *The History of the Last Trial by Jury for Atheism in England*, 7.
13. *Ibid.*, 7.
14. Cheltenham remains a "fashionable town" and is one of the most attractive of England's small cities (pop. 120,000). It boasts handsome commercial buildings and impressive homes built of Cotswold sandstone that shimmers in colours of cream and warm yellow. Its tree-lined streets and spas, popular still today, are reminiscent of Cheltenham's history as a leading Regency town.
15. Holyoake, *The History of the Last Trial by Jury for Atheism in England*, 8.

Chapter 5

1. Report of the Committee of the New Meeting Sunday Schools, May 18, 1840, cited in Sophia Dobson Collet, *George Jacob Holyoake and Modern Atheism*, 7.
2. William Galpin, Bishopsgate Institute, Holyoake 1:2, Letter, William Galpin, July 24. 1841.
3. "Sheffield Fair." *Sheffield Independent*, December 4, 1841.
4. Bishopsgate Institute, London, Holyoake 1:2., Letter, Walter Newall, July 15. 1841.
5. Bishopsgate Institute, London, Holyoake 1:2., Letter, William Galpin, September 2, 1841.
6. Dafoe, Daniel (1723–27). "Letter 8, Part 3: South and West Yorkshire." *A tour thro' the whole island of Great Britain*. Cited in *Oxford Companion to British History*, 859.
7. "The Socialists." *Bristol Times and Mirror*, December 4, 1841 The prison treadmill, a favorite form of Victorian punishment, was a large, wide wheel with steps which prisoners mounted to keep it turning. "It was a useless but exhausting task that fitted with Victorian ideals about atonement achieved through hard work," according to the BBC.
8. *Oracle of Reason*, undated, No. 4, 1.
9. The December 24, 1841, issue of the *Sheffield Independent* carries only one reference to Christmas and one to "the holidays." An item headed Christmas Presents reported that the Earl of Fitzwilliam had given his 1,010 employees (excepting domestic staff) each six pounds of beef and six pence to buy bread for their Christmas feast. The bounty went to plumbers, carpenters, gardeners, and other ranks. The New Queen Street Hotel advertised that the "Fat Ox," said to weigh 170 stone (2,300 pounds) had arrived and was being kept in a temporary shed "for inspection during the Holidays." There was also the "fat prize pig" of Mr. Weightman on exhibit, along with his silver medal.
10. Holyoake, *The History of the Last Trial by Jury for Atheism in England*, 10.
11. National Co-operative Archive, Holyoake House, Manchester, Letter #39, Wm. Galpin, April 13, 1842.
12. The Cheltenham Baths were among the town's main attractions, wealthy travelers having frequented them since a visit by the troubled King George III in 1778.
13. Holyoake, *The History of the Last Trial by Jury for Atheism in England*, 5.
14. *Ibid.*, 5.
15. *Ibid.*, 5. Trepanned is from trepan, a surgical tool resembling a carpenter's bit and brace.
16. *Ibid.*, 5.
17. McCabe, *The Life and Letters of George Jacob Holyoake*, Vol. I, 60.
18. "Atheism and Blasphemy." *Cheltenham Chronicle*, May 27, 1842.

19. Holyoake, *The History of the Last Trial by Jury for Atheism in England*, 8.
20. Close became Dean of Carlisle, in Cumbria in the far north of England, in 1856. He wrote some seventy books and pamphlets, few of them "considered of any permanent value."
21. Holyoake, *The History of the Last Trial by Jury for Atheism in England*, 8.
22. Holyoake, *Sixty Years of an Agitator's Life*, Vol. I, 149.
23. Holyoake, *The History of the Last Trial by Jury for Atheism in England*, 8.
24. *Ibid.*, 8.
25. The last man burned at the stake for heresy in England was Edward Wightman in 1612. Thomas Aiken, a 20-year-old Scottish student, was the last man hanged for blasphemy in the UK, in 1695.
26. *Sixty Years of an Agitator's Life*, Vol. I, 151.

Chapter 6

1. The two families and their properties remain intact today, the Grosvenors headed by the seventh Duke of Westminster, Hugh Grosvenor, and the Cadogans by the present Earl, Charles Cadogan, who is life president of Cadogan Estates. Ownership of much of London's most valuable properties is now in the hands of Middle East sheikhs. The president of the United Arab Emirates, Khalifa bin Zayed al Nahyan, is reported by *The Guardian* to have amassed property worth more than £5.5 bn, including the birthplace of Queen Elizabeth.
2. Holyoake, *The Life and Character of Richard Carlile*, 14.
3. Holyoake, *Sixty Years of an Agitator's Life*, Vol. I, 156.
4. *Ibid.*, 162. Holyoake contradicts this anecdote in *History of the Last Trial by Jury for Atheism in England* by stating, 67, that Mr. Carlile supplied the raspberry vinegar.
5. Only the façade of the Shire Hall of Holyoake's time remains today, serving as the entrance to the Eastgate shopping centre. Gloucester has struggled economically and depends on tourists who come to see the nearby Cotswold Hills. It main intersection has become a pedestrian mall and on Saturdays is crowded with shoppers. We stayed at the New Inn, occupying a fifteenth century building said to be England's oldest continuing late Medieval inn. Gloucester's docks district has retained its impressive warehouse buildings but its streets are occupied mostly by convenience stores, take-out joints, and vacant shops. The Gloucester Cathedral retains all its historic glory although in some respects the town exudes a general down-at-the-heels atmosphere.
6. The last person imprisoned for blasphemy in Britain was William Gott, jailed for nine months in 1921 after publishing pamphlets comparing Jesus Christ to a clown. Blasphemy was removed from English and Welsh law in 2008 but remains in force in Scotland and Northern Ireland.
7. McCabe, *The Life and Letters of George Jacob Holyoake*, Vol. I, 75.
8. Holyoake, *Sixty Years of an Agitator's Life*, Vol. I, 158.
9. *Ibid.*, 159.
10. Holyoake, *History of the Last Trial by Jury for Atheism in England*, 32.
11. This and most subsequent quotations from the trial are taken from Knight Hunt, *The Trial of G.J. Holyoake on an Indictment for Blasphemy*.
12. National Co-operative Archive, Holyoake House, Letter #60, G.J. Holyoake, August 9, 1842.
13. Knight, Hunt, *The Trial of G.J. Holyoake on an Indictment for Blasphemy*, 98.

Chapter 7

1. Holyoake, *History of the Last Trial by Jury for Atheism in England*, 67.
2. *Ibid.*, 68.
3. McCabe, *The Life and Letters of George Jacob Holyoake*, Vol. I, 80.
4. Holyoake, *History of the Last Trial by Jury for Atheism in England*, 71.
5. Holyoake, *Sixty Years of an Agitator's Life*, Vol. I, 168.
6. Holyoake, *History of the Last Trial by Jury for Atheism in England*, 74.
7. National Co-operative Archive, Holyoake House, Manchester, Letter #87, G.J. Holyoake, November 28, 1842.
8. Holyoake, *History of the Last Trial by Jury for Atheism in England*, 111.
9. *Ibid.*, 91.
10. William Paley, b. 1743 Peterborough, educated Christ's College, Cambridge; became archdeacon of Carlisle 1782, wrote

influential *Principles of Moral and Political Philosophy*; it and *Natural Theology* became major contributions to Enlightenment thought.
11. William Paley, *Natural Theology, or the Evidence and Attributes of the Deity*, 9.
12. Holyoake, *Paley Refuted In His Own Words*, 12.
13. *Ibid.*, 12. Paley's arguments were based on a teleological philosophy which teaches that evidence of design or purpose can be found in nature. According to this reasoning, design implies a designer, which in the case of the universe can only be God. In outlining the complex structures of living things, Paley linked such phenomena to the existence of a higher power. He was sued for plagiarism but the case was dismissed on the grounds that the watchmaker theory had been in general circulation for a very long time.
14. Henry Heatherington, b. 1792 London, apprenticed to Parliamentary publisher Luke Hansard; jailed for publishing weekly unstamped paper, *Poor Man's Guardian*, became a radical book publisher and supporter of Chartist and Owenite causes. He issued Holyoake's *Paley Refuted In His Own Words* as a 40-page booklet in 1843. Selling for 6d, it was Holyoake's fifth public work.
15. Charles White, *An Account of the Regular Degradation in Man, and in Different Animals and Vegetables* (London: C. Dilly, 1799), p134. https://archive.org/details/b24924507/page/n3.
16. Sophia Dobson Collet, *George Jacob Holyoake and Modern Atheism*, 9.
17. Holyoake, *Sixty Years of an Agitator's Life*, Vol. I, 176.
18. *Ibid.*, 176.

Chapter 8

1. Holyoake, *History of the Last Trial by Jury for Atheism in England*, 75.
2. *Ibid.*, 75.
3. *Ibid.*, 106.
4. National Co-operative Archive, Holyoake House, Manchester, Letter #96, G.F. Welch, May 26, 1843.
5. National Co-operative Archive, Holyoake House, Manchester, Letter #97, John Firmin, May 26, 1843.
6. McCabe, *The Life and Letters of George Jacob Holyoake*, Vol. I, 80.

7. Holyoake, *Bygones Worth Remembering*, Vol. II, 286–7.
8. Holyoake, *Sixty Years of an Agitator's Life*, Vol. I, 197.
9. *Ibid.*, 198.
10. *Ibid.*, 199.
11. *Ibid.*, 203.
12. McCabe, *The Life and Letters of George Jacob Holyoake*, Vol. I, 100.

Chapter 9

1. Holyoake, *Sixty Years of an Agitator's Life*, Vol. I, 205.
2. Holyoake, *English Secularism: A Confession of Belief*, 113.
3. *Leeds Times*, September 13, 1845.
4. Bishopsgate Institute, London, Holyoake 3:7 (Part 1), Unidentified newspaper, nd.
5. Holyoake, *Sixty Years of an Agitator's Life*, Vol. I, 78.
6. James Watson, b. 1799 Malton, moved to London; worked in Richard Carlile's bookshop, served six months for selling *Poor Man's Guardian*; ran Red Lion Square Co-op store, became radical publisher, selling stock to Holyoake 1854; first president London Secular Society.
7. Co-operative Archive, Holyoake House, Manchester, Letter #161, J. Watson, March 12, 1846.
8. *Ibid.*
9. Paul Eyre, historian of the Order of Oddfellows, Manchester, notes that Holyoake's essays still form the basis of the Degree Lectures that British Oddfellows use to illustrate the Order's values to members. The name Oddfellows, according to the web site of the Independent Order of Oddfellows, came about as follows: "That common labouring men should associate themselves together and form a fraternity for social unity and fellowship and for mutual help was such a marked violation of the trends of the times (England in the 1700s) that they became known as 'peculiar' or 'odd,' and hence they were derided as 'Odd Fellows.' Because of the appropriateness of the name, those engaged in forming these unions accepted it."
10. Holyoake, *Sixty Years of an Agitator's Life*, Vol. I, 207.
11. Also in 1846, Charles Darwin launched the *London Daily News*.

12. The acquittal led to a new catch-phrase signifying consternation, such as "What the Dickens are you up to?"
13. Co-operative Archive, Holyoake House, Manchester, Letter #630, G.J. Holyoake, n.d. 1854.
14. Co-operative Archive, Holyoake House, Manchester, Letter #244, S.D. Collet, et al, n.d. 1847.
15. Co-operative Archive, Holyoake House, Manchester, Letter #17, G.J, Holyoake, July 12, 1846. Frederick had died in 1844, age 23. Henry survived until 1881, age 56.
16. Co-operative Archive, Holyoake House, Manchester, Letter #567, Catherine Holyoake, April 12, 1853.
17. McCabe, *The Life and Letters of George Jacob Holyoake*, Vol. I, 155.
18. This same *Economist* ranks today as one of the world's foremost newsmagazines.
19. *Gloucester History*, No. 22, 2008, 11–17.
20. William Henry Ashurst, b. 1792 London, educated at a 'Dame School' articled to be a solicitor, became member of a Freethinking Christians sect, pamphleteer, and a member of the London Common Council.
21. Holyoake, *Sixty Years of an Agitator's Life*, Vol. I, 155.
22. McCabe, *The Life and Letters of George Jacob Holyoake*, Vol. I, 99.
23. *Ibid.*, 184–5.
24. *Ibid.*, 185–6.
25. Holyoake, *Sixty Years of an Agitator's Life*, Vol. I, 117.

Chapter 10

1. Merriman, John, *A History of Modern Europe: From the French Revolution to the Present*, 1996, 715.
2. "THE FRENCH REVOLUTION," London *Morning Chronicle*, February 28, 1848, p4, http://www.britishnewspaperarchive.co.uk.
3. This *Reasoner* slogan bore no relationship to the Communism of Karl Marx and Friedrich Engels, who only the week before had published *The Communist Manifesto* in London and Berlin. Holyoake says English Communists of his time "had a passion for industry, and sought only an equitable division of profits." Holyoake, *Sixty Years of an Agitator's Life*, Vol 1, 136.
4. "WHY HAVE WE HAD NO REVOLUTION IN ENGLAND?" *The Reasoner*, No. 1 (New Series), Vol VII, J. Watson, London, 1850.
5. Holyoake, *Sixty Years of an Agitator's Life*, Vol. II, 19.
6. *Ibid.*, 20–24.
7. Holyoake, *Bygones Worth Remembering*, Vol. I, 227.
8. *Ibid.*, 221.
9. Holyoake, *Sixty Years of an Agitator's Life*, Vol. I, 90.
10. McCabe, *The Life and Letters of George Jacob Holyoake*, Vol. I, 236.
11. *Ibid.*, 313.
12. *Ibid.*, 319.

Chapter 11

1. *Christianity and Secularism: Report of a Public Discussion Between Grant and Holyoake*, 1853, 40.
2. Holyoake, *English Secularism: A Confession of Belief*, 5.
3. Holyoake, *Sixty Years of an Agitator's Life*, Vol. I, 32. Catnach songs (the more correct term) were named after Jemmey Catnach, London street balladeer.
4. *The Reasoner*, December 3, 1851.
5. *The Reasoner*, December 10, 1851.
6. *The Reasoner*, January 14, 1852.
7. Co-operative Archive, Holyoake House, Manchester, Letter #489, G. J. Holyoake, April 20, 1853.
8. Holyoake, *Sixty Years of an Agitator's Life*, Vol. I, 260.
9. "Contemporary Literature of England," *Westminster Review*, July 1853, 129.
10. McCabe, *The Life and Letters of George Jacob Holyoake*, Vol. I, 137.
11. Holyoake, *Sixty Years of an Agitator's Life*, Vol. I, 137.
12. *The Reasoner*, March 5, 1851. Had Holyoake passed through the nearby town of Heanor, he could have encountered a woman calling out "Rag 'an bohns, rag 'an bohns." That woman was my great-grandmother, Catherine Argyle. Widowed at thirty-nine with seven children, she took on this lowliest of occupations and worked her way up to a shop of her own. Rag and bone collectors were the recyclers of their day, collecting rags for paper making, bones

for glue, and other household cast offs that could be put to further use.

13. "Lecture on Irreligious Books." *Carlisle Journal*, May 23, 1851. Jack Falstaff is a character in Shakespeare's comedy, *The Merry Wives of Windsor*. https://www.britishnewspaperarchive.co.uk/search/results/1850-01-01/1899-12-31?basicsearch=holyoake&exactsearch=false&retrievecountrycounts=false&newspapertitle=carlisle%20journal.

14. Holyoake, *Sixty Years of an Agitator's Life*, Vol. I, 248.

15. The first decennial census was carried out in the United Kingdom in 1801; the first formal census was the Domesday Book compiled in 1086, although a census of the "Men of Alba" had been conducted in the seventh century in Dal Riata (parts of Scotland and Northern Ireland), and by the Romans in the form of tax assessment records (none of which survive).

16. United Kingdom census records are online at https://ukcensusonline.com/.

17. Holyoake, *Bygones Worth Remembering*, Vol. I, 159.

18. Horace Mann, *Religious Worship in England and Wales*, 1854, 93.

19. Holyoake, *Principles of Secularism*, 25.

20. Holyoake, *Sixty Years of an Agitator's Life*, Vol. I, 260.

21. *Ibid.*, 79.

22. Holyoake, *English Secularism: A Confession of Belief*, 51.

Chapter 12

1. Holyoake, *Sixty Years of an Agitator's Life*, Vol. II, 95.

2. *Ibid.*, 12.

3. David Williams: *Mr. George Eliot: A Biography of George Henry Lewes*, 52.

4. "Lewes's Life of Robespierre," *The Reasoner*, July 18 and 25, 1849.

5. Co-operative Archive, Holyoake House, Manchester, Letter #567. Catherine Holyoake, August 8, 1849.

6. Co-operative Archive, Holyoake House, Manchester, Letter #333, Thornton Hunt, December 16, 1849.

7. Holyoake, *Bygones Worth Remembering*, Vol. I, 164.

8. John Stuart Mill, b 1806 Pentonville, Middlesex, educated at home by academically obsessed father; learned Greek at three, Latin at eight, grew up agnostic, his works esp. *Political Economy* and *On Liberty* established him as pre-eminent social philosopher. He held that one should be able to do anything they wish if it does not harm others.

9. Holyoake, *Bygones Worth Remembering*, Vol. I, 232.

10. Herbert Spencer, b 1820 Derby, ed. in father's school by teachers of Derby Philosophical Society; worked as sub-editor of *The Economist*, pub. *Social Statics* in 1851 predicting a libertarian withering of the state. A polymath, he came to be regarded as one of greatest philosophers of nineteenth century but his reputation declined rapidly thereafter.

11. In a 2007 poll of authors by *Time* magazine, *Middlemarch* was voted the tenth greatest literary work ever written. As part of the "Reclaim Her Name" program, *Middlemarch* has been republished under Mary Ann Evans's own name. Works by Ms. Evans and twenty-four other female authors are being republished under their own names. They are available for free download at https://nam11.safelinks.protection.outlook.com/?url=http%3A%2F%2Fwww.baileys.com%2F&data=02%7C01%7C%7Cc1bb945c1be44f0c1df08d83f2b0520%7C84df9e7fe9f640afb435aaaaaaaaaaaa%7C1%7C0%7C637328801279428849&sdata=lvt5AEpLjZ0JEnIy1qf4CkLMfpC9LY7zrZs3kLTJGaY%3D&reserved=0.

12. Garrison's anti-slavery views so outraged his fellow whites that he was, as Holyoake records, "dragged through Boston streets with a rope round his neck, and was imprisoned by the mayor to save him from being lynched." Holyoake, *Sixty Years of an Agitator's Life*, Vol. I, 97.

13. Holyoake, *Principles of Secularism*, 11.

14. *Ibid.*, 15.

15. *Ibid.*, 25.

16. *Ibid.*, 27.

Chapter 13

1. Holyoake, *Bygones Worth Remembering*, Vol. I, 173.

2. Florence Fenwick Miller, *Harriet Martineau*, 182.

3. Holyoake, *Bygones Worth Remembering*, Vol. I, 172. William Wordsworth,

a founding father of the school of British Romanticism poetry, occupied Rydal Mount until his death at eighty in 1850, two years before Holyoake's visit. The house afforded a view of both Windermere and Grass Lakes.
4. *Ibid.*, 171.
5. *Ibid.*, 172.
6. *Ibid.*, 173.
7. McCabe, *The Life and Letters of George Jacob Holyoake*, Vol. I, 288.
8. Holyoake, *Bygones Worth Remembering*, Vol. I, 175.
9. Holyoake, *Sixty Years of an Agitator's Life*, Vol. II, 128.
10. Harriet Martineau, *Harriet Martineau's Biography*, Vol. I, 79.
11. Letter, April 1, 1838. Darwin Correspondence Project.
12. Holyoake, *Bygones Worth Remembering*, Vol. I, 177.
13. Co-operative Archive, Holyoake House, Manchester, Letter #362, Harriet Martineau, March 4 1850.
14. Holyoake, *Sixty Years of an Agitator's Life*, Vol. II, 139. The efforts of feminists like Martineau, supported by Holyoake, would not gain women (over the age of thirty) the right to vote until 1918. They would have to wait a further year before winning the right to sit on a jury, serve as a magistrate, or take up such professions as the law and accountancy.

Chapter 14

1. Holyoake, *Life and Last Days of Robert Owen*, 11.
2. *Ibid.*, 10.
3. *Ibid.*, 26.
4. Podmore, *Robert Owen: A Biography*, Vol. II, 626.
5. "Death of Robert Owen." *The Globe*, London, November 19, 1858.
6. "Funeral of the Late Robert Owen." *Irish Advocate and Industrial Journal*, November 28, 1858.
7. Holyoake, *Life and Last Days of Robert Owen*, 15.
8. Holyoake, *The Principles of Secularism*, 22.
9. Royle, *Victorian Infidels*, 190.
10. Holyoake, *The Trial of Theism*, 174.
11. Holyoake, *Sixty Years of an Agitator's Life*, Vol. II, 45.

12. Holyoake, *The History of Co-operation in England*, Vol. I, 2.
13. *The Reasoner*, April 20, 1853.
14. Hypatia Bradlaugh Bonner, *Charles Bradlaugh*, Vol. I, 22.

Chapter 15

1. Bishopsgate Institute, London, Holyoake 3:3, 10, Invitation.
2. "Anderton's Hotel." *The Sanitary World*, July 5, 1844, 9.
3. Bishopsgate Institute, London, Holyoake 3:3, 13, speech text.
4. *Ibid.*
5. Bradlaugh Bonner, *Charles Bradlaugh*, Vol. I, 119.
6. McCabe, *The Life and Letters of George Jacob Holyoake*, Vol. I, 353.
7. *Ibid.*, vii.
8. Robert Malthus, b1766 Westcott, Surrey, educated Jesus College, Cambridge; ordained Church of England 1789; in 1798 published *An Essay on the Principle of Population*. It argued that the only checks on uncontrolled population growth were a higher death rate (hunger, disease, war) or a lower birth rate achieved through birth control, late marriage, and celibacy.
9. https://www.secularism.org.uk/uploads/a-chronology-of-british-secularism.pdf.
10. Holyoake, *History of the Last Trial by Jury for Atheism in England*, 17.
11. Holyoake, *Sixty Years of an Agitator's Life*, Vol. I, 117.
12. William J. Linton, *Threescore and Ten Years*, 164.
13. McCabe, *The Life and Letters of George Jacob Holyoake*, Vol. I, 345.
14. *Ibid.*, Vol. II, 18.
15. https://www.secularism.org.uk/uploads/the-national-secular-society-the-first-150-years-(1866-2016).pdf.
16. The London-based National Secular Society continues today as an active advocacy organization, its campaigns focused on strengthening secular education, eradicating religious influence in government, promoting equality and human rights, and monitoring global issues including blasphemy and religious oppression.
17. Holyoake, *Bygones Worth Remembering*, Vol. I, 81.

18. The 1870 Elementary Education Act provided for schools for children aged five to thirteen but backed off secular education. Nor did it make education free or compulsory; it consolidated church control of schools by giving them partial funding by the state. Public funding for secular education in church-run schools was finally included in the 1902 Education Act.
19. *Secularism, Scepticism, and Atheism*, 3.
20. *Ibid.*, 16.
21. *Ibid.*, 73.
22. McCabe, *The Life and Letters of George Jacob Holyoake*, Vol. II, 57–58.

Chapter 16

1. Holyoake, *Bygones Worth Remembering*, Vol. II, 182.
2. Holyoake, *Self-Help by the People; History of Co-operation in Rochdale*, viii.
3. Co-operative Archive, Holyoake House, Manchester, Letter #1005, Wm. Cooper, November 3, 1858.
4. Holyoake, *The History of Cooperation*, 267.
5. *Ibid.*, 269.
6. *Ibid.*, 270.
7. Holyoake, *The Co-operative Movement Today*, 181.
8. Holyoake, *Sixty Years of an Agitator's Life*, Vol. II, 149.
9. *Ibid.*, 150.
10. *The Reasoner*, XXX, No. 1, 1871, 2.
11. Holyoake, *Sixty Years of an Agitator's Life*, Vol. II, 294.
12. Co-operative Archive, Holyoake House, Manchester, Letter #1247, James Salisbury, October 29, 1858.
13. Edward O. Greening, *The Story of the Life of George Jacob Holyoake*, 31.
14. Arthur Trevelyn, b. 1802 Hartburn, Northumberland, second son of Sir Walter Trevelyan, gave up any claim to inheritance by marrying a working class girl. Holyoake says Trevelyan did not believe in temperance but in prohibition; he suppressed all the inns in his home village of Midlothian.
15. Holyoake; *Jubilee History of the Leeds Co-op Society*, iv.
16. Greening, *The Story of the Life of George Jacob Holyoake*, 31.

Chapter 17

1. Annie Besant may have wondered why this meeting place of freethinkers was called a Hall of Science. The term was, it must be admitted, a pretentious title first given to meeting places of Robert Owen's Society of Religious Rationalists. It was intended to set their halls apart from those of nonconformist churches, and was picked up by secularists for their meeting rooms. The first Secularist Hall of Science in London was in a leased building in City Road. When the lease expired in 1866, Bradlaugh formed a Hall of Science Company and leased the Old Street location. By 1876 some £1400 had been spent to improve and enlarge the structure, providing for a 1,200-seat main hall, a smaller hall seating 200, and a coffee shop and classrooms. By naming their premises Halls of Science early freethinkers were both dissenting from religion and reflecting the belief that things recognized in natural science warranted primary consideration. They also celebrated good music, fine art, and literature. Preoccupation with the social consequences of science would become known as scientism. Such a worldview is regarded pejoratively today for an excessive reliance on science as the main source of knowledge and human values. The record of the Holyoake-Bradlaugh debate of 1870 has Holyoake sneering at the Hall of Science label as "this kind of place in which we now meet, opposite a lunatic asylum, where people, so the enemy says, naturally expect to find us." Annie Besant, *Annie Besant: An Autobiography*, 80.
2. *Ibid.*, 62.
3. *Ibid.*, 82.
4. *Ibid.*, 15.
5. Bradlaugh Bonner, *Charles Bradlaugh*, 16.
6. McCabe, *Life and Letters of George Jacob Holyoake*, Vol. II, 81.
7. *Ibid.*, 83.
8. "The Prosecution of Bradlaugh and Mrs. Besant." London *Globe*, April 6, 1877.
9. Bradlaugh Bonner, *Charles Bradlaugh*, 22.
10. *Morning Post*, April 18, 1877.
11. Bradlaugh Bonner, *Charles Bradlaugh*, 21.
12. *In the High Court of Justice: The Queen vs. Charles Bradlaugh and Annie Besant*, 162.

13. *Ibid.*, 51.
14. *Ibid.*, 51.
15. *Ibid.*, 58.
16. *Ibid.*, 162.
17. *Ibid.*, 267.
18. *Ibid.*, 267.
19. *Ibid.*, 268.
20. Bradlaugh Bonner, *Charles Bradlaugh*, 26.
21. *In the High Court of Justice: The Queen vs. Charles Bradlaugh and Annie Besant*, 319.
22. *Ibid.*, 319.
23. *Ibid.*, 319.
24. Holyoake, *Sixty Years of an Agitator's Life*, Vol. II, 178.
25. Bradlaugh, *Charles Bradlaugh*, 30.
26. Besant, *Annie Besant: An Autobiography*, 81.

Chapter 18

1. In an act of goodwill, Charles Bradlaugh undertook to raise £650 to buy Austin's printing business on behalf of Charles Watts; when the trustee responsible for part of the funds absconded with the money, Bradlaugh made up the promised sum out of his own pocket.
2. Holyoake, *Secular Responsibility*, 13.
3. Holyoake, *Sixty Years of an Agitator's Life*, Vol. II, 303.
4. Holyoake, *The Trial of Theism*, 43.
5. "The Birmingham Education League." *London Evening Standard*, January 17, 1873.
6. Charles Darwin, *The Origin of Species*, 21.
7. Alexander Zevin, *Liberalism at Large*, 81.
8. Holyoake, *Bygones Worth Remembering*, Vol. I, 291.
9. McCabe, *Life and Letters of George Jacob Holyoake*, Vol. II, 19.
10. *Ibid.*, 49.
11. http://www.victorianweb.org/cv/gplbio.hyml.
12. *Edinburgh Daily Review*, June 16, 1879.
13. Holyoake, *Principles of Secularism*, 8.
14. *The Freethinker* has since published continuously, currently as an online publication: https://www.patheos.com/blogs/thefreethinker/.
15. In 2019 Humanists International ranked the United Kingdom 132nd of 196 countries in order of secularity. Canada was 123rd and the United States, 15th.
16. Edward Royle, *Victorian Infidels*, 292.
17. "New Forms of Free Thought." *The Secular Review*, February 4, 1877. Co-operative Archive, Holyoake House, Manchester, #2381.
18. McCabe, *Life and Letters of George Jacob Holyoake*, Vol. II, 164.

Chapter 19

1. Holyoake, *Travels in Search of a Settler's Guide-Book of America and Canada*, 9.
2. *Ibid.*, 6.
3. Holyoake, *Among the Americans and a Stranger in America*, 206.
4. Holyoake, *Travels in Search of a Settler's Guide-Book of America and Canada*, 6.
5. Holyoake, *Among the Americans and a Stranger in America*, xiv.
6. *Ibid.*, 35.
7. *Ibid.*, 73.
8. *Ibid.*, 88.
9. *Ibid.*, 93.
10. "The Father of Cooperation." *Providence Journal*, September 29, 1879.
11. Holyoake, *Travels in Search of a Settler's Guide-Book of America and Canada*, 101.
12. Holyoake, *Among the Americans and a Stranger in America*, 54.
13. They may have sighted the remnants of a comet identified by Mexican astronomer José Bonilla who counted 450 objects passing over the face of the sun. In 2011 astronomers estimated the fragments came within 600 km and 8000 km of Earth—a hair's breadth—and that a collision could have caused extinction of all life.
14. Holyoake, *Travels in Search of a Settler's Guide-Book of America and Canada*, 83.
15. *Ibid.*, 146–7.
16. Holyoake, *Among the Americans and a Stranger in America*, 211.
17. Holyoake, *Travels in Search of a Settler's Guide-Book of America and Canada*, 104.
18. Holyoake, *Among the Americans and a Stranger in America*, 127.
19. *Ibid.*, 192.
20. The Grange is in use today as an annex to the Art Gallery of Ontario.
21. *Travels in Search of a Settler's*

Guide-Book of America and Canada, 44. Canada's most prominent painter of Macdonald's time, Cornelius Krieghoff, painted just such snow-laden scenes. Later Canadian artists such as the Group of Seven expanded their oeuvre to landscapes and forests. As with many men of his era, Sir John A. Macdonald's reputation and legacy has taken a battering in this era of Black Lives Matter and Indigenous reconciliation. MacDonald was hailed for 150 years as the brilliant statesman who brought the colonies of British North America into Confederation in 1867 to form the Dominion of Canada. Biographer Richard Gwynn called Macdonald's accomplishments "staggering" but admitted he also was responsible for the Canadian Pacific Railway scandal, the execution of native leader Louis Riel, and the head tax on Chinese workers and exclusion of their wives. Macdonald has been condemned for his denigration of Blacks and his creation of a system of residential schools in which Indigenous children were sexually and physically assaulted by Anglican and Catholic priests. His statues have been vandalized or removed entirely and his name taken off buildings amid calls for a re-examination of his legacy in which the ills as well as the achievements of his life are recognized.

22. *Ibid.*, 74.
23. *Ibid.*, 125.
24. Co-operative Archive, Holyoake House, Manchester, Letter #2808, R.G. Ingersoll, January 1, 1883.

Chapter 20

1. Co-operative Archive, Holyoake House, Manchester, Letter #1884, G.J. Holyoake, August 14, 1869.
2. "Death of Mrs. G.J. Holyoake," *The Present Day*, Co-operative Archive, Holyoake House, Manchester, #2902, January 11, 1884..
3. Co-operative Archive, Holyoake House, Manchester, Letter #2900, Emily Tennyson, January 3, 1884; Letter #2911, Emily Tennyson, January 16, 1884.
4. "The Co-operators." *Manchester Evening News*, May 31, 1887.
5. McCabe, *Life and Letters of George Jacob Holyoake*, Vol. II, 203.
6. "The Prayers for Mr. Bradlaugh." *Northampton Mercury*, November 16, 1889.

7. Gandhi, according to Ramachandra Guha in *Gandhi Before India*, attended some of Bradlaugh's public meetings and met Annie Besant and Madame Blavatsky, the founder of Theosophy. Gandhi viewed Bradlaugh as one of the "most strenuous and picturesque figures" of British politics, a "self-assertive propagandist of Secularism and Republicanism," and a man who "came from the people and retained to the last some habits of speech which marked him out as a Londoner of the humbler classes." At Bradlaugh's funeral, Gandhi was struck by the fact that "a few clergymen were also present to do him the last honours."
8. Bradlaugh Bonner, *Charles Bradlaugh*, 421.
9. McCabe, *Life and Letters of George Jacob Holyoake*, Vol. II, 203.
10. Holyoake, *Warpath of Opinion*, 62.
11. Holyoake, *Bygones Worth Remembering*, Vol. II, 184.
12. Holyoake, *English Secularism*, 39.
13. The Victorians had it right—the new century did not begin until 1901. Their celebrations may have been reserved but they knew how to read the calendar and understood that a new century did not begin until the first year after the end of the previous one. This was a lesson lost on their descendants, who incorrectly saw the twenty-first century as beginning on the 1st of January 2000. We should have waited a year. Attitudes toward William Gladstone and his legacy also have changed. Amid worldwide indignation over anti-Black racism in 2019, the University of Liverpool moved to rename Gladstone Hall, a student residence.
14. Holyoake, *Bygones Worth Remembering*, Vol. I, 117.

Chapter 21

1. *The Western Mail*, Cardiff, Wales, July 14, 1902.
2. https://en.wikiquote.org/wiki/George_Holyoake.
3. Holyoake, *Principles of Secularism*, 28.
4. "The Career of Mr. George J. Holyoake." *Sunderland Daily Echo*, April 15, 1901.
5. McCabe, *Life and Letters of George Jacob Holyoake*, Vol. II, 295.
6. "George Jacob Holyoake, An

Interesting Birthday Party." *Gloucester Citizen*, April 21, 1903.

7. "An Hour With George Jacob Holyoake." *Brighton Citizen*, May 2, 1903.

8. McCabe, *Life and Letters of George Jacob Holyoake*, Vol. II, 304. As Governor General of Canada, Lord Grey donated a trophy for the Canadian football championship. The Grey Cup is still competed for by Canada's professional football teams and its playing makes for one of the country's leading annual celebrations.

9. *Ibid.*, 308.

10. Holyoake, *Bygones Worth Remembering*, Vol. I, 35–36.

11. The 1902 Education Act represented a step backward for Secularism in that it shifted control of schools from local school boards to regional authorities that would be made up largely of Anglican supporters. The battle was not so much over the reduction of religious teaching, as to who would provide it. Protest meetings were held throughout the country. In the village of Rhayader, Montgomeryshire, the Rev. M.J. Mills charged that "In every attempt to establish a thoroughly national system of education, the church had thrust its demand, and not the needs of the nation at large." *Montgomeryshire Echo*, July 19, 1902.

12. "Veteran Chartist. Death of Mr. G.J. Holyoake." *The Leeds Mercury*, January 23, 1906.

13. McCabe, *Life and Letters of George Jacob Holyoake*, Vol. II, 304.

14. McCabe, *George Jacob Holyoake*, i.

15. "Religious Changes Preceded Economic Change in the Twentieth Century," Damian J. Ruck et al, *Science Advances*, July 2018.

16. Canadian legal scholar John Peters Humphrey, first Director of the United Nations Division of Human Rights, was the principal drafter of the Universal Declaration of Human Rights. Co-author Renè Casson of France received the Nobel Peace Prize partly for his work on its final draft. The Declaration was adopted by the United Nations December 10, 1948. Of the UN's then 58 members, 48 voted in favour, eight abstained (Saudi Arabia, South Africa, and the Soviet bloc) and two did not vote. The Declaration is a largely aspirational document, committing member states to freedom of religion but omitting any reference to the right to live free of religious belief. The omission could be seen as a failure to recognize that those who identify as humanists—agnostics, atheists, other freethinkers—also warrant protection of their beliefs.

Epilogue

1. Holyoake, *The Trial of Theism*, 174.

2. "Half of Americans Say Bible Should Influence U.S. Laws." https://www.pewresearch.org/fact-tank/2020/04/13/half-of-americans-say-bible-should-influence-u-s-laws-including-28-who-favor-it-over-the-will-of-the-people/.

3. "Trump Steadily Fulfills Goals on Religious Right Wish List." *Associated Press*, August 20, 2019.

4. "Trump Boosts School Prayer, Faith Groups As He Rallies Base." *Associated Press*, January 16, 2020.

5. "William Barr Speech on Religious Freedom Alarms Liberal Catholics." *The Guardian*, October 20, 2019.

6. "Cross is Not Secular." https://www.freethoughttoday.com/vol-36-no-06-august-2019/ruth-bader-ginsburg-cross-is-not-secular.

7. "Ignorance won—can we return to reason?" https://www.huffpost.com/entry/ignorance-won-can-we-return-to-reason_b_58233104e4b0334571e0a3a0.

8. "A Secular State for a Secular People." https://andrewcopson.com/2018/09/1972/.

Bibliography

By George Jacob Holyoake

Among the Americans, and A Stranger in America. Chicago: Belford, Clarke & Co., 1881. https://archive.org/details/in.ernet.dli.2015.87257/page/n6.

Bygones Worth Remembering, Vols. I–II. London: T. Fisher Unwin, 1905. https://archive.org/details/bygonesworthrem04holygoog/page/n10 (Vol. I) https://archive.org/details/bygonesworthreme02holyuoft/page/n8 (Vol. II)

The Cooperative Movement Today. London: Methuen & Co., 1891. https://archive.org/details/in.ernet.dli.2015.90683/page/n5.

English Secularism: A Confession of Belief. Chicago: Open Court Publishing, 1896. https://archive.org/details/englishsecularis00holyiala/page/n8.

The History of Co-operation in England. London: T. Fisher Unwin, 1908. https://archive.org/details/in.ernet.dli.2015.90572/page/n3.

The History of the Last Trial by Jury for Atheism in England. London: James Watson, 1850.

The Jubilee History of the Leeds Industrial Co-operative Society. Leeds: General Co-operative Offices, 1897.

Life and Last Days of Robert Owen. London: Holyoake & Co., 1859. https://books.google.ca/books?id=5ApPAAAAYAAJ&pg=PA1&source=kp_read_button&redir_esc=y#v=onepage&q&f=false.

Paley Refuted in His Own Words. London: Heatherington, 1843. https://archive.org/details/thehistoryofthel36799gut.

The Principles of Secularism. London: Austin & Co., 1859 and 1870. https://archive.org/details/principlesofsecu00holy/page/n3.

Public Speaking and Debate. London: T. Fisher Unwin, 1895. https://archive.org/details/in.ernet.dli.2015.24584/page/n7.

Secular Resoonsibility. London: Trubner, 1873. https://books.google.ca/books?id=d8IwAQAAMAAJ&pg=PA13&dq=secular+responsibility&hl=en&sa=X&ved=0ahUKEwj9s8q1oafoAhWEhOAKHTqeD68Q6AEIKDAA#v=onepage&q=secular%20responsibility&f=false.

Self-Help a Hundred Years Ago. London: Swann Sonnenschein & Co., 1888. https://archive.org/details/selfhelphundredy00holyuoft/page/n4.

Self-Help by the People: History of Co-operation in Rochdale. London: Holyoake & Co., 185.

Sixty Years of an Agitator's Life, Vols. I–II. London: T. Fisher Unwin, 1893–1909. https://archive.org/details/cu31924055813988/page/n9 (Vol. I). https://archive.org/details/sixtyyearsofagit02holyuoft/page/n6 (Vol. II).

Travels in Search of a Settler's Guide Book. London: Trubner & Co., 1884. https://archive.org/details/travelsinsearch01holygoog/page/n3.

The Trial of Theism. London: Holyoake & Co., 1858. https://archive.org/details/trialoftheism00holy.

Other Authors

Berman, David, *A History of Atheism in Britain*, London: Croom Helm, 1988. https://archive.org/details/georgejacobholy00collgoog.
Besant, Annie, *Annie Besant: An Autobiography*. London: T. Fisher Unwin, 1893.
Bonner, Hypatia Bradlaugh, *Charles Bradlaugh*, Vols. I–II. London: T. Fisher Unwin, 1894. https://archive.org/details/charlesbradlaugh01bonn/page/22.
Bradlaugh, Charles, and Besant, Annie, *In the High Court of Justice: The Queen V Charles Bradlaugh and Annie Besant*. London: Freethought Publishing Co., 1877. https://archive.org/details/queenvcharlesbra00brad/page/n5/mode/2up.
Collet, Sophia Dobson, *George Jacob Holyoake and Modern Atheis*. London: Trubner & Co., 1855.
Copson, Andrew, *Secularism: Politics, Religion, and Freedom*. Oxford: Oxford University Press, 2017.
Daiche, David, and Flower, John, *Literary Landscapes of the British Isles*. London: Paddington Press, 1979.
Darwin, Charles, *The Origin of Species*. New York: P.F. Collier & Son, 1909.
Dawkins, Richard, *Outgrowing God: A Beginner's Guide*. London: Bantam Press, 2019.
Delic, Zijad, *Islam in the West: Beyond Integration*. Ottawa: University of Ottawa Press, 2018.
Goss, Charles William F., *A Descriptive Bibliography of the Writings of George Jacob Holyoake*. Charleston, SC: BiblioBazaar, Reprint, 2009.
Grant, Brewin, and Holyoake, George, *Christianity and Secularism: Report of a Public Discussion*. London: Ward & Co., 1853.
Greening, Edward Owen, *The Story of the Life of George Jacob Holyoake*. Manchester: Co-operative Union Ltd., 1917.
Grugel, Lee E., *George Jacob Holyoake*. Philadelphia: Porcupine Press, 1976.
Guha, Ramachandra, *Gandhi Before India*. Toronto: Vintage Canada, 2015.
Harvey, Rowland Hill, *Robert Owen: Social Idealist*. Berkeley: University of California Press, 1949.
Hopkins, Eric, *Birmingham: The First Manufacturing Town in the World*. London: Weidenfeld & Nicolson, 1989.
Howe, Catherine, *George Jacob Holyoake's Journey of 1842*. Studly, Warwickshire, History into Print, 2012.
Hunt, Knight, *The Trial of George Jacob Holyoake on an Indictment for Blasphemy*. London: Anti-Persecution Union, 1842.
King, Steven, *Writing the Lives of the English Poor, 1750s–1830s*. Montreal: McGill-Queen's University Press, 2019.
Laxer, Emily, *Unveiling the Nation: Secularism in France and Quebec*. Montreal: McGill-Queen's University Press, 2019.
Linton, William J., *Threescore and Ten Years*. New York: Charles Scribner's Sons, 1894.
Mann, Horace, *Religious Worship in England and Wales*. London: George Routledge & Co., 1854. https://archive.org/details/censusgreatbrit00manngoog/page/n5.
Martineau, Harriet, *Biography of Harriet Martineau*. Paris: Ulan Press, Reprint, 2012.
McCabe, Joseph, *George Jacob Holyoake*. London: Watts & Co., 1922.
_____, *Life and Letters of George Jacob Holyoake*, Vols. I–II. London: Watts & Co., 1908. https://archive.org/details/lifelettersofgeo01mccaiala/page/n7 (Vol. I). https://archive.org/details/lifelettersofgeo02mcca/page/n3 (Vol. II)
Merriman, John, *A History of Modern Europe: From the French Revolution to the Present*. New York: W.W. Norton, 2009.
Miller, Mrs. F. Fenwick, *Harriet Martineau*. London: W.H. Allen & Co., 1884.
Morgan, Mary S., *Charles Booth's London Poverty Maps*. London: Thames and Hudson, 2019.
Newsome, David, *The Victorian World Picture*. New Brunswick, NJ: Rutgers University Press, 1997.
Owen, Robert, *The Life of Robert Owen*. London: G. Bell & Sons Ltd., 1920.
Paley, William, *Natural Theology, or the Evidence and Attributes of the Deity*, London: Richard Griffin and Company, 1855.

Podmore, Frank, *Robert Owen: A Biography.* Vol. I. New York: Appleton, 1907; Vol. II, London: Hutchinson & Co., 1906.
Rectenwald, Michael, *Nineteenth-Century British Secularism: Science, Religion and Literature.* London: Palgrave Macmillan, 2016.
Royle, Edward, *Victorian Infidels: The Origins of the British Secularist Movement, 1791–1866.* Manchester: Manchester University Press, 1974.
Sharlet, Jeff, *The Family: The Secret Fundamentalism at the Heart of American Power.* New York: Harper, 2008.
Taylor, Charles, *A Secular Age.* Boston: Belknap Press, 2007.
Yeo, Stephen, *Victorian Agitator: George Jacob Holyoake.* Brighton: Edward Everett Root, 2007.
Zevin, Alexander, *Liberalism at Large: The World According to the Economist,* London: Verso, 2019.

Index

Adams, George 46, 55, 61, 66, 68, 81
Adams, Harriet 46, 55, 61, 68, 81
Adams, John 195
Adams, John Quincy 195
Age of Reason 120
Agnostic 185
Ahmed, Rafida Bonya 229
Albert, Prince 88, 123, 209
Ambleside 136, 142
America 192–193, 202
American Humanist Association 220, 224, 226
Analysis of the Influence of Natural Religion 157
Anderton's Hotel 152
Anglican Church 36, 165, 228
Anglican Church, Thirty Nine Articles 150
Anne, Queen 98
Anti-Corn Law League 101–102
Anti-Persecution Union 64, 84–85
Ashurst, William Henry 103, 113, 132, 144
Associated Press 196
Association of All Classes of All Nations 32, 36, 40
Ataturk, Mustafa Kemel 227
atheism ix, x, 5, 52, 54–55, 58, 63, 78, 81, 83, 99, 103–104, 106, 114, 116, 129, 131, 133, 140, 142, 145, 150, 154, 156–157, 160–161, 166, 169, 173, 185, 188
Atheon 92
Attwood, Thomas 23, 33, 41, 235n6
Austen, Jane 28, 55
Austrian Empire 107

Bagehot, Walter 185
Bangladesh 229
Barker's Review 155
Barlow, Thomas 209
Barnum, E.E. 194
Barr, William 224
Bartram, James 59, 67

Bataclan 228
Bate, Frederick 89
Beardsley, Aubrey 207
Bear's Head Hotel 144
Beecher, Rev. Mr. 195
Belcher, James 35
La Belle Epoque 194
Beneath the Starry Arch 203
Berman, David 157
Bernard, Dr. Simon 108–110
Besant, Annie ix, 139–140, 172–181, 207
Besant, Frank 172
Bharatiya Janata Party (BJP) 229
Bibi, Asia 229
Bible 53, 139, 223
The Bible: What It Is: Being an Examination Thereof from Genesis to Revelation 150
Biden, Joseph R. 225
Biographical History of Philosophy 129
Bird, Dr. George 184
Birmingham 11, 13, 29, 33–35, 55, 64, 74, 81, 99, 106, 109, 117, 124, 143, 147, 165, 186
Birmingham and Gloucester Railway 45
Birmingham Education League 185
Birmingham Gazette 40
Birmingham Missionary Society 40
Birmingham Political Union 22–23
Birmingham Post 76
Bishopsgate Institute 217
Bissett's Magnificent Guide to Birmingham 14
Black Dwarf 63
Blaine, James G. 197
Blanc, Louis 107, 132
Blasphemy 5, 52, 83, 188, 219
Blavatsky, Helena 181
The Blind Watchmaker 79
Boer War 222
Bologna 202, 205
Booth, Charles 213
Boston 195

Index

Boston Index 190, 193
Boston Liberator 133
SS *Bothnia* 193
Bottomly, Mr. 213
Bradlaugh, Charles ix, 3, 6, 140, 149–151, 154, 157–161, 166–168, 172–181, 186, 188–190, 204; death 206
Bradlaugh, Hypatia 180, 207
Bramwell, Lord Chief Justice 179
Bright, John 102
Brighton 203, 205, 207, 216
Brighton Gazette 213
Bristol 29, 52, 55, 57, 96, 139, 202
Bristol Times and Mirror 52
British Association for the Advancement of Science 104
British Empire 202, 208, 210, 222
British Ethical Union 220
British Secular Union 188
British Social Attitudes Survey 227, 233*Intro.n*4
British tax system 17*n*13
Britons 202
Bromley, William 31
Bronte, Charlotte 129
Brooklyn Bridge 194
Brougham, Lord 137, 144
Bryant & May 181
Budge, William 86
Burgess, Elizabeth 100
Burns, Geoff v
Burns, Robert Lodge 94
Bury 122
Bush, George W. 223

Cambrian Railways, 211
Campbell, Dr. Hugh 184
Canada (Dominion of) 199
Canada First 199
Canterbury, Archbishop of 19
Capper, R. 59
Cardiff *Western Mail* 212
Carlile, Richard ix, 2, 34, 62–63, 65, 69, 74, 82, 100–101, 115, 140, 150, 154, 157, 174, 217
Carlisle 121
Carlisle Journal 121
Carter, Brudenell 184
SS *Catalonia* 192, 200
Catholic Emancipation 187
Census, 1851 122
Chambers' Journal 36
Chapman, John 132–133
Charles Bradlaugh 180
Charlie Hebdo 228
Chartist Union 33, 103, 145, 174
Chautauqua Lake 196

Cheltenham 29, 45–47, 236*ch*4*n*14, 55, 57, 61, 75, 81, 83, 158
Cheltenham Chronicle 58–59, 67–68
Chicago Times 197
Chilton, William 75, 82, 86, 99, 125
China 230
Christ 196
Christian 63, 70, 120, 169, 173, 182–183, 185, 188–189, 204, 223, 228–229
Christianity 5, 110, 119, 157, 161, 188, 196, 227, 229
Christmas 236*ch*5*n*9
A Christmas Carol 86
Church of England 52, 116, 184, 187, 190, 222, 227
Church of the Holy Saviour 227
Churchill, Winston 128, 207
Civil War (U.S.) 198
Clark, John 153
Clinton, Hilary 223
Close, the Rev. Francis 55–56, 58
Cobbett William 149
Cobden, Richard 102
Cockburn, Sir Alexander 177–178
Coleridge, Sir John 128
College of Propaganda for Secularism 147
Collet, C.D. 125, 203
Collet, Sylvia Dobson 79–80, 100
Combe, George 25, 235*ch*2*n*10
Communisn 239*ch*10*n*3
Comte, August 134
Congressional Freethought Caucus 224
Connecticut City Railroad 195
Conservative Party 205
Constitution, U.S. 225
Cooke, Thomas 202
Cooper, Bransby 73, 76, 80
Cooper, Robert 147, 150
Cooper, William 163
Co-operative Colony Aid Association 194
Cooperative Congress 205, 214
Co-operative News 193
Co-operative Union 166, 211, 215
Copson, Andrew vi, 230
Cornell University 196
The Counsellor 155
Covid-19 221
Cowan, James, Sr. 100
Cowper Street School Rooms 119
Crawford, E.H.J. 98
Crawford, John G. 152, 158
Crimean War 98, 101, 222
Cumbria 121
currency, 19th century vs 21st 234*n*22

Dafoe, Daniel 51
Dale, David 19

Index

D'Arusmont, Guillaume 90
Darwin, Charles 77, 79, 132–134, 139, 141–142, 178, 185
Darwin, Erasmus 141
Dawkins, Richard 79
Denmark 107
Department of Education, U.S. 224
Derby 147
Derby, Lord 186
Derbyshire 34
Devon 109–110
Dewsbury, Yorkshire 205
Dickens, Charles 11, 86, 98, 137, 140, 231
Dickers, Stefan v, 215
Dickinson, John 94, 96–97
Disraeli, Benjamin 165
Donne, John 221
Douglas, Frederick 198
Dragoon Guards 150
Drysdale, George 155
Dutch 203

Eagle Foundry 17, 21–22, 26–27, 33, 39, 42, 81, 234n1
Earl Grey, Lord 23, 214, 217
The Economist 102, 132, 185, 220
Edinburgh 106
Education Acts 160, 184, 215, 245n11
Edward VII, Kind 209
Egypt 202, 226
Eisenhower, Dwight D. 223
Elements of Social Science 155
Eliot, George 28, 134, 140–141, 216, 238ch12n11
Emerson, Ralph Waldo 195
The Emperor 113
English Excursionists 112–113, 154
Equality Act 219
Erdogan, Recep Tayyip 227
Erskine, Mr. Justice Thomas 65–66, 68, 70–73
Eugenie, Empress 110
Euston Station 61, 105
Evans, Mary Anne 133
Evans, Stephen 227
Every Woman's Book 63
Every Woman's Book or What Is Love? 174

The Family 223
The Family: The Secret Fundamentalism at the Heart of American Power 223
Farrah, Frederick 101
The Fellowship 223
A Few Words on the Christian Creed 150
Fielding, Henry 146
Firman, John 84
First Amendment 224

Fleet Street House 98, 100–101, 112, 147, 152–153, 155
Florence, Mass. 195
Fly Sheet 98
Foote, George Wm. ix, 185, 188
Forder, Robert (Bob) vi, 1
Fordham University 227
Foreign Enlistment Act 112
Formation of Human Character 30
Forster, W.E. 139
France 202, 227
Francis, Pope 222, 226
Fraser, Col. James 176
Free Inquirer 80
Free Religious Society 196
Free Thinker 188
French Second Republic 107
The Fruits of Philosophy: An Essay on the Population Question 174, 176–177, 187
Fry, Alfred 31

Galpin, William 50, 54, 68, 89
Gandhi, Mohandas K. 181, 206, 244n7
Garibaldi, Giuseppe ix, 108, 111–113, 153, 205
Garibaldi Fund 110, 112–113
Garrison, Lloyd 133
German Confederation 107
Germany 205
Gifford, Sir Harding 177
Gilded Age 193
Ginger's Hotel 108
Ginsberg, Ruth Bader 225
Gladstone, William E. ix, 2, 98, 135, 165–166, 180, 186, 190, 199, 203, 205, 209, 217
Glasgow 92–93, 95, 106
Glasgow Herald 95
Glenn, Ellen v
Gloucester 40, 61–62, 64, 77, 90, 103
Gloucester County 189
Gloucester Gaol (Jail) 59, 72–73, 76–77, 81, 88
Gloucester Shire Hall 237ch6n5
Gloucestershire 55, 59, 102
Godin, Jean-Baptiste 205
Golden Green Crematorium 215
Golden Spike 194
Good, the Rev. James J. 195
Gorsuch, Neil 224
Graham, Sir James 61, 74
Grand National Consolidated Trades Union 32
Grant, the Rev. Brewin 119–120, 133
Great Exhibition 123, 202
Great Western Railway 143, 211
Greeley, Horace 163
Greening, Edward 156, 166, 169, 212, 215

Index

Greenock 93
Grote, George 157
Groves, Richard 12
Guelph, Ont. 199
Guterres, Antonio 230

Habeas Corpus Act, 15, 233*n*7
Hagia Sophia 227
Hall, Robert 32
Hall of Science 50, 87, 99, 134, 172–173, 206, 242*ch*17*n*1
Hansard, the Rev. Septimus 186
Hansom, Joseph 89
Harvard University 195
Hawke, William 14
Hawkins, Blisset, Dr., 77
Hayes, Pres. Rutherford B. 198
Heatherington, Henry 65, 97, 154
Heidegger, Martin 221
Henry VIII 218
Herald of Progress 97
Highgate cemetery 125, 203, 216
A History of Atheism in Britain 157
History of Fleet Street House 147
History of Philosophy 13
Holland 202
Hollick, Frederick 25, 42–43, 194
Holyoake, Austin (brother) 82, 101, 160, 178, 183
Holyoake, Caroline (sister) 76, 95
Holyoake, Catherine (Groves) (mother) 13–14, 18, 101, 168
Holyoake, Edward 195
Holyoake, Eliza (sister) 18, 168
Holyoake, Elizur 195
Holyoake, Emilie (daughter) 103, 192–193, 199, 213–214, 217
Holyoake, Eveline Ellen (daughter) 51, 76, 92, 101, 122, 213
Holyoake, Francis (Frank) (son) 214
Holyoake, George (father) 1, 18
Holyoake, George Jacob ix, 1, 4–7, 11–18, 27–38, 41, 44, 46, 51–52, 54–58, 60, 82–84, 86–87, 90, 92, 94–96, 99–103, 105–106, 108–126, 128–144, 146–147, 149–162, 165–167, 173–176, 178, 181–191–222, 231; *The Advantages and Disadvantages of Trade Unions* 52; *Among the Americans and a Stranger in America* 193; blasphemy trial 61–71; on boyhood 11–16, 20, 23; *Bygones Worth Remembering* 214; co-operative movement 4, 162–163, 165, 169, 185, 202–205, 211; *English Secularism: A Confession of Belief* 200–201, 208; *Handbook of Graduated Grammatical Exercises* 87; *History of Co-operation in England* 163, 184; *History of Co-operation in Rochdale* 163; *History of Fleet Street House* 147; *The History of the Last Trial by Jury for Atheism* 81, 100; imprisonment 72–80; *The Liberal Situation: Necessity for a Qualified Franchise* 159; *The Life and Character of Richard Carlile* 62; *Mathematics no Mystery, or, the Beauties and Uses of Euclid* 100; Mechanics' Institute 25, 33, 43, 55, 102, 194, 211; *The Origin and Nature of Secularism* 208; *Paley Refuted in His Own Words* 84; *Practical Grammar* 87; *The Practical Philosophy of the People* 125; *Principles of Secularism Illustrated* 128, 134, 208, 212, 220; *Rationalism: A Treatise for the Times* 96, 205; *The Reasoner*; secularism; *Secularism: Self-Help by the People*; *Self-Help a Hundred Years Ago* 205; *Travels in Search of a Settler's Guide-Book of America and Canada* 193; *Sixty Years of an Agitator's Life* 27, 63, 117, 168, 208, 214; *The Trial of Theism* 147; *A Treatise for the Times* 96; Universal Community Society of Rational Religionists; *The Uselessness of Prayer and the Impossibility of Proving the Existence of God* 146; *The Warpath of Opinion* 207; *see also* Eagle Foundry
Holyoake, Helen (Eleanor Williams, 1st wife) 36, 39, 76, 81, 95–96, 122–123, death 203
Holyoake, Horatio (brother) 82
Holyoake, Jacob (G father) 12
Holyoake, Madeline (daughter) 44, 51, 75–76, 81
Holyoake, Malkus (son) 100
Holyoake, Malthus (son) 96, 122
Holyoake, Manfred Griffyn (son) 87, 92, 122
Holyoake, Mary Jane (Parsons, 2nd wife) 205, 214, 217
Holyoake, Matilda (sister) 18, 168
Holyoake, Maximillian Robespierre (son) 100–101, 122, 124–125
Holyoake, Selina (sister) 82
Holyoake, William (brother) 82, 217
Holyoake Lecture 219
Holyoake, Mass. 195
Home Rule 205
Hornblower, John 32
Hornblower, L.G. 44
The Hour and the Man 137
House of Commons 101, 188
House of Lords 24, 116, 187, 228
House of Representatives 224
Household Education 141
Household Narrative of Current Events 98

Index

Huddersfield 145
Huffman, Jared 224
Hughan, James 121
Huguenot, 139
Hull 94
Humanists International 220, 229–230
Humanists UK 219
Hungary 107, 227
Hunt, Henry 34
Hunt, Knight 64
Hunt, Leigh 130
Hunt, Seth 195
Hunt, Thornton 103, 130–132, 141
Huxley, Thomas Henry ix, 133, 135, 142, 185

Icke, William 27
Illustrations of Political Economy, 137
The Impeachment of the House of Brunswick 168
Independent Order of Oddfellows (IOOF) 94, 96, 141, 238*ch*9*n*9
India 229
Indian National Congress 181
Industrial and Provident Societies Act 163
Industrial Revolution 231
Ingersoll, Robert G. x, 197, 200
Innocents Abroad 193
The Investigator 85, 146, 150
Irish Church 165
Islam 229
Italy 205, 215

James, the Rev. John Angell 17, 119
Jane Eyre 129
Jeffery, Henry 86
"The Jew Book" 52
Jewish Relief Act 188
John Street Institution 105
Johnson, Dr. Samuel 117
Jones, the Rev. Samuel 74–75
Jubilee History of the Leeds Co-operative Society 168

Kalley, Dr. Robert 85
Kansas City 200
Kavanagh, Brent 224
Kensal Green cemetery 142
King William IV 24
Kingston, Ont. 199
Knowlton, Dr. Charles 174
Kossuth, Louis 107, 124

Labour Representation League 148
Lacité 228
Lamb, William 85
Landor, Savage 132

Las Vegas 196
Law, Harriet 139–140
The Law of Population: Its Consequence and Bearing Upon Human Conduct and Morals 179
The Leader 103, 131–133, 146
Leeds *Northern Star* 100
Leeds *Mercury* 216
Leeds *Times* 93, 97
Leicester 204
Leicester Secular Society 214
Lewes, Agnes Jervis 130, 133, 141
Lewes, Charles Lee 131
Lewes, George Henry 103, 129–133, 135, 141, 216
Lewes, John Lee 131
Lewin, Sarah 100
Liberal Party 186
The Liberal Situation: Necessity for a Qualified Franchise 159
Liberty Counsel 224
Life and Labour of the People of London 213
Life and Letters of George Jacob Holyoake 218
Life in the Sickroom 142
Life of Goethe 131
The Life of Maximilien Robespierre 129
Linton, William J. 132, 158
Liverpool 93, 144, 200
Local Government Act 190
London 61–62, 93, 106, 109, 125, 130, 138, 142, 144, 150, 166, 189, 200, 202–203, 215
London and Birmingham Railway 61
London and Southwestern Railway 88
London Courant 96
London *Daily News* 178, 216
London *Evening Standard* 185, 216
London *Globe* 144
London *Morning Chronicle* 23, 34, 105, 216
London *Morning Post* 176
London Secular Society 147
London *Star* 215
London *Sun* 213
London *Telegraph* 216
London *The Times* 178, 209, 215
Louis Philippe, King 88
Lowe, John 200
Lucretius 157
Lush, Mr. Justice 176

Macdonald, Sir John A. 199, 243*ch*19*n*21
Machiavelli, Niccolò 221
Macron, Emmanuel 228
Madras 182
Maitland, Mr. 56
Malthusian League 156, 179, 241*ch*15*n*8

Manchester 34, 87, 94, 99, 106, 122, 166, 187, 202, 205
Manchester, Bishop of 187
Manchester Evening News 205
Manchester Secular Society 147
Man's Nature and Development 142
Marquess of Queensbury 160, 186, 209
Married Women's Property Act 190
Martineau, Harriet x, 132–142, 147, 203
Martineau, James 142
Marx, Karl 123
Mason, Captain 72, 76–77
Mayhew Henry 62
Mazzini, Giuseppe 108, 111, 205
McCabe, Joseph x, 6, 79, 218
McCarthy, Cormac 221, 230
McCulloch, Sophie v
McKinley, Pres. William 209–210
Medill, Joseph 197
Melbourne, Lord 41
Mellor, Justice 177
Mersey River 200
Mexican 200
Middlemarch 133, 141
Milan 202
Milholen, Layla vi
Mill, John Stuart 147, 156, 163, 183, 186
Modi, Narendra 229
Molesworth, W.N. 124
Montmorency Falls 199
Montreal 199
Moral Physiology 174
Mormonism 93
Morrison, Walter 184
Mosely, the Rev. Thomas 18, 69
The Movement 86–90, 92–93
Moxon, Edward 65
Mubarak, Bala 229
Mulroney, David 230
Muslims 227, 229–230
Mutz, P.H. 33

Naples, Kingdom of 144
Napoleon 15
Napoleon III 107–108, 110, 153
Nash, David 140
National Association for the Promotion of Social Science 144
National Catholic Register 226
National Co-operative Union 217
National Day of Prayer 225
National Labour Equitable Exchange 31
National Liberal Club 208, 214
National Portrait Gallery 207
National Prayer Breakfast 223–224
National Reformer 154–159, 172–173, 176, 188

National School 150
National Secular Association 155
National Secular Society 2, 147, 159, 172, 186, 188, 206, 219, 241n16
Natural Theology or Evidences of the Existence and Attributes of the Deity 77
The Necessity of Atheism 157
Nehru, Jawaharlal 181
New Harmony 30, 56, 88
New Lanark Mill 19–20, 30
The New Moral World 40, 54, 96–97
New York 194
New York Daily News 196
New York Herald 196
New York Mail 196
New York Times 196
New York Tribune 104
New Yorker 149
Newall, Walter 51
Newcastle 120
Newcastle Star 100, 104
Newell, the Rev. Dr. 59
Newman, Cardinal 132
Newman, Francis 132
Newspaper Stamp Abolition Committee 98
Newtown, Wales 143–144, 211
Niagara Falls 137, 195, 199
Nicholas, Tsar 30, 107
Nicholls, Charles Frederick 119
Nigeria 229
Nineteenth Century 214
Norman, Sharon vi
Northampton 99, 188
Norton, Caroline 85
Norwich 142
Nottingham 120, 147

Oath Keepers 225
Ogden, Mr., 73
On the Laws of Man's Nature and Development 141
On the Nature and Existence of God 173
On the Nature of Things 157
On the Origin of Species 79, 133, 185
Opium Wars 166, 222
Oracle of Reason 52, 54, 57, 61, 69, 75, 79, 82, 85–86, 99
Orange Free State 209
Orban, Viktor 227
Orsini, Felice 108, 110
Orthodox Observer 227
Ottawa 199
l'Ouvreture, Toussaint 137
Owen, Robert x, 2, 5, 18, 32, 34, 41–43, 69, 88, 92, 102, 114–115, 144, 148–149, 154, 211–212; *see also* Association of All

Classes of All Nations; Grand National Consolidated Trades Union; National Labour Equitable Exchange; New Harmony; New Lanark Mill; Universal Community Society of Rational Religionists
Overbury, J. 59
Owen, Robert Dale 143–144, 174
Oxford Movement 40
Oxford University 185

Paddington Equitable Co-op Society 167
Paine, Thomas, 34, 63, 115, 121
Paley, Dr. William 77–79, 238n13
Pall Mall Gazette 216
Palmerston, Lord 42, 153
Panic of 1873 194
Papanikolaou, Aristotle 227
Pare, William 36, 89, 144, 163, 233ch3n14
Paris 148, 205
Paris, Touzeau 174
Parker, the Rev. John Graham 150
Parliament 204, 228
Parliamentary Oaths Act 160
Parsons, Gertie 205
Paterson, Thomas 51, 86
Paty, Samuel 228
Pearce, Henry 59
Peel, Sir Robert 42, 63, 102
Pelosi, Nancy 224
Pemberton, W.B. 43
Pen, Marine le 227
Pentecostalism 219
Pentrich Revolution 15
People's Press 100
Peterloo massacre, 34, 50, 63, 98
Pew Institute 223, 228
Philadelphia 195
Phillips, Wendell 195
Philosophical Union 27
Philpotts, Dr. Henry, Bishop of Exeter 40, 55
phrenology 25
The Pickwick Papers 230
Pinching, Mr. 59
Plant, James 44
Pooley, Thomas 128
Poor Laws 33
Poor Man's Guardian 149
Pope, J.H. 199
The Positive Philosophy 134
The Present Day 204–205
Principles of Political Economy 163
Propagandist Press Committee 208
Prophet Mohammed 228
Protestantism 188
Proud Boys 225

Providence, R.I. 195
Pulsky, Francis 107

Q Anon 225
Quakers 188
Quebec 116, 227, 229
The Queen vs Charles Bradlaugh and Annie Besant 177
Queenwood 51, 56, 88–89, 94, 99
Quincy, Josiah 195
Quran 227

Ranthorpe 129
Rationalist Press Association 208, 214
The Reasoner 97–99, 106, 111, 118–119, 122, 124, 128–129, 138, 141, 147, 149, 152–156, 158, 166, 174
Reconstruction Era 194
Reform Acts 22, 33, 41, 98, 133, 186, 203
Reform League 131, 159, 165
Reformers Memorial 142
The Refutation of Deism 157
The Report of Religious Worship 123–124
Representation of the People Act 203
Republican 167–168, 209
The Republican 63, 149
Republicanism 167
River Severn 211
Robespierre, Maximilien 101, 124, 130
Rochdale Society of Equitable Pioneers 148, 163
Roebuck, John Arthur 63, 69
Rogers, Samuel 52
Roman Catholic 205, 222, 226
Roosevelt, Franklin Delano 128
Roosevelt, Theodore 197, 210
The Rotunda 63, 84
Royal Navy 202
Russell, George 117
Russell, Lord 144
Rutherford, the Rev. J.H. 120
Ryall, Malthus Q. 62, 86, 92

St. George's Church 187
St. James Gazette 213
St. Martin's Church 12, 18, 41, 69
St. Peter's Church 150
Salisbury, James 167
Salvation Army 156
Sante Fe 200
Sarte, Jean-Paul 221
Sayer, Rev. Andrew 77–78
Second Boer War 208
Second Italian War of Independence 113
Secular Hymns for Sunday Schools and Secular Gatherings 146
Secular Responsibility 183

258 Index

Secular Review 188, 190
The Secular World and Social Economist 158
secularism 115–119, 122, 124–126, 128–129, 132–135, 138–140, 145–148, 153, 160, 162–163, 165, 169, 181, 184–190, 200, 204, 208, 212, 218–222, 224, 226–227, 229–231
The Secularist 187–188
Shaen, William 158
Sharlet, Jeff 223
Sharples, Eliza 140, 150
Sheffield 29, 51, 99, 109, 119, 154, 158
Sheffield Free Press 119
Sheffield Independent 51
Shelley, Percy Bysshe 65, 157
Sherwin's Political Register, 34
Shoreditch 113
Shrewsbury 143, 211
Sickert, Walter 207
Simmonds, William 176
Smith, Prof. Goldwin 199
Smith, Joseph 93
Smith, Samuel 14
Social Economist 166, 212
Society for the Diffusion of Useful Knowledge, 31, 137
Society in America 137, 141
Soundy, Frances 31
South Africa 209
Southwell, Charles x, 29, 52, 54–55, 57, 65, 85–86, 93, 140, 154, 157
Speckhardt, Roy 226
The Spectator 87, 128, 132
Spencer, Herbert 132, 133–135, 142, 205
The Spirit of the Age 103
Spooner, the Rev. Richard 40
"Springtime of the Peoples" 105
Stamp Act 98–99, 106, 153
Staver, Mat 224
Suicide Act 219
Sunday League 148
Supreme Court (U.S.) 194, 224
Switzerland 107

Taft, Albert 217
Tax on Knowledge 148
Taylor, G.W. 156
Taylor, Joseph 109
Ten Bells Inn 65
Tennyson, Emily 203
Tennyson, Lord Alfred x, 135, 18, 203
Test and Corporations Act 187
Thames River, 143
theosophy 181
Through Storm to Peace 181
Tlaib, Rashida 224
Tolpuddle Martyrs 32, 94

Toronto 199
Tours, France 202
Tower Hamlets 148
Trafalgar Square 159, 168
Transvaal 209
Travelling Tax Abolition Committee 204
Trevelyan, Arthur 168
Truelove, Edward 150, 160
Trump, Donald 224
Trussel, Dr. 196
Turkey 218, 227
Turkish baths 145
Turley, William J. 152
Twain, Mark 193
Twelve Years in a Monastery 218
Twentieth Century 244n13
Two Sicilies, Kingdom 107–108
Tyndall, John 135

Ulster Conservative 95
Union of Ethical Societies 219
Unitarians 36, 141
United Kingdom 116, 169, 184, 189
United Nations 220, 230
United States 116, 189
Universal Community Society of Rational Religionists 5, 40, 43, 50–51, 55, 68, 83, 85, 87–88, 92, 99, 114, 143, 147, 174, 211
Universal Declaration of Human Rights 220, 245n16
University College London 117
University of London 103
University of Notre Dame 224
Urquhart, David 42, 145
The Uselessness of Prayer and The Impossibility of Proving the Existence of God 146

Van Burl, Captain 42
Vereide, Abraham 223
Victoria, Queen 41, 88, 123, 146, 186, 202, 209, 215
Victorian Age 194
Vietnam War 189
Volturno River 113

Walpole, Charles 168
War Chronicle 98
Washington, D.C. 196
Watson, James 96, 100
Watson, Sarah vi
Watt, Charles 174, 188
Watts, John 36, 101
Westminster Review 120, 132–133
White, Charles 79
Whitehaven 121
Wilks, Thomas 101

Williams, Eleanor 35
Wilson, James 102
Windsor, Deborah vi
Woburn Buildings 122
Woman's Journal 141
Worcester 29, 43–45, 81
Worcester Journal 41
The Worker 194
Workingman's Reading Club 121
World Mission Day 226

World War II 222
Worthington, John Hugh 141
Wright, Daniel 42
Wright, Frances 90

Xinjiang 230

Young Husband's Book 37

Zola, Emile 162

www.ingramcontent.com/pod-product-compliance
Lightning Source LLC
Chambersburg PA
CBHW021350300426
44114CB00012B/1162